BOY

David Wagner

ISBN-13: 978-1466231054

Boy

To my wife Pamela and my daughter Emma

Boy

Chapter One

The greatest story ever told began with the birth of a child, it would therefore seem wrong to begin with my birth as if it were an event of importance. So I will begin with the status quo. As I reach the biblical allotment of seventy years I look back in wonder at the number of people, places and events that fill a person's lifetime. Mine has been filled with all kinds of men and women from public names to gangsters, titled ladies to women of the oldest profession. I have found employment in over forty occupations in forty-five years ranging from cleaning indescribable filth from trawler bilges to managing projects worth millions of pounds, from fairground roustabout to Shakespearean actor and theatrical director, managing along the way love affairs and loving relationships that resulted in three marriages and two children. I have lived in mansions and hovels in luxury and in poverty.

Did I waste my life? I cannot say but I believe that my wanderlust and lack of stability could be traced to my childhood and that it left me a hopeless radical; perhaps that leads in a respectable way to talk of my arrival.

I was born into a world at war and, according to my mother, my birth began in an ambulance speeding through the bomb torn streets of the South Wales city of Cardiff with the driver cursing Adolph Hitler as he was forced to make constant detours to avoid bomb craters and rubble and my mother cursing the pain.

It was the beginning of the fourth decade of the twentieth century; the century that saw more sweeping world changes than any other with two worldwide wars, several economic depressions, the dawn of the space age, the end of and the birth of a number of nations. The second of the two worldwide wars was well under way in1941; the city had experienced air raids only a couple of weeks before and clearing up was still uncompleted on the day that I decided to make my entrance.

The ambulance eventually reached the maternity wing of Saint David's Hospital and after long hours of painful labour for my poor mother I was born on the late morning of the Second of June 1941. I weighed in at fourteen pounds two ounces this was and I believe remains a record weight for the hospital. My weight might have been due to the numerous bottles of fizzy lemonade that my mother drank during her pregnancy and it is no small wonder that I did not literally "pop" out, it was however a difficult delivery and she was grateful for the gas and air mixture made available to her - to quote her, 'I was so desperate for its comfort that they had to fight to take the mask away from me.'

As she lay resting following her delivery the woman in the next bed engaged her in conversation and got around to asking what name she intended for me, my mother told her that she planned to name me Alun. The woman paused and then asked if my mother would be very kind and call me David because her baby had been stillborn and she had planned to call him by that name.

My mother was and remained all her life one of the most softhearted persons that I ever met; she did not even hesitate, 'Of course I will, love,' she said and so I was named after a dead child, perhaps not the most auspicious of beginnings.

The hospital in which I was born was, like every second building in Cardiff it seemed, named after the patron saint of Wales and at its rear was the high Victorian wing that was known to locals as The City Lodge - this grim fortress like edifice was in 1941 the local workhouse. Few people today realise that the workhouses existed as late as the nineteen-forties but the Workhouse Act abolishing them was not passed until 1947 and did not come into full effect until 1948.

My mother could not have dreamed that when she took me from the hospital wing in 1941 she would be taking back to the workhouse wing in 1947 but that was far into the future; for the present she returned with me to a small terraced house in the nearby coal port of Barry Docks.

The house was rented by my grandfather, James (Jim), and shared with my maternal great grandmother Sarah Ann; the latter died when I was two years old and I remember nothing of her. I do remember my grandfather or Grampie as I knew him. He was then in his mid sixties, a small neat white- haired person who doted on my mother and in turn on me. He was a man whose life had been marred by a number of tragedies but - in my memory - he had a gentle and caring nature despite the cruel blows that life had delivered.

Born in 1878 Grampie had been orphaned in his early teens and sent with his only brother, Bill, to live with a spinster aunt in Barry, here he displayed a wickedly mischievous nature and finally disgraced himself by using his air gun to shoot holes in a neighbour's large bloomers as they hung on the washing line - a heinous crime in late Victorian Britain. To escape the condemnation of his aunt and her neighbours he enlisted, or was persuaded to enlist in the army.

In 1898 he saw action in his first major battle when the British Army led by General Kitchener fought the Mahdi at Omdurman or as Grampie's brother was to tell me, '...he fought the fuzzy-wuzzies with Kitchener.' Omdurman was the battle in which the last cavalry charge of the British army took place a charge in which a young officer named Winston Churchill took part and described so vividly in his book "My Early Life."

Grampie rose to the rank of warrant officer and during a period of leave in Britain met and married his first wife a Cardiff girl. He returned with her to India where she became another garrison wife and bore him twin children, a boy and a girl. They must have endured separations caused by army life one in particular when he was posted to a small fort in the Khyber Pass - as he described it to my mother, '...it was a square mud hut about eight feet by eight feet with a nearby well for water and a telegraph.'

His only companion was a large black Labrador dog. With this dog he sat guarding a large stretch of empty mountain for six months and passed the time by making elaborate beaded cushions from scraps of old uniform and pins and beads that he had acquired in the bazaar. We still owned several of these when I was a young boy and they were true works of art; unfortunately they were lost in our wanderings and I have no family mementoes from Grampie.

Shortly after his return from the fort duty an outbreak of cholera hit the city of Agra where they were based. His wife was an early victim and she lies buried in the British Cemetery at Agra - as a small boy I recall seeing the sepia coloured photograph of her large tomb in the heavy black leather bound scrapbook that belonged to my grandfather. The tomb was surrounded by a tall iron fence ('...to keep off wild animals' my mother explained to me). The scrapbook was later lost following our eviction from the family home.

To protect the twins from cholera he put them on a ship bound for Britain and the security of his aunt's home - unfortunately, the cholera sailed with them and along with a number of passengers and crew the twins fell prey to the disease, died and were buried at sea. When told the news Grampie went insane with grief, absent without leave and lived like a native in the bazaar district for several months; he was finally found living talking and looking like a local; he was returned to his regiment, reduced to the ranks and sent to another hill fort. He later went on to work his way back to the rank of Sergeant but not to his previous rank.

Upon his demobilisation from the army he returned to the town of Penarth near Cardiff and shortly afterwards met my grandmother, Bertha; she was just twenty and in service to a local family, he was almost thirty and her mother disapproved strongly of soldiers.

In those far off days when Rudyard Kipling penned the poem "Tommy" with its lines: "For it's Tommy this, an' Tommy that, an' Chuck him out, the brute! But it's "Saviour of 'is country" when the guns begin to shoot;" He knew what he talking about, despite centuries of war and colonial conquest where British servicemen had fought gallantly and died bravely for their country ordinary soldiers and sailors of Victoria's army and navy were considered rogues and ne'er-do-wells and not welcomed in polite society.

My grandmother defied her mother's objections to Grampie and became his wife in 1908. To support her he took up work as an insurance agent. She soon became pregnant and a son, Ronald David, was born in 1909; he died in 1910. In April of that same year my mother was born, she was named Dorothy May but she was usually called, Dolly - you will notice that I did not say 'christened' Dorothy May that is because, despite being born into a Christian family, she was never christened or baptised neither for that matter was any of her children.

Childbirth in those hard Edwardian times took place at home and was a risky business with high mortality rates. My grandmother was to add her name to those death lists; she remained weak following a difficult confinement and when her mother, who was living with them, went up to see her the following morning she found her kneeling on the floor beside the bed leaning forward with hands clasped in an attitude of prayer surrounded by a pool of blood - she had haemorrhaged and quietly bled to death whilst praying.

Tragedy had hit Grampie again and my great grandmother blamed him for her daughter's death cursing him and vowing to make him suffer until the end of his days. Despite her hatred she offered to live with Grampie and help bring up my mother; he accepted and in his grief poured his devotion on my mother worshipping the air she breathed and refusing her nothing within his power.

My mother was also loved and pampered by her two uncles, Fred and Bill, who lived with them and when they went off to serve in The Great War she would look forward to them coming home on leave and opening their kit bags to reveal gifts for her in the shape of French dolls or other foreign toys. When they dressed to return to the front line she would help them wrap their legs in puttees layering them carefully and tucking them in at the top, this made her feel very important. Her pride in her soldier uncles was echoed by her pride in Grampie who had re-enlisted at the outbreak of war and was serving as a recruiting sergeant.

Time passed and my mother's uncles returned home from the war, married and moved away from the family home. Left with my mother and my grandfather my great grandmother kept her word and until her death over thirty years later spent every day calling Grampie names such as 'Murderer' and 'Wife Killer' and making his life as unbearable as she could, her worst trick being her ongoing attempts to turn my mother against her father by telling the child that he had murdered her mother and that he was a monster. He endured her abuse by resorting to whistling cheerfully when his temper threatened to get the better of him.

In truth any monstrous deeds were performed by great grandmother who possessed a fierce temper. As a child my mother had long ringlets that fell down to her shoulders, these were not natural but the end product of hours with a pair of curling tongs, the tongs were heated in an open fire until hot enough to scorch newspaper. On one occasion when curling my mother's hair with a very hot curling tongs my great granny lost patience with the child's fidgeting and laid the tongs across the top of her bare leg scarring her badly and shouting as she did so, 'There, that will teach you to fidget, madam.'

My mother carried the scar all her life and would sometimes show it when telling the story. On the good side my great grandmother waited on her hand and foot, dressing her like a little fashion doll and not expecting or allowing the child to perform any chores or household tasks - consequently on reaching maturity she could not even boil an egg.

I do not know if the tension in her young life was to blame but my mother would tell and repeat a strange tale; at the age of about nine or ten she caught measles and was confined to bed for some days. One afternoon she was awoken by a noise and sensed that she was not alone, looking down to the foot of the bed she saw the figure of Satan sitting there complete with cloven hooves horns and pitchfork; paralysed with terror she stared and heard the Devil say, 'I will always be with you, Dorothy.'

She screamed and closed her eyes tightly, when she opened them again her grandmother had rushed in and the apparition was gone. The old lady told her not to be so silly and my mother eventually went back to sleep, the strange thing is that when she next looked in a mirror a bright red three-pronged fork had appeared on her left cheek it faded with time but never completely and it remained on her cheek until her death. She always said that she had received the visitation because she had not been christened - this did not, however, prompt her to have any of us christened.

Despite the domestic stress she remained a bright intelligent girl and used to take great pleasure in helping Grampie, who called her by the affectionate name, Pigeon. One of her chores at an early age was to place Grampie's horse racing bets for him; off-course betting was illegal in Britain and remained so right up until 1960. The way that bookies got around the law was to post 'runners' on street corners and in other public places these runners would accept cash bets and betting slips and pay out any winnings. Punters would write out their betting slip using a pseudonym – my mother's was 'Oxo' and she told me that it had been Grampie's.

With your permission a little geography might be of help here - our street, Regent Street was on a hill running down towards the dock's area but the district was separated from dockland by the main street of the town that cut diagonally across the bottom of our street. Once you had crossed that main street you found yourself at the top of a steep hill running down to the dock's entrance. This street, Thompson Street was a no-go area at night with frequent knife fights and policemen patrolled it in pairs but it was harmless enough during the day. The roads were unmetalled dirt and the sidewalks were wooden planking - shades of the old Wild West.

As my mother told it she would clutch the betting slip and cash tightly in her hand to conceal it and crouching down on her scooter she would race down her street with ringlets flying pausing only to cross the main street, here she was frequently stopped by a jolly red-faced Irish policeman named Sergeant Skelly. Holding his hand out as if stopping traffic he would stop her and enquire in a broad brogue, 'and where might you be heading, Dolly?'

Sergeant Skelly knew my mother well because Grampie, who spoke several Indian dialects fluently, served as an interpreter in the local courts whenever an Indian sailor was being tried and knew every member of the local constabulary - there again so did most local residents, a 'bobby' as they were called could remain on the same beat for years and watched the kids grow up taking an interest in the ups and downs of the lives of the residents on his patch. My mother when stopped would reply innocently,

'I'm going to meet my dad from the club, Sergeant Skelly.' (Grampie was a steward at the Thompson Street Club of The Royal and Antediluvian Order of Buffaloes) 'Ah, yes,' would answer Sergeant Skelly, 'and what is that in your hand, my dear?'

At this point my mother would tighten her grip on the money and dodging around the Sergeant's long legs scooter off down the steep hill of Thompson Street, '...hell for leather.' She placed many bets and this little scene was re-enacted on many occasions, both parties deriving much amusement from it.

For the benefit of younger readers I should point out that in the Edwardian era the piano was the chief source of home musical entertainment for many people and those who could afford to own an instrument would gather around it whilst a family member or a guest played the popular songs of the day or the classics.

Grampie bought my mother a piano when she was quite young, it was her most treasured possession and she devoted herself to the lessons he paid for, becoming an accomplished pianist at an early age. She went on to pass the highest exams and could proudly put the letters L.R.C.M and L.R.A.M after her name.

Although her performance of the great piano classics was, in my opinion and in many other opinions, of concert hall quality she also loved popular music; her favourite pianist being a man named Charlie Kunz whose virtuoso touch on the keys made the sound appear to swell and subside according to his feeling for the piece. In later years she earned a living as a piano teacher, played with a dance band and performed in a number of concerts.

By the time that she reached her teen years she had become an attractive young woman pursued by local Lotharios who met with small success against the combined defences of a protective father and a shrewish grandmother. She was so shielded that, at the age of twenty-one, she believed that kissing a boy could make you pregnant - it was truly another world.

Perhaps to distract her or to compensate in some way for being over protective my great grandmother would take my mother to the local cinema, or 'picture palace' as it was called, to see the latest silent movie. There my mother would swoon over her hero Rudolph Valentino. There was one snag in this treat, my great grandmother had never learned to read and she would make my mother read the movie's speech insets out loud to her, demanding that she spoke louder and louder to overcome the old woman's deafness and the playing of the pianist who provided a stirring, dramatic or romantic accompaniment to the film.

As my mother told it she would end up almost shouting and they were threatened with violence by other members of the audience on many occasions and even threatened with eviction by the management on several. When Valentino died suddenly my mother was one of the millions of women world wide who mourned him and she claimed that she did not eat for a week and grieved for months.

At the age of eighteen with the help of my grandfather she overcame my great grandmother's resistance and took a job as pianist in a local dance band. She loved playing with the band and developed a crush on the drummer a young man who played under the name Scarlett Ball. He was more protective of her than any parent but died suddenly (ironically of scarlet fever) leaving the band without a drummer and mother without her first love and her protector - she left the band soon after. She always said it was another example of what my grandfather called 'The Family Curse.'

She also played in local concerts and for political rallies. People took their politics seriously in those days and held frequent public meetings and rallies. She was a staunch Conservative and on one occasion when she had spent the evening playing for a Labour Party event she was asked to play the anthem; she began playing "God Save The King"; the party organiser stopped her saying, 'No, No. "The Red Flag."' she told him in plain terms just what she thought of his anthem and left the hall - I do not think she was paid for that night but her honour was satisfied.

Having broken the ties of her grandmother's apron strings she began to go out in the evenings with a girl friend named Kitty. Her escapades with Kitty were innocent and their favourite pastime was to go down to Barry Island of an evening and flirt.

The town of Barry was zoned into three parts: Barry Town, Barry Docks and Barry Island. The Island as it was called was literally a small island joined to the town by a man made causeway. It boasted several golden sanded beaches complete with large flat topped gothic columned shelters and a large funfair - it was the Blackpool of South Wales and immensely popular with holiday makers and day trippers but at night it became the playground of the local lads and lasses.

The boys would gather on top of the beach shelters some seven metres high and as the girls paraded giggling beneath the shelter a boy would shine a torch beam down suddenly - the rule was that if a girl was caught in the spot she must give that boy a kiss and they could end up dating although this was rare.

My mother and Kitty were still playing this harmless little game when they reached their early twenties and had enjoyed a number of pleasant cinema dates as a result. One night my mother was caught in the torch light and as she waited to pay the forfeit she saw a tall Welsh Guardsman approaching, his dress cape slung across one shoulder. He claimed his kiss and with it my mother's heart, she fell instantly and madly in love: he was a handsome man; tall and slim with broad shoulders and a pencil thin film star moustache.

After a short and passionate courtship they decided to wed; both my grandfather and my great grandmother objected for different reasons - he distrusted the young man and she detested soldiers. Nevertheless, they went ahead and on a fine summer day in 1934 they presented themselves at Cardiff Registry Office where my mother received a shock; when the Registrar read out Alec's family name it was not the name by which she knew but a German name.

'You've made a mistake,' she told the Registrar, 'that's not his name.'

'Shut up. It is,' said the groom.

'That's a German name!' shouted my mother, 'I'm not marrying a Hun!' and she stormed out of the office.

Eventually she was coaxed into returning and the wedding went ahead. Like her mother before her she had married a soldier against her parent's wishes she was twenty-four years old and she soon came to regret her decision. Alec left the army soon after their wedding and went to work in a butcher's shop but he only lasted there for a short time and there followed a long spell of unemployment.

They were renting a small house and it was furnished with items from my grandfather's house including my mother's beloved piano. Alec's desire to work was not as strong as his desire for social climbing and through a friend he became embroiled with a local clergyman who saw him as a sort of protégé, neither my mother nor my grandfather approved of this clergyman whose German origins and comments led them to believe he was a Nazi sympathiser.

Alec's film star looks belied his nature and he grew increasingly morose and prone to angry outbursts. One day my mother got into a fierce argument with him and received a beating, the first of many, it left her black and blue and she had to hide from her family for some time in case they tried to become involved.

It was around this time that she discovered that she was pregnant. Alec demanded that she have a back street abortion but she refused and his cruelty increased. One day he told her that he could murder her and nobody would ever know that he had done it, claiming that he could give her a heart attack by shock tactics. She was terrified of him because he would hide in dark corners and, screaming like a madman, leap out on her; she soon became a nervous wreck. He vowed to keep it up until she either went mad or died from heart failure and said that he would succeed because she would never know where he was hiding or what he would do.

The financial situation steadily worsened as Alec spent more and more time with the Reverend Leichner and less and less time seeking casual work, eventually my mother was forced to call on what was known as Parish Relief. There was no Welfare State in those days and Parish Relief was a handout from the Parish Purse for those in dire straits, there was a condition to it, however, it was 'Means Tested.'

A man from Parish Relief came to visit the house and made an inventory of all goods and furnishings, he then told my mother which items she must sell before she could be considered eligible for relief - the first item was her beloved piano. She told me that she cried as it was taken away and she never forgave Alec for putting her in the position of losing it. Up until that time she had not told my grandfather of her plight but when he noticed that the piano was missing she broke down and confessed her poverty, that was when Grampie began giving her small sums of money each week on the condition that she did not tell her husband or give any of it to him.

Alec kept up the pressure on her and several months into her time he finally bullied her into undergoing an abortion; abortions were illegal and dangerous because the quacks that performed them did so in a rough unsanitary way, the result being a high risk of the death of the mother.

After the operation, if it can be called such, the abortionist gave the foetus to Alec and patched my mother up roughly before disappearing; she lay in her bloodstained bed half conscious as Alec left the room carrying the child. When he returned he was as white as a sheet and shaking, 'It was a boy, Dolly,' he said 'and he was perfect.' He knelt by the bed buried his head in his hands and began to sob uncontrollably.

'It was what you wanted,' she said. He raised his head a look of utter despair on his face and said, 'When I pulled the flush he turned and looked up at me. Oh, God forgive me.' She told me many years later that it was at that moment that any love she might have felt for him died.

When in my maturity I played the part of Alfie in the Bill Naughton play of the same name there was a scene in which one of his lovers has an abortion. Alfie stands alone on stage an imaginary foetus in his hands and cries as he tells how perfect the child had been. I was complimented on my tearful performance but in truth I was not acting I was thinking of my long dead brother.

On the financial front things improved when Reverend Leichner gave Alec a job as his secretary, the only snag was that he began to drink and when drunk he became violent, his anger often prompted by my mother's inability to cook. He would often ask her if she expected him to eat such a heap of pig swill and then throw the plate of food at the wall.

My mother was by now several months into another pregnancy and one violent night she told him that she was leaving him and ran out through the rear of the house - he caught up with her in the back lane knocked her down and then kicked her in the stomach. Leaving her to crawl back into the house on her own he went to bed and collapsed in a drunken stupor.

My sister, Marina, was born with epilepsy something that my mother claimed was due to that kick in the stomach. I will refrain from recounting the cruelest and the most sordid of that wicked man's crimes against my mother, sufficient to say that he plumbed the depths of cruelty and depravity.

At first Marina's epilepsy was not detected but when it eventually was the doctors recommended that she be placed in an institution known as "An Epileptic Colony" this was, in my view, similar to a leper colony inasmuch as it performed the function of removing victims of epilepsy from society under the pretext of providing special care for them. The colony was in Chalfont Saint Giles, England and was for my mother an unreachable distance away from South Wales; so, apart from rare holidays, Marina was not to see my mother or return to family life for sixteen years.

Chapter Two

The Second World War broke out and Alec, being a reservist, was amongst the first to be called up. A year later he was captured by the Germans and despite the cruelty that she had endured at his hands my mother must have retained a bond of affection for him because she would tell a story relating to his capture; on the night that it occurred she dreamed that she was in a darkened cobbled street and heard the sound of German jack boots marching towards her, she then heard shots and Alec's voice crying, My God, they've got me, Dolly. When he returned to her at the end of the war she asked him what his thoughts had been at the time of his capture and he replied, 'I said, My God they've got me Dolly.'

This was in the future, however, and as the war outlook for Britain grew grimmer my mother had plenty to cope with because she was pregnant with me; I was the result of the wartime shortage of nylon stockings. To make ends meet my mother accepted the billeting of an armaments worker, a young Wolverhampton man named George. According to her he was a few years younger than she and quite handsome; he was also a lady's man and tried on a number of occasions to have his way with her, to no avail.

Then on a day when she was feeling particularly alone he came home with a pair of nylon stockings, something that my mother, like most young women in wartime, could only dream of. 'They're for you,' he said, 'on condition that I put them on you,' and so I was conceived, another unwanted love child – although that is really a misnomer because there was no love involved.

George was assigned to another port soon after and never knew that he had left me behind him. I cannot find it in my heart to condemn my mother, she had suffered years of abuse in a loveless marriage and must have been desperate for affection.

On my birth she wrote to Alec in his prisoner of war camp and confessed her betrayal of him. It must have been a cruel blow for a man in his situation but he forgave her and agreed to adopt me through the army adoption scheme.

How far back does memory go? Some people claim to remember as far back as their pre-birth time in the womb. A good many of my friends can, they claim, remember back to their first year. I cannot recall my first year, or the second, or the third and I believe that many a person's recollections of infant years are simply subconsciously recalled stories that they were told as a child.

I am told that I had all the usual childhood ailments such as chickenpox, measles and so on; I also had convulsion fits. At the age of three months I began to have one fit after another and my mother lost count. I was turning blue by the time the family doctor arrived and he immediately demanded a large bowl filled with very hot water and one filled with cold water; stripping me naked he plunged me into the hot water and held me there for a second or two. He then removed me and plunged me into the cold water. He continued with this drastic remedy until the fits ceased and I have no doubt that he saved my life.

That my earliest recollections are few is probably due to gripe water, this popular indigestion remedy for children was at that time made from a base of alcohol and to pacify me my mother would fix a rubber teat onto a bottle of the liquid and let me get on with it; I must have spent the first couple of years of life in a happy alcohol induced daze.

One memory is, however, distinct. I remember waking up in the deep well of the feather mattress and sensing that I was all alone in the dark room with its threatening shadows; I was terrified and began to scream loudly, then I felt my mother's arm around me, knew her warmth, smelled her scent and was safe. I sobbed into her side as the dawn filtered through the Venetian blinds that hung in the bay window of our room. I remember her tired voice as she attempted to lull me to sleep by singing "The Old Lamp Lighter" a popular song of the times.

My mother's scent was like the scent of burnt sugar, a scent that I have since concluded is the natural smell of woman, the only smell to compare with its wonder is the smell of the earth after a summer rain shower and I think it a shame that so many women disguise it with manufactured perfumes.

In 1943 my great grandmother caught pneumonia and died; as I mentioned earlier I have no memory of that lady and she was certainly a lady, living a life governed by moral and religious doctrine and strict rules of etiquette, something that she passed on to my mother who was called the lady by her working class peers - behind her back of course.

My mother would tell me the story of her grandmother's death: as a young girl Sarah Anne, my great granny's name although her family called her Saranne, had fallen deeply in love with a midshipman named John and they had hoped to marry, her parents, however, had other ideas considering their daughter far too good for a common sailor.

Sarah Anne, unlike her daughter and granddaughter, bowed to their wishes and John sailed away. When she met the socially acceptable land worker John her parents blessed their union and she became Mrs. John Bagley but she never forgot her first love.

As my great granny lay dying with pneumonia my mother would give her frequent sips of brandy to revive her, when the doctor discovered this he told her that she was being cruel and should let the old woman go naturally. My mother did as she was told and the old lady slowly declined until late one night when my mother, sleeping as I have said in the downstairs parlour, heard a noise from the front hall; cautiously opening the door she discovered her grandmother standing in her night gown before a wide open front door.

'Oh, God, Mum,' she cried, 'what are you doing?'

'It's all right, Dolly,' said the old lady, 'I was talking to John.'

'Let's get you back to bed before you catch your death of cold,' said my mother and she led her back upstairs.

I think that the irony of that last remark was lost on my mother because she always told of it with a straight face. When she had the old lady safely in bed she asked her what she had been doing and she replied,

'I heard a loud knocking on the front door and when I came down the stairs I saw the sun shining brightly through the fanlight above the door, when I opened the door it was the brightest daylight that you ever saw and my John was standing there.'

'You mean my granddad?' asked my mother, referring to John Bagley.

'No, no, *my* John, my sailor John,' said my great grandmother. 'I opened the door, Dolly, and he was standing there in his midshipman's uniform just as he was on the day that I last saw him. Oh, the sun was so bright and he looked so handsome and he said, "I've come for you, Saranne" and then you came out and he vanished and it was all dark.'

'You must have been dreaming, Mum,' said my mother. 'You'll feel better in the morning.'

'I won't be with you in the morning, Dolly,' replied the old lady. 'I'll be with my John.'

At that point my mother began crying and her grandmother told her to go back to bed and not to worry about her. The next morning she found her grandmother dead; there was a smile on the old lady's lips as if she was completely at peace.

Some of my happiest early memories are of moments with my Grampie and I recall his snowy white hair and quick manner. He slept in a large high backed armchair in front of the black iron range and fireplace in the kitchen - by then the extra bedrooms were allocated to lodgers - and he always had a cat on his lap, Grampie loved cats and despite a constant nagging from my mother he always had four or five strays under his wing.

Even when angry and I heard him so on occasions, particularly when he heard my mother getting cross with me as she did frequently having inherited her grandmother's quick and fiery temper, Grampie never swore not even a 'bloody' or a 'damn.' My mother would say that he was proud of that fact saying that swearing was the last resort of the ignorant and that never in his life had he resorted to it - how I wish that I could make the same claim.

In those days it was every boy's ambition to own a pocket knife, or a penknife as we called it, the bigger the better and if it had several blades and a 'thing for taking stones out of horse's hooves,' you were the cock of the walk. Grampie owned a two bladed silver pen knife and he told me that it would be mine when I was old enough to use it. He would sharpen it using the top flagstone of the steps that ran up from our small back courtyard to the long narrow back garden as a whetstone. Spitting on the stone to provide lubrication he would briskly work the edge of the blade against it, testing the sharpness periodically with his thumb, when he was satisfied he would produce an old handkerchief from his pocket and wipe first the blade and then the step - if that step is still there it will have a worn edge as a result of years of knife sharpening.

One day, following a sharpening session, Grampie said,

'Davie, I'm going to teach you how to make a bow and arrow like the ones the Fuzzie Wuzzies use.'

I didn't have a clue what a Fuzzie Wuzzie was but it sounded like a good game. We went up the garden where he cut a long stick from a shrub. He then cut several smaller and thinner twigs and sitting down on the top step he proceeded to peel the bark off the long stick leaving a small portion un-peeled in the centre Next he produced a length of thick string and formed the stick into a bow, the thinner twigs soon became arrows and I received my first lesson in archery at the expense of a poor old rhododendron shrub. I realise now that I was lucky to be born in that pre-electronic age when people found time to educate children in the pleasure that could be gained from simple toys.

He would sometimes bring out his scrap album, this was a large black leather bound volume resembling the large bibles that you sometimes see in a church, it was quite thick with a great many pages containing drawings, photographs, valentine cards, birthday cards, cuttings, coloured scraps and even pressed flowers.

The Victorian cards were exquisitely decorated in the most subtle of colours and the ones that I liked best were the embossed ones where I could run my fingers over the flowers and feel their shapes. Near the front of the book were several brightly coloured pastel drawings of Arabian Desert scenes with pyramids and palm trees Grampie explained that these were drawings that my mother had made as a child,

'Aren't they good' he would ask and, 'Oh, yes, Grampie,' would come from a little boy impressed with his mother's cleverness. Further on in the book were several large sepia photographs of a grave at Agra, 'That is where my first wife is sleeping,' said Grampie, 'One day when I go to heaven they will put me there alongside her.' He was not to get his wish and lays buried in the cemetery at Barry far from his beloved India and his first love. The album like everything else of my grandfather's including his war medals, his silver pocket knife and his gold hunter pocket watch and chain was not destined to be mine.

After my great grandmother's death Grampie took over the tenancy of the house and as much out of sympathy for their plight as the need to help with the rent he took in a couple who had fled from Nazi Germany, a Mr. and Mrs. Steiner. To accommodate the Steiners my mother and I were moved down into the front parlour that had been turned into a bed-sitting room for the purpose.

My memories of that time are fragmented and mainly of trivial events or occurrences I do, however, vividly recall my first misdeed: it happened when I must have been about four years old, my mother had a friend name Mrs. Dubrovnik who had a daughter, Lily, about my age and she would bring Lily with her on her visits so that we could play together. On one occasion my mother had the idea of making a tent for us out of the counterpane by propping it up with a broomstick, Lily and I crawled in and for a while we chattered away as kids do, then for what reason I do not recall as I do not recall who began the game, we began to explore each other's anatomy in great depth.

For some time we each examined the other's most intimate zones with the innocence of two curious puppies. It was obvious to me that Lily had met with an accident to her groin and I examined her injuries. As I sympathetically explored she began to giggle and cried out that I was tickling her. Suddenly my mother alerted by Lily's giggles threw back our tent and discovered our game; there was no doubting the nature of our escapade. 'Ohh! You dirty little bastards!' she screamed, dragging me from bed to floor. Mrs. Dubrovnik in a state of shock meanwhile stood by wringing her hands and muttering over and over again, 'Oh, My God, Oh, My God.'

My mother grabbed the first weapon to hand, unfortunately that happened to be the tent prop stick, and began beating whatever part of my wriggling form came within reach - thankfully she had but little room in which to swing it. She was out of her mind with rage and embarrassment. I believe that she might have done me a serious injury had not Grampie, alerted by my screams, burst in and taken the stick from her - that did not prevent her from kicking me and screaming further abuse - finally she subsided into tears and Grampie removed me from the scene. I never saw Lily or her mother again and I never forgot that day.

Although certain painful incidents stand out I am sure that my early childhood was mainly a happy one; traffic was almost non-existent and like all the other kids I played in the street almost from the time that I could walk, looking up to the older kids with awe and respect because they played many games that we toddlers were only allowed to watch and long to be a part of.

Most girls - and boys - owned a steel hoop; these were made of solid steel bar about a half an inch thick formed into a circle about a yard in diameter, they were bowled along by hand or by means of a small steel rod one end of which was coiled loosely around the hoop. The best thing about the hoop was the dull rumbling noise it made as it was bowled along. The hoops disappeared towards the end of the war and can only guess that they were melted into weapons for the war effort, it would be quite something if Lily Dubrovnik's hoop ended up as part of a fighting tank.

I so badly wanted a hoop but never owned one. I did, however, have a life-sized stuffed toy Wire Haired Terrier mounted on a four-wheeled base and pushed by a wooden handle and I would race down the pavement alongside the hoop rollers usually ending up arse over tip when my Terrier hit an uneven paving slab.

Our street's paving slabs were large flagstones laid irregularly so that the join of any two met the centre of the slab to each side and they provide the pitch for a game that we call Hecksle, probably from the local term 'heck' for hop, but the rest of the world called Hopscotch. The numbers on the slabs were drawn with lumps of broken chalk ornaments because at that time funfairs gave chalk figurines as prizes and if, conveniently, a kid broke one of them he or she had a lifetime's supply of white chalk. Little kids weren't allowed to play Hecksel but we would draw out our own pitch and happily hop along ignoring all rules.

Another game was swinging on a lamp post, Barry still had the old Victorian gas lamps and a lamplighter on a bicycle would pedal around the town at dusk and dawn lighting and extinguishing the flame with a long pole. I was fascinated by the lamplighter, perhaps because my mother had sung the song about him so often. The lamp posts had two protruding arms just below the actual lamp and kids would tie a rope to one of these with a short stick tied to the rope's end for a seat. They would then swing out and around the post until the rope had wrapped itself to its end unwind it and swing again.

Both girls and boys alike played Whip and Top. The wooden top was like a small inverted conical beehive and had a steel stud embedded in the pointed end. This top would be set spinning by a twist of the wrist and then kept in motion by use of a small whip made from short stick and a long leather boot lace. The kids would colour the flat end of the top with chalks so that it blended into a pattern as the top spun and they would use the whips fiercely and with no regard for bystanders. Today's health and safety brigade would be appalled but I could assure them that the onlookers were in far more danger than the top spinners.

A more lethal game was called Tip-Cat, a sort of rounders in which the batting person would have a flat round bat similar to a table tennis bat but a bit larger and a short length of stick the thickness of a man's forefinger that had been sharpened to a point at either end. With the fielders in position the batter would lay the 'cat' on a flat surface and then strike it hard on one pointed end using the edge of the bat, the 'cat' would leap up into the air and the batter would try to hit it as far as he or she could they would then try to score runs whilst the fielders grabbed for the flying 'cat.' If you had any sense you tried to avoid the viciously pointed missile and waited until it had landed.

Then there was the great sport of pestering American soldiers and sailors or 'Yanks' as most of us called them. These generous good hearted men must have been sick of gangs of scruffy kids following them around yelling, 'Got any gum, Chum?' I do not, however, recall an instance of rejection by them or bad temper from them. Everyone, with the exception of a large proportion of British men who feared that they would lose their women to those handsome strangers, loved the yanks. Several of my mother's friends had American boyfriends and we benefited indirectly from their largesse in the form of unobtainable rationed goods

Life was not all play, kids were expected to do chores and run errands from the earliest age and the wonderful thing was that parents could let their children run free or send them on errands alone without the fear that pervades today's society. One of my chores was polishing the big black range in Grampie's kitchen, this was polished to a gleaming finish by means of a product call 'Zebo Polish' the tin adorned with the picture of a zebra, it was I believe a mixture of alcohol and black lead - probably highly toxic and amazingly is still available in a modern form (non-toxic of course).

I had watched my mother polishing the range with its large oven and black iron fender and plagued her to let me use the wooden handled polishing brushes, one day she allowed me to have a go and like the kids encouraged by Tom Sawyer to paint his aunt's fence I jumped at the chance. I must have been all of four years old when I ended up with the job. I wasn't unhappy about the situation, I liked the smell of 'Zebo' and loved to see the shine appearing when the finishing brush was applied although by completion I was as black and shiny as the grate

Another chore was taking up the ashes - all heating was by means of a coal fireplace and every room including bedrooms had such a fireplace, although not all were used daily. Coal was also used in the kitchen range for cooking and usually delivered by way of the front door, the coal man traipsing through the house to the coal house a 112lb sack of coal balanced over one shoulder whilst the householder gave warning directions such as, 'Mind that picture,' or, 'Don't catch that corner.' On his return to the coal cart the empty sacks would be thrown down on the front pavement as proof of quantity delivered for it was bought twenty or more sacks at a time and unscrupulous coal men were known to throw down a sack or two that had never made the journey to the coal house but a canny housewife would stand at the door counting.

I liked to watch the coal men, one man on the flat bed of the horse drawn coal-cart would pull a sack to the edge and another man wearing a leather shoulder protection would back in to it and grasping the rope handle effortlessly heave its weight up onto his back then, one handle over his shoulder the other handle of the open sack pointing up into the air off he would go; coal was cheap but rationed and housewives were as vigilant as hawks when counting sacks. When as a young man I was obliged to heave similar weights up onto my shoulder I often thought of those hard working coal men and smiled.

Those fires that were used needed cleaning out the next morning and this meant that the larger cinders from the fireplace and the small ash and small cinders from the ash pan below had to be removed. The large cinders were saved to be used in kindling the next fire but the small ash was carried out to the back lane and tipped; this sounds like anti social behaviour but in fact it was a community service because none of the back lanes were tarmac surfaced and they were all surfaced with cinders that bedded down as hard as any manufactured preparation. The idea was that you selected an area of lane that had a pothole or thin covering and you spread your cinders on that patch and trod them down, the big drawback from a kid's point of view was that if you fell when running down the lane, your knees received a severe gravel rash wound with the resulting pain. Large galvanised steel rubbish bins were left out once weekly for the 'dustman' but refuse was minimal in those days of fresh produce and paper wrappings that could be used for fire lighting.

Every morning my mother would listen for the loud cry of 'Milko-o!' Then she would send me out to the milkman with a large white jug, her ration book and instructions on how much to buy; milk like most other essentials was strictly rationed. The milkman like so many other street traders drove a horse drawn flat-bed cart in the case of our milkman a low one laden with tall shiny steel milk churns. If you asked him for two pints of milk he would take a long handled steel milk dipper of a certain size from several that hung on the lip of a churn, take the lid off a churn, dip down into the creamy milk and with a twist of his wrist and a flourish that never failed to excite me send a long stream of milk down over a gap of several feet into the jug - I never saw him miss and I often followed him up the street just to see him perform. At each halt he would throw the reins over his horses head so that they trailed on the ground and the horse would stand patiently lifting and lowering his feet like a policeman waiting on a corner.

Another such horse belonged to the rag and bone man whose street cry is almost impossible to put into words it was something like Ra-bowl-ee-o! For a good bundle of old clothes or rags he would give you a goldfish in a large jam jar, these poor fish never lived long because we would only feed them bread crumbs and the oxygen in the jar was limited but when he came around every few weeks we would optimistically hope that this latest fish would live for ever.

The knife grinder rode a bicycle and would sharpen the household knives or scissors to a razor edge for a few pennies. His grindstone was mounted on the back of his bike and he would swivel his seat around pull a lever to engage the gears and pedal like mad to set the wheel spinning. Sparks would fly like miniature fireworks and he would hum a little song as he worked although only he could hear the tune over the noise of the grindstone. Every now and again he would test the blades edge on a blackened thumb and when satisfied he would hand the now lethally sharp knives back to a four-year-old child, collect his pay and begin on the next set. There was always a queue at his bicycle and he must have made a good living for a small outlay.

A major street event in my young life was the visit of the One Man Band. If you were playing in the street as we usually were you could hear him coming and we would run indoors and beg our parent to give us a few coppers for him because he wouldn't't begin to play until the collecting cup that hung from his accordion held enough money but when it did he made the most glorious racket. It wasn't always the same man but each one had a similar range of instruments, to get a good picture of him watch the classic film "Mary Poppins" in which actor Dick Van Dyke appears on one occasion as a One Man Band.

These bandsmen always had a large base drum hanging on their back and usually a pair of cymbals inside their knees, the drumstick was operated by a long string from one heel and a small set of crash cymbals was operated by a string from the other heel, cymbals were tied one to each elbow and a harmonica and a bugle fastened to a sort of cradle that sat on their shoulders to complete the ensemble they would carry an accordion or a piano accordion. It might be a trick of memory but I can only remember them singing one song "MacNamara's Band."

Once he had the money secured the Bandsman would stamp his foot shout, 'A-one-a, two-a, three!' and he would be away singing loudly, "Oh my name is Macnamara; I'm the leader of the band!" He needed to bellow over the banging of his drums and crashing of his cymbals. When he reached the end of his song his audience, mostly kids, would cheer him loudly - we were not demanding - and that would inspire him to even greater efforts. During the song he would provide a harmonica break for a few bars and then begin bawling out the words again, by the time he'd finished his lengthy performance he would be red in the face and running with perspiration but the applause he received would have delighted any Covent Garden star. He would then bang the drum two or three times and march out of the street giving a ragged encore.

Another band that featured largely in my early years was the band of the local Sea Cadet Corps, led by a drum major named Monty, who was the hero of boys and girls alike. They marched through the town with bugles and drums on all civic and public occasions. Monty carried a tall mace with a large silver head and he would twirl it and twist it in the most amazing fashion. More impressively he would throw it high into the air at frequent intervals. Up it would spin propelled by his arm and its weight higher than the surrounding buildings, it would then appear to hang there for a second before descending for a perfect catch from the thrower; Monty's mace twirling always drew applause from the onlookers and I fondly remember him and his band of young men marching proudly in their smart navy uniforms, belts and gaiters gleaming white in the sunlight.

As much as I enjoyed the street play and the visits of the traders there were moments of unhappiness, I was particularly disliked by and constantly the victim of revilement from a neighbour, an Irish woman named Mrs. O'Rourke, who detested me and made no secret of it. I once overheard my mother telling her friend Kitty on one of her visits that Mrs. O'Rourke had said that I was the bastard child of the devil and would come to a bad end.

'She's barmy,' said Kitty, 'she keeps her shroud folded up under her bed.'

'Yes I know,' whispered my mother, 'and she washes and starches it so that it will be nice on the day.'

I asked my mother what a bastard child was and she told me it was a child who did not know the name of its father. 'Am I a bastard child, Mum?' I asked. 'No,' she replied, 'I knew the name of your father.' My mother later told me that around the time of my birth Mrs. O'Rourke had been delivered of a boy who was been born 'deaf and dumb' as the saying was. Like my poor sister he had been taken away to a special residency. She blamed herself, my mother said, because during an air raid whilst pregnant she clapped her hands over her mouth and her ears and believed that caused her son to be born afflicted. Whatever the reason that woman hated me and wasted no opportunity to make my life difficult. She would still expect me to run errands for her if only for the chance to find fault with me.

I ran errands for several neighbours to the shop at the top of our street usually to buy something small like a box of matches or a gas mantle. Safety matches were unheard of and the two popular brands were "Swan Vestas" also called "The Smoker's Match" and "England's Glory" with its patriotic picture of a World War I Dreadnought on the front. Matches were not regarded as dangerous for a child and any would be juvenile arsonist could obtain a plentiful supply at any time.

Electricity had not yet reached our street and an essential for our household lighting was the gas mantle a small china ring that clipped onto its metal equivalent on the household gas jet, below the ring was a small woven bag impregnated with some chemical and although they could be handled when new once they had been put in place and ignited the bag turned to a fragile white crystal that glowed with a white heat and turned the dim gas jet into a brilliant white light almost as bright as a modern electric lamp (we made do with candles in the bedrooms.)

Between listening intently to the chatter of my mother and her friends, learning from Grampie, running errands, playing in the street and following street entertainers my early years were quite full and mainly happy and I was blissfully unaware of the global tragedy that was World War Two. One major family event occurred soon after my great grandmother's death, my mother had lived a lonely life for several years and in the autumn of that year she met, fell in love with and became pregnant by a Swedish soldier named Erik.

When I was older she would talk about Erik. 'He was so handsome,' she would say. She would recall that he had china blue eyes and a mass of blonde hair and that he was so gentle - gentleness in a man must have been an attractive feature after the physical abuse she had suffered. When her delivery was due she disappeared from my life and I went to live with Kitty, I was probably with her for about six weeks but I completely forgot my mother.

Some weeks later Kitty led me into her front parlour to greet a strange woman, who wore a blue pinafore dress,

'Look who's here,' David," she said.

The woman reached out and pulled me into a tight embrace and I burst into tears not recognising my own mother.

I never saw my little sister, whom my mother named Sonja after Sonja Henie the famous Scandinavian skating star, because she was adopted from the hospital and my mother never saw her again; in her later years she would talk about her baby girl, how beautiful she had been and how she longed to see her just one time but she never did and - respecting my sister's privacy I have made no serious attempt to trace her. Following the "tears" incident I quickly realised that this was my beloved mother and was happy again.

Apart from my mother an early love was a tiny elderly creature named Mrs. Adzed, I never knew her first name she was simply Mrs. Adzed and always will be; that does not diminish her importance in my life or the affection that I felt for her. She carried with her the scent of lavender, peppermints and talcum powder, and she must have been in her seventies. I suppose that there was at some time a Mr. Adzed, but I never met him or heard him mentioned - not that his presence would have occurred to me, I was after all only five years of age.

Mrs. Adzed was like a little Victorian doll she was scarcely much taller than me, clad head to toe in black she might have stepped out of a novel by Dickens. I recall vividly her neck high ankle length lace embroidered dress and how shiny her pointed-toed patent leather shoes were with a strap across each instep fastened by a tiny bright button. Her silvery white hair was bound back in a bun and surmounted by a small black bonnet pinned in place with large hat pins.

She was a Bristolian by birth and she would chatter away to my mother about Bristol and her life there, one tale stands out in my memory; she had sent me on an errand up to the corner shop - oh yes, five year olds were sent out on messages and shopping trips without a care in those happy days of innocence and pre-nanny state times - when I returned and handed over her bag of sweets and couple of coppers change she dropped a sweet in my mouth and told me that I was a good boy and that I reminded her of a little boy who had run her errands in Bristol.

'He always brought my change back and never loitered or lost anything. He's a famous man now,' she said, 'and his name is Cary Grant but I knew him as little Archie Leach. I can see him now in his woollen jersey and shorts; his socks were always down around his ankles.' It would be years before the significance of her tale dawned on me but the description could have been of any boy on our street. This was long before the age of the fashion conscious child and in our world dress was standard and plain.

Boys wore a vest and an undergarment called a liberty bodice (a misnomer because it was thick, stiff and tightly binding) with a plain cotton shirt and grey flannel short trousers held up by over the shoulder suspenders called braces or a brightly coloured elasticated belt with a "snake" buckle – the pockets of these trousers were always bulging with the treasures of boyhood such as marbles, pen knives, bits of string and any shiny object that took a boy's fancy. This clothing was topped by a long sleeved woolen jersey in winter or a garishly patterned "Fair Isle" sleeveless pullover. The only concession to fashion was the belt that came in a number of bright striped colours.

Girls wore vest, liberty bodice and navy blue bloomers with a plain or patterned cotton dress and a woolen cardigan. Most boys wore lace up boots and girls patent leather strap over shoes in winter; boys and girls wore sandals in summer. Neither boys nor girls were given any say in their dress. We had no say in our dress but wore what we were told to wear.

Mrs. Adzed introduced me to the world of art and gave me my first lesson, she could not have known how largely art was to figure in my life and although, due to infirmity, I can no longer hold a paint brush or pencil and, lacking the talent or determination of Renoir who had a brush bandaged into his hand, I just do not bother (a very small loss to the art world). I can, however, still appreciate beauty and fine art and sometimes dream of that first naive lesson. She came to visit one day struggling with a blackboard and easel having set it up she told me that it was mine and that she was going to teach me to draw pictures. She produced a box of brightly coloured chalks (all colours are bright when you are young and only become common place if you allow age to dull your vision and imagination)

'We are going to draw a sea scene,' she said. 'First, we'll draw the sky.'

Many years have passed since that wonderful afternoon, but I can still feel the excitement of watching her as she slowly, with much explanation, drew a seascape on the blank black surface of the board. I leaned against her knee as, seated on the edge of a dining room chair. She first selected a blue stick of chalk and using its broad side began to sweep bright blue strokes across the upper half of the board this she continued until the top half was sky; then, wetting a finger with the tip of her tongue, she rubbed out small circular patches of the sky and filled them in with white. She stepped back,

'Clouds,' she said in a satisfied tone of voice.

I was fascinated by this magic and watched in spellbound silence. 'Now for the sea' and she quickly drew a line of inverted vees in green representing the peaks of waves, she drew another line of the same just below the first and carried on until she reached the bottom of the board. At this point she paused stood back and looked at me for comment, I had none and could only stare at here Mrs. Adzed smiled,

'Now, what sails on the sea?' She asked.

'Ships!' I had seen pictures of ships and felt proud of my knowledge.

'You are a clever boy. Now we will draw a ship.'

Out came the white chalk and it was used to create two large triangular sails perched atop the line of the waves. She then used brown to draw a long thick line just below the sails, a line rising to a pointed bow at each end. She stood back again,

'Can you see what is missing?' She asked.

I was too astounded at her achievement to answer.

'We need seagulls.'

41

The white chalk and a series of elongated 'm' shapes corrected the omission and the work was complete. I have stood in admiration before great works of art but never have I felt a greater respect or excitement than that I felt when I stood before that blackboard on the day that Mrs. Adzed drew the sea. That sweet lady was soon to disappear along with all things good and secure following the death of Grampie.

I hope that she found another little boy to teach and inspire.

Chapter Three

My fifth birthday arrived and it was time to begin my schooling. On one bright summer day my mother took me through the narrow ash surfaced back lane that was a shortcut from our street to the local school, although the school had always been a short distance away it had never been a part of my sphere of activities and I was stunned by the size and grandeur of this great red brick building with its many tall windows.

We entered a through a large double door and I was immediately aware of the smell of chalk, polish and the other scents that go into making up the indescribable and unforgettable smell of a school; there is nothing quite like it and even sixty years later I can walk into a school and be transported back to my first day in the classroom.

The classroom was like any one of a multitude of classrooms, a large double blackboard on one wall, high windows masked to discourage distracted pupil's attention, walls covered with brightly coloured drawings and paintings and row upon regimented row of small two-seater desks. Most of the desks were occupied but, after she had introduced me to my classmates, my teacher led to a vacant seat next to a blonde haired boy, 'This is Peter,' she said, 'He will show you what to do, David.'

Peter was a kind and patient desk mate and during the course of the morning he showed me where the modelling clay and bricks were kept with which we re to amuse ourselves and during playtime he stuck by me and shielded the new kid from the rougher elements in the playground.

At lunchtime I ate the jam sandwiches that my mother had wrapped in a brown paper bag for my lunch and had a free bottle of milk to wash them down with. In those days of scarcity and food rationing there was no such thing as a 'packed lunch' containing the variety and quantity that you see today, kids usually had jam sandwiches or very rarely cheese sandwiches (cheese was rationed) but as I did not know any better in I never felt deprived in any way and I really enjoyed the free milk.

After lunch I returned to the classroom and Peter produced sheets of paper with squared divisions on them, he then showed me how to form the letters A B C in the boxes. I was enjoying this game when I felt a pang of discomfort in my lower stomach; my bowels were reacting to the excitement and the milk, bread and jam. I attempted to hold back nature's complaining demands not having been told that I could ask to go to the lavatory (my mother insisted on lavatory, saying that the word 'toilet' was common). I bravely fought the losing battle for goodness knows how long and then nature won out over shame and fear and let loose the floodgates, the result was disgusting and I was horrified and mortified. Peter edged away from me and a child in the next aisle put her hand up crying,

'Please, Miss.'

The teacher approached and wrinkled her nose. Then with a look of utter disgust distorting her pretty face she took me by the arm and led me to the door, 'Go home. You filthy little beast,' she hissed and pushed me into the hallway.

How clearly I remember my shameful progress from the school and down that lane, I now believe that in addition to my ignorance of toilet procedure I must have had some type of stomach bug because my griping pain continued all the way home and I was in an awful mess by the time I knocked at the front door.

My mother opened the door, 'What are you doing home so early?' she asked and then wrinkled her nose, 'Oh, My God! she cried, "Get up those bloody stairs!" hurling me in front of her and half throwing half kicking me up to the bedroom,

'Don't sit on the bed!' she screamed, 'Just stand still!' and I froze in fear of her wrath. She then proceeded to peel my clothing from me, muttering threats and obscenities as she did so and holding each garment at arms length she dropped it onto a sheet that she had spread on the floor; there were quite a few items to remove, like most kids I wore the full combination of vest, liberty bodice, a white long sleeved shirt and a knitted sleeveless pullover - no wind would blow on me.

'Don't move!,' she shrieked and left the room.

I stood there naked, shivering in shame and fear until she returned with a bowl of water and a flannel. She washed and dried me and comforted by the warm water and its cleansing powers I began to feel better. After another admonishment for me to stand still she grabbed the sheet together with my clothing and left the room again. Once more I stood naked alone and cold but relaxed glad that the worst was over.

My mother returned shortly and she was carrying the leather tipped suspenders or braces that were used to hold up my trousers, as soon as I saw the leather thongs and the look in her eye I began to back away from her but she was too fast for me. Grabbing my arm tightly enough to leave bruises that lasted for days she threw me down on the bed and began to lash me with the leather end of the braces,

'No, Mum!' I yelled, 'No, Mum! Please don't!'

She could not hear me because she was beside herself with rage and the fact that for every hit she gave my struggling body she gave herself a hit on her hands did not help matters. How long the beating lasted I cannot tell but I ran out of the strength to scream and struggle and could only lay there sobbing and gasping for breath; finally I heard Grampie's voice crying,

'Good grief, Dolly, what are you doing to that child?' Seeing that she was not going to stop he grabbed her arm and said, 'That's enough, what do you want to do kill him?'

My mother came slowly to her senses and began to call me all the dirty little bastards under the sun, she was still shouting at me as Grampie led me from the room and took me down to the kitchen where he wrapped me in one of his cardigans in front of the fire. I carried the bruises and weals from that beating for weeks and never forgot it. Another odd side effect was that I can recall nothing of my early schooldays following that awful afternoon.

When my mother was in good humour - and that was most of the time - she would sit with me in front of the fireside and tell stories about our family many of which were about the supernatural, there was a tradition of oral history on her mother's side and Grampie had also told my mother many tales about his life and family. I cannot recall all of these yarns and do not think you would want to read them, one or two, however, stick out in my memory.

My grandmother's grandfather was a man named John Rees who lived in the small Welsh village of Penmark. He was a devout man, a lay preacher who would walk ten miles each way on a Sunday to deliver a sermon but he was also a heavy drinker who frequently staggered home from the pub blind drunk. One night after a particularly heavy drinking session he was making his way home across a large field known to the locals as 'The Devil's Field', so called because there had been several suicides by hanging from the old tree that stood in its centre; he had crossed this field hundreds of times man and boy and knew every inch of it.

He made his way across the field in the dim light cast by the moon and headed for the gate that led to his home lane it was not there, or at least he could not find it. Muttering drunken grumbles he began to move around the tall hedgerow seeking the exit and found himself back at the entrance, he carried on moving around the edge of the field stumbling and muttering and this time could not even find the entrance. By now he was sobering up and decided that his problem was drink and that he might as well wait for the dawn, so he went and sat under the old tree. He began to nod off but was awakened by a voice apparently coming from the tree,

'Go on hang yourself,' said the voice.

He shook himself and after a while settled down again but no sooner had he done so than the voice came,

'Hang yourself, you old sinner, you're no good to anyone. They'd be better without you.'

It was then that he saw the small shadowy figures leaping and cavorting around him and the tree, indistinguishable as human or animal but undoubtedly evil and malicious. He became a very frightened man and began to pray loudly, asking God for protection. This appeared to silence the voices and frighten off the figures and he leaned back against the tree trunk exhausted but as he settled himself it all began again and went on throughout the long night.

With the coming of dawn he arose and dragged his tired feet towards the exit gate; there it was where it had always been. He made his way up the narrow lane that led to his cottage and as he turned the final corner he stopped dead in his tracks; in the lane before the entrance to his home stood a small hearse with two white ponies standing in the shafts their heads adorned with tall white plumes.

He ran past the hearse and burst into the cottage calling out his wife's name and when she rushed out of the kitchen startled by the panic in his voice he asked her what was happening.

'Happening?' the poor woman enquired.

'What in God's name is that hearse doing outside our house?'

She looked out of the front door and turned to him quietly, 'There's nothing outside, my love,' she answered gently.

Eventually they agreed that he had been imagining things and his panic subsided. Two weeks later their youngest child died suddenly and when the small child's hearse arrived it was drawn by the two white ponies with their plumed head dresses. I would like to report that she ended the story by saying that John Rees became a teetotaller: that was not the case but although he continued to enjoy his strong ale he always took the long road home from the pub.

Another story that my mother was fond of telling was the one about the Marquess. She claimed that a powerful Marquess, whose name would be instantly recognised by any Welsh person, had taken advantage of an ancestor of ours who was in his service and made her pregnant. He had then married her off to his Gilly who had accepted paternity. My mother said that when they died the Marquess paid for an expensive funeral for each in turn together with headstones. If the story is true I can claim descent from Mary Queen of Scots but the throne is safe because I will never know the truth of the tale.

My mother's stories helped many a long evening hour to pass for there was no television or such in those days the only home entertainment of that nature being the Wireless Relay Radio that stood on the windowsill in Grampie's kitchen. The Wireless Relay was a precursor of today's cable television the signal being relayed by wires from a large aerial mast. It cost something like sixpence a week and gave you listening access to the BBC Home Service and the BBC Light Programme.

Grampie allowed me to listen to the radio with him and we would sing along to the popular wartime songs - I knew the words of "Run, Rabbit. Run, Rabbit, Run, Run, Run" before I knew what a rabbit was. I was made to be silent for the news, however, and the Prime Minister's speeches - Winston Churchill was held in the highest regard in our house, his words being almost regarded as sacred text. I recalled those days many years later when I played the role of Churchill on stage, intoning those same speeches in what I hoped was an acceptable facsimile of his inimitable delivery.

My fondness for the stage probably began around that time when, near the end of the war, I was taken to my first pantomime. It was "Aladdin" and it was staged in the local Welfare Hall a large Nissan hut with a small proscenium stage at one end. Seating was provided by long narrow wooden benches, scenery was made of garishly painted cardboard, an upright piano acted as orchestra, the costumes were all home made and lighting changes were accompanied by electrical arcing and curses from the wings. I was entranced from the Dame's first entrance to the last drawn out notes of 'Now Is The Hour' with which they closed the show. My throat hoarse from yelling, 'oh, no you don't!' or, 'oh, yes. he does!' I left the hall captivated by the theatrical experience and pantomime in particular.

As a grown man writing for the stage I have scribbled and seen staged many of my pantomimes including "Aladdin" but none ever will or ever could compare to that magical amateur performance at The Colcot Welfare Hall, Barry. (Curious footnote: although I was to leave the area and not return for over thirty years, I ended up marrying the daughter of that wonderful pantomime's hilarious Dame and we have shared thirty-five happy years together.)

On a summer day in my fourth year I went out to play in the street and saw that hanging from a lamp post bar, that usually held a rope swing, was a life sized dummy figure made from old clothing tied and stuffed, its head made from a stuffed white pillowcase had a face crudely drawn on its front to represent a moustached man with a lick of hair hanging down on his forehead; the figure was suspended by a noose around its neck and years later I realised it represented Adolph Hitler.

The European phase of World War Two had ended, it was V.E. (Victory in Europe) Day and the effigy was a part of the celebrations. That night my mother took me up to the Town Square, it was only a short walk from our street but it took some time because the pavement and the road was a mass of people shoulder to shoulder singing and dancing. I felt scared by those thousands of bodies, I had never seen more than a handful of people before and the noise was tremendous with people blowing horns and rattling wooden football rattles. The Town Hall was lit up by a large V made of lighted coloured lamps and reaching two stories high. If the pavements had been crowded the square was impassable and after greeting and embracing one or two friends my mother took me back home.

The victory celebrations were closely followed by the street parties. Throughout the nation streets were decorated with red, white and blue bunting and national flags; tables of all description covered with white bed sheets as tablecloths were laid down the middle of the street and chairs were brought out from every house. It was a superb example of the community spirit fostered by war, for a common enemy brought people closer together although that does not seem to apply today try as governments might to find a common enemy or even create one.

Rationing was still in full force but food that had been scarce for years miraculously appeared on dishes ranged down the length of the tables. Blancmanges, jellies, cooked ham, real dairy butter, tarts and pies there was everything that people had been without for years and it is likely that a great deal of it was black market and even more of the food donated by the ever generous

American troops stationed around the district. Large jugs of fizzy lemonade for the kids and beer for the grown ups completed the feast. A piano was dragged out and I believe that it was my mother who struck up a nonstop medley of popular songs: "Roll Out The Barrel", Knees Up Mother Brown" and "Okey Cokey".

I was seated at a table and asked what I wanted to eat by a kindly woman. The adults were all serving the kids and making sure that they had plenty of everything, laughing when a boy or a girl failed to recognise food that they had never seen before. After the food had been consumed and I mean totally consumed the tables were cleared away and the dancing and singing began.

Regrettably, the street party has, with rare exceptions, disappeared from our lives, probably because it would breach some regulation or other, but it was a major event in my childhood and was not repeated until the coronation of Queen Elizabeth the Second. That party was the last in my experience and appeared to spell the end of such community events.

A few months later these victory scenes were repeated with the difference that the lights spelled out a V J to celebrate victory over Japan. My mother must have been really happy because she hated Germans and Japanese with a passion that remained with her for life, even in her last years she called the Germans Nazis pronouncing it (as did her hero Winston Churchill), 'Narrzzees' and the Japanese were Little Yellow Perils. I cannot condemn her for that when I remember that her generation had seen two World Wars and suffered in and from both.

Apart from the street festivities the end of the war did not greatly affect my young life, Double British Summertime was to continue for some years and kids could and in my case did play outside until eleven o'clock at night. The summer of 1945 was as lovely as were all the summers of my early years.

Do not listen to anyone who says that the long golden summers of those years were a trick of memory; they were not, they lasted from April to September and boys in their short sleeved shirts and grey flannel short trousers and girls in their short cotton dresses were as brown as berries, thanks to the hours that we spent playing outdoors.

During the summer of the year following victory my sister, Marina, came home for a short holiday, at the time my mother was working washing dishes in a Greek owned fish and chip restaurant on Barry Island. She would take Marina and me to work with her and I loved the smell of the frying fish and chips and their taste, cooked in Greek olive oil. She worked with a young deaf and dumb man who would sign his passion for her with his hands and who, to clear us out of the way, give Marina and me a shilling apiece to go and play on the nearby fun fair.

I always made a beeline for the helter skelter that great tall lighthouse like structure with its spiral staircase inside and its spiral slide outside, Marina would help me climb the twisting staircase clutching my square of coconut matting to sit on and make sure that I was seated safely before launching me with a gentle shove. It cost three pennies a time and we soon used up our eight turns or two shillings worth and returned to impede the progress of my mother's admirer.

In what was probably desperation to get rid of me - Marina was quite happy to go and sit on the wide golden sands of the beach - my mother's would-be suitor took me out to the back lane, gave me several empty matchboxes and showed me where to find caterpillars in the hedge that ran along one side of the lane. Poor caterpillars, I was more ruthless than any African big game hunter in my pursuit of their tiny fat green bodies dropping each victim into a matchbox with a dock leaf for food and then going back to the hunt. I would like to think that my mother, who when not in a temper was tender hearted, later released them into Grampie's garden where they could feast on his shrubs and flowers.

At the end of summer Marina returned in tears to confinement in the epileptic colony but before she left my sister spent her remaining pocket money on a gift for me, a brightly coloured lead miniature of a cowboy on a rearing white horse. I could not believe my eyes, he was magnificent one hand waving aloft a white Stetson his red neckerchief blowing in the wind (as I had seen a few western films by then) I could almost hear his cry of, 'Yippee!'

I took my cowboy everywhere with me, I even took him to bed - a mistake - he ended up being sent to the laundry with the sheets and I never saw him again. He was the forerunner of an army of lost possessions because my life was soon to change dramatically and permanently.

Before that change, however, another took place, Alec returned from his lengthy imprisonment by the Germans. He was seven stones in weight at six feet three inches tall and my mother was horrified at his appearance. He told her that he had been on the thousand mile death march as the Germans marched their prisoners away from the advancing Allied armies, he cried as he talked and she later told me that her heart went out to him, nevertheless she had to tell him about Sonja and naturally he took the news hard. In order to give them time together to heal the rift in their marriage I was sent to stay with his family in a nearby village.

Alec's parents lived in a large three-storied house and I slept with one of my cousins in his attic bedroom, the stairs were steep and because I was nervous I would descend each morning for breakfast by bouncing from step to step on my bottom. Breakfast consisted of porridge oats with cream and as much sugar as you liked followed by kedgeree, bacon, eggs, sausages and kidney accompanied by thickly buttered toast (and this in the days of food rationing).

You may wonder why I remember this in such detail, it is simply because I had never seen breakfast served from a line of chafing dishes spread along the top of a long sideboard - I could not reach the sideboard and so I was given whatever I asked for by my older cousin and I asked for everything - how anyone moved after such a spread I cannot say but following breakfast we would dress and go down to the nearby beach.

There are times in life when one comes close to heaven on earth, I can recall very few but the first trip to that small shingle beach is one. My cousin, Jeanette, led our small party myself, two male cousins who were a year or two older than me and Jeanette herself who was about ten years of age.

The path to the beach was bounded on one side by a tall hedgerow and on the other by the wire fence of a meadow, the day was hot and the still air was disturbed only by the wings of countless butterflies, busily buzzing bees and the periodic emergence of panic stricken birds from the hedge, flapping desperately to lure the intruders away. The scent of the hedgerow bulging with wild flowers was so heady to my young senses that I turned my head as I walked so that I would not miss any of it, that scent was mingled with the smell of the meadow grass and its flowery field mates.

The sun shone, my head spun with the heat and intoxication of nature's perfumery and I was speechless with happiness as my cousins chattered merrily on their way. Jeanette, however, smiling down at me as if she knew how I was feeling stayed close holding my hand. I was disappointed when the path abruptly ended and we found ourselves at the top of the beach but soon found myself distracted by the rock pools and the other distractions on offer.

I have passed that small lane many times but I have resisted the desire to walk down it certain that it would hold no magic for a cynical old man and happy to retain the memory of a sunny day so many years ago.

When I returned from my short holiday Alec was no longer in residence and only when I was much older did my mother tell me that he had met another woman and gone to live with her, he obviously could not forgive my mother for two betrayals; she and Alec were divorced within the year and it was to be over twenty years before I saw him again.

The next two years passed without incident that I can recall except for Margaret a girl about fifteen years of age who would baby-sit for my mother; I recall Margaret as if she had left me only yesterday. I liked her because she was pretty with a mass of tight blonde curls and a ready smile and she was fun, knowing lots of chasing games and engaging me in wrestling bouts on the big bed.

One day following a heated wrestling bout she grew quiet and lay back on the pillows her face flushed. Her legs were wide apart, her knees bent, her dress up around her waist. She looked at me silently for a moment. I saw that she was not wearing underwear and gazed at the base of her stomach where a cluster of soft blonde down covered the vee between her sun-browned thighs. She saw me staring,

'Do you like that, David?' she asked, 'Am I pretty?'

I nodded.

'Come here, my love,' she said and held out her arms.

She took my hand and guided it to her. On that mystic day I learned to touch the softness and warmth of womanhood and as I did so I myself experienced a hitherto unknown warmth in the pit of my stomach. The pleasure was all too short because Margaret heard my mother returning home and quickly covered herself holding her finger to her lips and whispering,

'Our secret.'

I was happy with our secret and felt closer than ever to my dear Margaret. I never told anyone of our game, there was never any call to do so and we never played it again. As I grew older and realised what had happened on that warm afternoon I could not find anything but good in the memory and I certainly did not feel that I had in any way been violated, I believe that warm hearted sensuous Margaret wished only to share pleasure with me and I love her for that.

I do not approve of the horrid practise of paedophilia and the above is not meant to endorse it but I believe that like a later incident in my childhood the episode with Margaret was the spontaneous reaction to a situation by a healthy young girl who had just begun to experience the power of her budding sex hormones.

Chapter Four

Grampie's health had not been good for some years, he had suffered a stroke in his forties and had since been living with one lung. On a morning in November 1947 my mother went in to wake him and found him dead in his armchair, his favourite cat sleeping on his lap.

The undertakers arrived and Grampie was laid out in the middle bedroom on a long trestle table whose sides were hung with black drapes. I was taken up to see him and to kiss him goodbye, such being the custom in those times. My grandfather looked as if he was sleeping and when I kissed his cheek it was cold and rough with slight beard stubble that was odd because he had always been scrupulous about being clean shaven. The next time that I passed through the middle bedroom, because that was the only way to the bathroom, Grampie was covered by a white sheet and I lifted it to see him again touched his cold cheek and then carefully laid the sheet back.

A thought has occurred to me whilst writing the above; never in all our years together did I think to ask my mother what became of Grampie's beloved cats. I hope that they found loving homes and were not abandoned to fend for themselves and return to the forlorn state of hunger and cold that Grampie had rescued them from.

On the morning of the day following Grampie's death I found my mother with Mr. Grey, she was alternating between crying and shouting; one moment she would be sobbing loudly and then she would suddenly stop crying begin swearing. My first instinct was to think that I had done something wrong, had she seen me peeping at Grampie? I realised it was not me when I heard her shouting about "Them".

'Hush, Dolly,' said Mr. Grey, 'They will hear you.'

'I don't care if they do, the...' she screamed and launched into another stream of invective using many words that were foreign to my young ears. I crept away not wanting to be included in whatever it was annoying her.

On the day after Grampie's funeral my mother and Mr. Grey began taking ornaments down from the mantelpiece and elsewhere and wrapping things in old newspaper. When I asked what she was doing she sat me down and told me that we were going on holiday. When I was old enough to understand she told me the story. The day after Grampie's death she had gone to see the landlord and asked him to transfer the tenancy to her name.

'I'm sorry, Dorothy,' he said, 'but I've given it to Mr. and Mrs. Steiner I didn't know you wanted it and they did offer to pay a higher rent.'

My mother was benumbed to hear that the Ackerman's had repaid Grampie's kindness by stealing the tenancy whilst he lay dead in the house, when she asked them why they had played such a dirty trick on her they replied

'We had to protect ourselves,' and they hid away refusing to talk about the matter.

I have never been able to feel the same degree of pity for refugees that my friends feel because I know from our experience with the Steiners how selfish and grasping hardship and insecurity can make such persons. It was some years later that I discovered that I too had been sold out that same week. My grandfather had often shown me a shiny wooden box that he kept in the kitchen cupboard containing his gold hunter pocket watch with its gold chain with a number of gold sovereigns dangling from it, it also held his army medals,

'One day these will be yours' he would say 'mind you look after them.'

When my mother opened the box after his death she also found over three hundred pounds in notes, a substantial sum in those days, enough to buy a small house had my mother only been aware of it but she had never been brought up to think in terms of owning property. Then, on the day before the funeral and at a time when she was beside herself with grief and rage at being betrayed by the Steiners my grandfather's nephew called

'I hope this is not a bad time, Dolly,' he said, 'but Jim promised his gold watch and his medals to me and I thought I might take them.'

'Oh, did he?' said my mother and she handed them over to him together with the silver pocket knife.

We left Regent Street with a large brown suitcase and a collection of string handled paper carrier bags and Oh how I grew to hate those carrier bags, it was usually my job to carry the bulk of them whilst my mother lugged the suitcase and when I was allowed to put them down the insides of my fingers would red and numb and there would be deep white grooves across them where the strings had cut in. The furniture and household furnishings went to the Steiners, my granddad's scrapbook and the smaller household belongings were left with Mrs. O'Rourke – my mother never went back for them and my final link to my grandfather was lost.

For some weeks we tramped around South Wales going from hotel to hotel and boarding house to boarding house, I often found myself left alone with strangers whilst my mother went out seeking work and permanent accommodation.

On one evening I was left in bed reading my Rupert Bear Annual and the story of "Rupert and The Red Indians." I fell asleep and began to dream that the Indian braves were chasing me. Whooping and yelling they came at me flourishing their knives and tomahawks. I was awakened by a voice shouting my name and found myself on the wet pavement with the landlady shaking me and calling my name. I had been sleepwalking for the first time in my life but not the last as, when under stress, I would periodically sleepwalk with varying severity for some years, one of the later episodes almost ending in tragedy.

It was about then that I became obsessed with the prospect of death, not my death but my mother's death. I would lie awake in the bed that we shared listening to her breathing I would then imagine that it had stopped and leaning over I would pinch her sharply on her arm. She would wake abruptly and quietly murmur,

'Don't pinch mummy, David. It hurts.'

I must have been a really mixed up six-year old and she later told me that on many mornings she would wake with bruises all over her upper arm; thankfully she resisted the urge to strangle the little sadist who shared her bed. The weeks went by and the high cost of hotel bills and eating in restaurants was draining her small capital, then one late December day as we sat on the top deck of a bus going nowhere in particular except on to the next hotel my mother turned to me and said,

'We are going to see Mr. Grey.'

We caught the next bus to Cardiff and walked the city streets to a small cu-de-sac near the railway sidings, one of a number of such small streets in the Cathays district each street with an entrance from the main road and the opposite end blocked by the high fencing of the railway. My mother found the terraced house that she sought and knocked with the large knocker that might once have been shiny brass but had turned black with age and want of polish. The door was opened by a middle aged man wearing a flannel vest and black trousers held up by a belt and a pair of wide braces, his face was lined and he had not shaved for some days. He glared at us,

'Yes?' he barked.

'Hello,' said my mother, 'Does Mr. Grey live here?'

'Who wants him?'

'Would you tell him it's Dolly,' she said.

The man called back into the dark interior, '...there's someone to see you!' He shouted, using Mr. Grey's given name, a name that escapes recall because he was always just Mr. Grey to me.

Mr. Grey came shuffling out, 'Dolly!' he cried and to the unshaven one said, and 'I told you that they would be coming, this is Dolly and David.'

At this the man's face broke into a welcoming grin revealing a mouthful stained teeth, 'Meg,' he called into the house, 'they're here.'

'Well bring them in,' shouted an unseen woman and in we went.

The long dark hallway was made even darker by thick layers of brown paint and it led through to a small kitchen at the rear that was not much lighter than the hallway; it being obvious that the small window had never seen the window cleaner's rag. The room was lit by a small electric bulb the single twisted flex also powered a radio whose power lead was draped around the ceiling like some bald Christmas festoon.

A woman with uncombed hair sat in a chair before a coal fire a cigarette hanging from her lips and four unwashed kids sat at a newspaper covered table playing with a set of dominoes. She squinted at us through her tobacco smoke. My mother who must have been heartsick and perhaps guilty at finding herself in the middle of such abject poverty began to thank them for taking us in.

'Would you like a cup of tea, love?' interrupted the woman in a kind tone.

'Oh, yes please,' said my mother.

'Righto,' said the man, 'let's get some clean newspapers on that table.'

The kids, shoving each other and showing off as children will in front of strangers threw the dominoes into a large red 'OXO' tin and one kid grabbed the table covering crumpled it into a ball and threw it on the fire. The paper caught fire with a roar sending a ball of flame up the chimney and causing the woman to lean back from its heat and swear under her breath.

'Silly little bugger!' cried the man and smacked the child on the side of her head; she cried a loud, 'Oww!' more for effect than from the pain and began to help her brothers and sister who were laying newspapers out on the table.

The woman disappeared into the back scullery and re-entered carrying a large tray on which sat a number of empty jam jars. She put the tray down on the table and I saw that several of the jars had a coloured or multicoloured length of knitting wool tied around the neck.

The woman placed a jar before me half filled with milky tea, it lacked a winding of wool and noticing my look to my mother said, 'We've all got our own jar in this house, We'll sort you out some wool later.'

I had never drunk from a jam jar before and I am sure that my mother had not; I soon discovered that there was an art to it, if you held the body of the jar the heat hurt your fingers, you had to hold it just above the neck on the rim and then it did not burn you. Within a day or two I had adapted to their ways and become a part of the Grey family, demonstrating a facility for adaptation to my surroundings of which I was totally unconscious but something that was to become the predominant part of my nature and stand me in good stead in later years. My knees were as black and scraped my nose and as runny as any of the other kid's and I was proud owner of my own wool-marked jam jar.

I slept with the Grey youngsters, five to a bed, in a bedroom lit by a small night light (now known as a tea light) that spluttered out halfway through the long cold night but as there were no curtains to the window the glow of the city's street lamps provided almost as much light. Our two pillows were bare of pillow cases the striped ticking obscured by years of dirt and sweat with the exception of the corners that retained a vestige of the original colour.

The feather mattress was equally devoid of covering and the sharp ends of feathers pierced the fabric in places and irritated any exposed skin until the victim changed position and changing position was constant as us five kids fought over the four ex-military greatcoats that served as bedding. The trick was to get a leg down each sleeve of a coat, which was not only warmer but it made it more difficult for your neighbour to grab it. When dawn came the bare window was covered in a thick coating of frozen breath and the first one up would draw pictures in it with a dirty fingernail.

Breakfast was - and the menu never varied - a jar of hot sweet tea and a doorstep of bread generously coated with gravy streaked beef dripping sprinkled with salt; how well I remember the delicious taste of such dripping, unavailable now due to healthy eating restrictions. After breakfast we would be sent out to find our own amusement. Favourite was the railway bridge, this long narrow footbridge led from the end of the street out across countless railway siding lines to the engine sheds, the bridge had steel handrails held up by crossed steel struts and if you stood on it as a great steam locomotive ran beneath you would be enveloped in a cloud of steam so dense that you could taste it and you felt as though you were on a cloud.

We never tired of this game and one or the other would shriek as an engine approached, whereupon we would race along the bridge to get in position above its track. I like to think that the train drivers knew of our game and played along with us by pushing their engine to make lots of steam because few trains passed without the great cloud that we desired and sometimes they would even blow the train whistle, a real treat.

Another activity that occupied us for hours was playing in the ruins of bombed houses. There were still a number of these not cleared of their rubble and a place where treasure in the form of personal objects lost by the poor householders could be found. Cutlery, chinaware, kitchenware were all useful for playing at house and our imaginations were lively. I do not think we could have been called juvenile looters because we never removed a find from the site.

I was always saddened by the walls that survived the building's destruction; these one dimensional rooms still retained their character with wallpaper, fireplaces and often a picture or two hanging drunkenly on torn wallpaper. I imagined the people who had lived there and thought of how sad it was that their private world should be exposed for everyone to see (strange thoughts in a six year old).

I spent Christmas 1947 in that little house by the railway sidings and lost my innocent belief in Father Christmas when one of the boys who had insisted that Santa did not exist nudged me awake to see our parents creeping in with our Christmas Stockings, I don't recall being distressed by this discovery I was more interested in seeing what was in my stocking; today's children would be bitterly disappointed by our meagre hoard but we did not know any better and so we were excited and happy.

That year in addition to a few sweets, nuts and a tangerine in the toe I had a small tin clockwork army tank that shot sparks from its gun as I pushed it along every surface in reach until the small flint that provided the spark was worn to nothing. I do not know just how long we stayed with the generous and warm hearted Grey family and I would happily have remained in their home but my mother decided to move on although we had nowhere to go.

The first evening away from the shelter of the Greys was cold and wet. We walked along the embankment near the old canal in central Cardiff I was carrying the string handled bags that were slowly disintegrating in the rain obliging me to carry them in my arms and I began to complain as only a miserable wet kid can.

Finally my mother agreed to sit on a public bench. She sat there hunched over and silent. I sat looking up at the raindrops as they fell through the trees, raindrops lit by the phosphorescent orange street lamps of Cathays Park thinking how pretty they were. My mother began to cry quietly, which scared me and I tried to comfort her talking all sorts of childlike drivel about the rain being pretty and how nice it was being out in the night.

'Don't worry, Mum,' I said, 'I'm here.' I was to say those exact words to her some fifty years later as she lay in a cold hospital room dying of kidney failure - "Don't worry, Mum, I'm here." They were as pointless and hopeless then as they were on that wet evening in the park. She continued to sob quietly and I cuddled into her shoulder. I looked up when I heard a male voice enquire, 'Are you all right, love?'

It was a young man carrying a large umbrella that he held over us sacrificing himself to the rain. My mother gave some incoherent reply through her tears and the young man sat down next to her.

'If there is anything I can do to help?' he said. Gradually she unburdened herself and told him our story. 'You need a cup of tea, love,' said the student, for that is what he turned out to be.

Carrying the suitcase he led us to an All Night Cafe one of those long since disappeared havens where one could find warmth and shelter for as long as a mug of tea could be nursed. He told us that he was a student in lodgings near to the university and that his landlady would never allow him to take us in. '...but,' he said, ' I could sneak you in after she has gone to bed and let you out early before she is up.'

'Oh no, I couldn't let you do that,' she said, 'You would be thrown out if she caught you.'

'She won't know if we are quiet,' said the young man. He turned to me, 'You can be quiet like a mouse, can't you?' I nodded, I was not long on words as a child and people would often ask, "Cat got your tongue?" Mrs. O'Rourke always said that I was slow witted.

The young man wrote down directions on the back of a cigarette packet and told my mother to wait until after midnight. We were not to worry he said because he would be looking out for us and then he left. Several hours and a couple of mugs of tea later we left the cafe and she traced the route to the boarding house, as it happened it was not too far away. On the way she made me go down a lane and pee,

'Just in case,' she said.

We reached the street soon after, 'I think this is it.' she whispered as we stood in front a large bay windowed house in the long terrace of silent sleeping bay windows. We tiptoed up the tiled front path and paused, then the front door opened silently and our young friend was there. He led us into the front parlour and closed the parlour door. 'I can't put the light on,' he said, 'but the street lights stay on all night.'

I could see by the dim light from the street lamps that the room was furnished with a large three-piece suite and our friend dragged the two armchairs together front to front to make a sort of a box bed. 'This will do for you, David,' he said, 'and I hope that you can manage on the settee, Dolly. You won't be able to use the bathroom because it's on the second floor and she'd hear you.'

She assured him that we would not need it and with a whispered 'Goodnight' he disappeared closing the door softly behind him. I was excited and scared as I took my shoes off before crawling fully clothed into my armchair bed. My mother kissed me goodnight and I lay there listening to my breathing and smelling the dust on the uncut moquette covering of the chairs. I began to doze, suddenly from somewhere in the house a clock chimed loudly. My heart nearly stopped and it was all that I could do to prevent myself shouting for help. I lay there wide awake waiting to hear the footsteps of the landlady and it seemed like hours before I closed my eyes only to be awakened immediately by a hand shaking me gently, it was my mother.

'Come on, love,' she said, 'we've got go.'

Go, I had only just gone to sleep; it could not be time to go but it was. We trudged sleepily back to the cafe where, although it was still night, the cafe clock told us that it was morning. After a fried breakfast and another cup of tea we took to the streets again and ended up sitting on another bench whilst my mother had a 'think.' I didn't care how long she took to think, I knew that I did not have to carry the hated bags when she decided to sit down. After a long sit she rose to her feet,

'Come along,' she said and off we went to the bus station.

A short bus ride later we were out down in a long road where tarmac covered driveways led up slight inclines to modern detached houses. My mother had obviously been there before because she began walking purposefully up the road.

'Where are we going, Mum?' I asked.

'We are going to see my cousin, your Uncle Russell,' she replied, 'and I want you to be on your best behaviour because he is the head of the NSPCC (The National Society for the Prevention of Cruelty to Children) and if you are naughty he'll put you away.'

I did not have a clue about the NSPCC or whatever she'd said and I certainly did not know how prophetic her words would turn out to be.

Some distance up the road we turned in to a driveway and I found myself standing in a rather ornate porch before a stained glass door. The bell was answered by a tall smartly dressed man with short neat blonde hair and a narrow moustache.

'Dorothy!' he exclaimed 'What on earth brings you here?'

'I need help, Russell,' she said, 'and I couldn't think of anyone else to turn to.'

'You had better come in,' he said, leading us through the hallway to his study.

'This must be your boy. What is your name, Son?' I told him. 'Well, David,' he said, 'your mother and I have to talk so you come over here and you can play trains on my desk.'

He led me to a big roll topped desk whose top was rolled down and from a drawer produced a handful of brightly coloured wooden blocks. 'Look,' he said, 'you can run them along the grooves, you see, just like trains one a track.' He left me playing with the blocks and sat with my mother on the far side of the room. They were talking quietly and I could only guess that My mother was repeating the story of our misfortune to him. Then she began to raise her voice,

'No,' I heard her say, 'No, that's not what I came to you for.'

'I'm sorry, Dorothy,' he said, 'I have to think of the boy.'

'I *am* thinking of him, they'll take him off me.'

My ears pricked up and fear began to creep up my back it was becoming an all too familiar feeling.

'I'm sorry,' he repeated, 'I've no other option.' With those words he got up and left the room.

'Oh My God,' my mother muttered, 'Oh My God.'

'Are you all right, Mum?' I asked. Her manner was scaring me.

'I should never have come here,' she said, 'Never.'

I crossed to her, 'I'm scared, Mum,' I said, 'I don't like Uncle Russell.'

She wrapped her arms around me, 'Don't be scared. You'll be all right,' she said. I could hear Uncle Russell talking on the telephone in the hall. 'Can we go Mum?' I asked. 'I don't think he will let us, love,' she said softly.

Now I was really scared; were we this man's prisoners? I had read about wicked people in my Rupert books and stories of

Rupert and his chums being held prisoner fuelled my already over imaginative brain to a state approaching panic.

'I want to go, Mum,' I whined.

'Hush,' she said, 'I am trying to listen.'

At that moment my uncle returned. 'It's all arranged,' he said, 'I'll take you in my car.'

'Oh please no,' she said, 'anything else but that place.'

'Now be sensible, Dorothy. You know it is the best thing for you and the boy and it's only a temporary measure.

'It's the Workhouse, Russell. How can you put your own family in the Workhouse?'

'It is not called the Workhouse now, it is called The City Lodge,' he said.

'Call it what you like,' she said, 'it is still the Workhouse and once you are in there you stay there.'

'Nonsense,' he retorted and picked up the suitcase, 'Come on, David we're going for a nice ride.'

We stood in the drive way whilst he got his shiny black car from the garage, my mother was muttering unintelligible words of pain and fear and the more she muttered the more scared I became. I remembered what she had said about Uncle Russell putting bad boys away but could not think of anything bad that I had done. On the journey he talked to me ignoring my mother and asking me about my school, my games and my friends. I was too scared to answer his questions and sat next to my mother clutching her arm.

'You will make lots of new friends where we are going now,' he said.

'No he won't.' snapped my mother. That did it, I had begun to calm down but I shot back up to silent panic level.

'Come along now, Dorothy,' he said, 'you're frightening the boy.'

The car turned in between two grey granite pillars and drove down past several tall buildings made of the same stone; the buildings five stories high were forbidding with row upon row of square featureless windows. An adult would have made an immediate comparison to a prison but I could only think how nasty this place looked. We parked in a small courtyard towards the rear of the complex and Uncle Russell carrying my mother's suitcase led us through a plain door and into a long corridor with white tiled walls and more of the same on the floors.

We reached a small office where two apron-clad women were leaning over a desk. Uncle Russell went over and spoke quietly to them. One of the women looked at me, 'I'll take the boy while you register them,' she said and suiting action to words she took my arm. 'Come on, David,' she said and began to pull me into the corridor. Silent fear suddenly became loudly vociferous panic and I struggled screaming for my mum. Emotions are so much stronger in childhood before they become dulled by age and usage and the terror that I felt at being taken away from my mother by these strangers reduced me to a state of near collapse. Obviously the staff of The City Lodge were accustomed to such a reaction and totally lacking in imagination.

'We'll have none of that,' said the woman, 'You'll do as you are told, my lad.' Clutching my arm in a grip that must have left bruises she half dragged half pulled me along a corridor. I was still yelling, kicking and struggling when we reached the children's dormitory with its long rows of empty iron beds. Another woman appeared,

'This is David,' said my gaoler, 'perhaps you can calm him down.'

The new woman caught hold of me by both shoulders glared closely into my face and said, 'Shut Up!' It had the desired effect and I subsided into sobbing gasping for breath between sobs.

'Would you like a jam butty?' The new woman asked and taking my silence for a yes, 'Well sit there and be quiet,' as she pushed me down onto a wooden stool. I sat there numb, my world had crashed around me and I had no way of coping with it. The woman came back with a thick breaded jam sandwich on a plate. 'That's better,' she said, 'you'll be all right now.'

All right or not I had arrived in the Workhouse or The City Lodge as it was then known, the only change being in the name. To say that the Workhouse bore any resemblance to the Dickensian model would be wrong but the regime was still harsh and it did have many rules that must have dated back to those times. One rule said that inmates could not discharge themselves without having a proven address to go to and some means of support; another said that all adult inmates must work within the system – my mother was put to work scrubbing floors and emptying bedpans in the hospital section. Hands that could bring to life the magic of Chopin and the other great composers soon became hardened split and reddened by being plunged into a solution of lye.

As a juvenile inmate I was not obliged to work and did not stay long on the main dormitory. I had been scratching since leaving the Greys and it turned out that I had impetigo and had several large sores that itched fiercely and so, impetigo being a highly infectious disease, I was taken to the isolation ward. This ward was in a long single storied building with large windows overlooking a small lawn, it snowed on the day I was admitted and I was able to watch the healthy junior inmates building a snowman and having snowball fights, how I envied their fun but impetigo was highly infectious and the garden doors were securely locked.

I missed my mother terribly and would spend hours laying on my bed my heart breaking with longing for her, I found that it helped to stretch up and clutch the iron frame of the bed (I am sure that a psychologist would make something of that). One day I heard a tapping on the window and there she was standing in the snow beckoning me over, luckily, there were no matrons present and we were able to hold hands through the window.

After that day she would visit almost daily and she was never caught. She told me that she was working hard to get us out of there and writing to every housekeeper advertisement that she could, the difficulty being the cost of writing materials and postage but with the help of a few kindhearted nurses in the hospital wing she was able to apply for a number of posts and eventually she was lucky; she was offered the job of live-in housekeeper to a miner and his three sons, the job was in the town of Risca and we were soon on the bus together with suitcase and carrier bags.

Chapter Five

My mother's new employer lived in a semi-detached house on a large council estate and although it was yet another stranger's house it was warm and welcoming after the City Lodge.

Mr. Jenkins and his three grown up sons worked down the local coalmine, they were polite and respectful to my mother and the sons treated me as if I were a younger brother playing games with me buying me comic books and sweets (I realise now that they must have used much of their sweet ration on me.)

My mother's duties were light because the wonder of pit head baths had removed the need to provide baths of hot water for miners home from work and her heaviest duty was the washing that was done in a large copper boiler in the outhouse.

We had been living with Mr. Jenkins for some weeks when I went down with jaundice (quite a severe attack I believe because my mother said that my eyeballs were the colour of buttercups) and I was once again quarantined but this time in our bedroom. The young doctor who attended me had a caring bedside manner and in addition to his gentle and kindly way with a child he was generous bringing with every visit the gift of a glossy coloured sticker-book, I had never seen such things before and the books completely took my mind off my confinement.

When I think back I am humbled by the kindness of people that my mother and I met during those troubled days and wish there was some way in which I could repay them, my mother attempted to repay them in later years by never turning away a person in need and when I remonstrated with her she would remind me of the kindness that we had received.

I had been in bed for about a week when I heard a commotion downstairs and the sound of people rushing about and doors slamming, I lay there desperately wanting to know what the rumpus was about and finally losing my patience I called for my mother, a few minutes later Mr. Jenkins came into the room looking worried and red faced.

'Where is my Mum?' I asked.

He paused 'Your Mummy has been taken ill, son' he said, 'and she has gone to hospital to get better.'

My heart sank and I began to cry. 'Don't cry, boy,' said that kind man, 'she won't be away for long and I'll take care of you.' He was true to his word and for the next few days he and his sons spoiled me waiting on me hand and foot, but it was not to continue for long. My mother had given herself a twisted hernia lifting a heavy bath of washing and she had been close to death when they reached the local hospital, as it turned out she would spend six months in hospital convalescing from the operation.

Some days after my mother had been taken to hospital Mr. Jenkins came into the room accompanied by a tall man in a business suit. 'This is Mr. James,' he said, 'and he's going to take you to a nice place where you'll have lots of friends your own age. Won't that be nice, David?' No, it would not be nice because I had heard the lots of friends story before,

'I'd like to stay here, please,' I said.

'Now come along, David, you can't stay here,' said the man, 'These good people can't afford to take any more time off work to look after you,' and, despite my protests, I soon found myself sitting in another shiny black car on my way to another strange place. In fairness to Mr. James he did his best to sell me on the idea of my new home promising me lots of fun and treats and telling me how much I would like it.

After what seemed like a long journey we arrived at The Sunlight Homes; a cruel misnomer for that cold institution. It was evening and I was quite tired as this was the first time that I had been out of bed since my illness began, I should have remained in convalescence for several more weeks but that did not seem to occur to my protectors.

The Homes was a long row of two storied red bricked buildings with connecting doors between each to form a continuous whole. Each house was approached by means of a short flight of stone steps leading into a small dark courtyard and then you entered the building through a small entrance door; the courtyards were to be a feature of my life there but I was not to know that on the day that I arrived. The first person we met was a dark haired woman dressed in a crisply starched navy blue uniform, her black hair was tied back in a bun and I do not ever recall her wearing make up, her name was Miss Kate Pugh matron of the Homes. Miss Pugh took my hands in hers and smiled down at me,

'Hello,' she said, 'what do they call you?' I replied and she drew me in to her,

'You'll be happy here, David,' she said, 'and you will make lots of new friends.' By now I was fed up with the 'new friends' speech but I did not have the nerve or the gumption to comment so I just stayed silent breathing in the woman scent of her. After a few moments she detached me and handed me over to another uniformed woman saying,

'Take David and give him his supper.'

She turned with a wide smile to the man and they were conversing in quiet tones as I left. Kate Pugh had a special smile that, as I discovered, was reserved for visitors and inspectors; she was in fact that worst kind of a sadist - a smooth tongued one.

The new woman led me through into a large hall furnished with several lines of long scrubbed wood tables and benches. On one table was a plate of bread, a knife, a saucer of butter and a dish of jam together with a large mug. The woman sat me down saying,

'Help yourself, love. I'll go and get you some cocoa.'

She took the mug and left whilst I tucked into the food. After a while she came back with my cocoa, very hot and sweet. I had almost finished when Kate returned. 'Come on,' she said, 'Time that you were in bed.'

On the way up to the dormitory she cautioned me to be quiet because all the other children were asleep. The dormitory a replica in size and shape to the big dining hall was filled with row upon row of iron beds each occupied by a silent sleeper. Moving between the rows Kate found an iron cot with drop down sides,

'You'll sleep here,' she said, 'There is your nightie. Get into bed when you have changed.'

She left and after donning a rough flannel Wee Willie Winkie nightie I was soon in bed and fast asleep. How long I was asleep I do not know but it must have been long enough to reach a dream state and I began to dream; I was standing in front of a porcelain lavatory pan my legs pressed up against its cold front and I was desperate to pee. I pressed up to the pan and began to empty my bladder. The relief was intense.

Suddenly I felt myself being picked up into the air and heard a woman's voice shouting obscenities I had wet the bed in my sleep. As it turned out there were two women, one of them Kate, and they lifted me up in the wet bedding like a baby being delivered by the stork, terrified and only partly awake I was swung through the air and carried I knew not where. Enveloped in the wet bedding I could not see a thing and could scarcely breathe. Dumped down on a cold surface I lay there bundled up and afraid to move. I heard Kate's voice,

'We'll teach you to pee our bed, you little bastard!' (bastard was in my experience a favourite curse word of the time.)

The other woman joined in,

'You filthy little pig!' (A change from bastard.)

From within my cocoon of bedding I heard the sound of taps running and after a little while I was bundled up aloft again but only for a few seconds before I was dropped. I felt myself hit the water and for a brief moment the bedding protected me, then the scalding hot water reached my skin and I screamed as I had never screamed before. Struggling to unwrap myself and escape the pain I only succeeded in half drowning myself, gulping down the hot water and choking on it.

The two women had dropped me into a bath of near scalding hot water and they stood there as I screamed. I must have woken up the entire building and when they returned me naked to a bare bed I was aware of rows of small heads peeping at me as I lay sobbing and crying for my Mum. Eventually I fell asleep and luckily had no further urinary dreams; to this day I cannot tolerate a really hot bath or shower.

I was awakened the next morning by the clanging of a hand bell, boys were darting about the room in various states of dressing some of them were returning from the scene of my night time torture carrying towels and wash bags. Someone had dressed me in a clean nightie during my sleep. At first I could not make out where I was and it came slowly back to me as I lay there watching the activities.

'Wakey, wakey,' said a voice from behind me. It was one of the matrons - the monster who had only hours before traumatised me was now all sweetness and smiles.

'Come on. Up you get, sleepy head.'

She dropped the side of the cot and I swung my legs out. She turned to a boy, 'Peter, you and Richard can show David where everything is and make sure that he washes properly.'

A slightly built fair haired boy came across as she left. He smiled,

'I'm Peter,' he said.

'And I'm Richard,' said another boy who had followed him across. I was seeing double, the boys were identical down to the last feature and, never having seen twins before, I was bemused and must have stared at them because Peter who led in everything said,

'We're twins.'

The twins showed me where my locker was, a green steel ex army cupboard that contained a towel, a wash bag with flannel soap and tooth brush together with tin of tooth powder and after helping me to wash, brush my teeth and dress they took me down to the day room.

My most vivid memory of the bathroom in The Homes is of the tooth powder that came in a small tin with a picture of a fairytale castle on the front and the proud label 'Gibbs Peppermint Dental Powder.' I believe that it was made from kitchen scouring powder coloured with green mildew because its taste was foul and lingering and it left your teeth feeling gritty for hours afterwards. The twins patiently endured my spitting and retching on experiencing Mr. Gibbs's wonder product and they were to prove the truth of the 'you'll make friends' promises because they quickly became the closest friends I had ever known in my young life.

Once downstairs they disappeared to perform their morning duties and left alone I sat at one of the long tables watching as several children scrubbed the wooden table tops with large scrubbing brushes and bowls of soap and water. If I thought that I was going to sit there until I was served breakfast I was mistaken. A matron soon spotted me and I was led out into one of the stone flagged courtyards where a couple of children armed with shoe polishing kits were kneeling on the flagstones surrounded by lines of hobnailed black boots.

Following the example of my workmates I learned how to dip a brush into the Cherry Blossom polish and apply it to a boot; following which the footwear was polished to a high shine with another brush, not forgetting to brush the hobnail studded soles. There must have been about thirty to forty boys in our block and there were that number of pairs of boots, each pair tied together by its long laces. The worst part was being obliged to put one hand inside a boot to hold it whilst polishing because they were invariably damp with cold stale sweat.

I cannot think that my help was welcomed that first day because the need to explain and demonstrate everything to me must have slowed the process considerably but my performance improved as the days passed and I was soon pulling my weight; which was just as well because none of us received our breakfast until the boots were cleaned and inspected. I never learned to enjoy kneeling on the cold flagstones and do think that they could have provided mats but I did learn to take pride in achieving a high shine on the boots. I later graduated to scrubbing wooden tables and floors in addition to the boots and – do not ask me why – was taught to knit. It could be said that this particular State institution provided a well rounded education.

Breakfast - and like the Grey's breakfasts I do not recall it ever varying - consisted of porridge with a thick slice of bread and margarine together with a large enamel mug of tea and a dessertspoonful allowance of sugar in a paper twist. You could use the sugar on your porridge, on your bread, in your tea or all three if you wished but spreading it that far had no effect so most kids opted for one of the three. After breakfast we queued to hand in our plates spoons and mugs, thankfully we younger ones were spared the washing up, and we were then lined up and inspected. After this we were expected to sit in the day room and amuse ourselves quietly until it was time for school.

On weekends and summer evenings we were allowed out into the nearby park or allowed to play on the mountainside that was only a short distance away. We always went in groups with a couple of the older kids in charge who were responsible for getting us back on time. In the park we were recalled for meals or bedtime by the ringing of the hand bell but how the kids in charge achieved this on the mountain I do not know. The school lunches and the weekend lunches at the homes were so forgettable that I cannot describe them.

The park that adjoined the Home's complex was like our back garden and we would rush to play on its green lawns at every opportunity. Well maintained with clean pathways, neat flower borders and leafy trees it was also a favourite picnic area for local families and on a sunny day its lawns would be decorated with brightly coloured picnic rugs and table cloths.

Answering an urge to rekindle childhood memories I recently revisited The Sunlight Homes and the park. The Homes appeared unchanged and was now a hostel for the homeless but the park, with its gates chained and padlocked to prevent incursion by drug addicts and other delinquents was a sorry sight. I looked through the bars of the gates to observe the once sweeping lawns overgrown and littered, the trees barren with broken branches and the paths potholed and rubbish strewn. I turned away saddened, wishing that I had stayed away and enjoyed my childhood memories of that once lovely haven of joy. So much for sixty years of progress.

On schooldays we were lined up in twos and marched off in a crocodile with boots clattering and (great fun) striking sparks from the paving stones to the local school, once inside the playground we were allowed to disperse but never did so because the local boys hated the 'Homies' and never failed to take an opportunity to make us suffer.

The locals were a tough bunch and play times could have been difficult had not the older 'Homies' been equally tough, I saw my first fight at that school with one of our boys and a town lad rolling around kicking, punching and biting. After a while it ceased to be a novelty and, unless it was a particularly bloody affair, most of us just went about our games.

The worst fights occurred when a group of us met a group of town kids on the mountain side, then stones and bottles or any other missile to hand would fly and no one was exempt. I returned to the homes on many occasions with a lump or a cut caused by failing to duck but nothing was said unless we had torn our clothing, then we suffered Kate's anger.

Kate's favourite instrument of punishment was a switch made by binding the long mountain rushes together in a sort of besom without a handle. She would make you bend over a chair so that your trousers were stretched tightly across your bottom and apply the switch viciously often hitting the back of your bare legs. The louder that you yelled the longer and harder she hit and you learned to suffer in silence if you did not wish to prolong your suffering.

On one memorable evening having suffered a beating from Kate I decided to run away. I had no idea where I was going or how I would get there but I was filled with thoughts of Rupert Bear type adventures and headed off up the mountainside as fast as my short legs would carry me. My mistake had been to forget the local kids. I reached a rise in the track and saw them. There were about six or seven of them all bigger than me.

I turned and began to walk nonchalantly back down the track; at first I thought that I had got away with it as I ambled back towards safety but I had not taken more than a few steps when I heard a chorus of screams from behind and turning saw the gang in full pursuit. I ran but they were too fast for me and caught me easily. I was pulled to the ground and a couple of hefty louts sat on my arms and legs. Although terrified, I decided to remain silent as they glared down at me.

'You're a home's bastard,' said a large boy, 'Do you know what we do to home's bastards?'

I said nothing knowing that any appeal would be wasted and not being sufficiently street wise to think up a retort.

'We drown'eds them,' said the boy, who must have been the leader.

At this point they all began shouting and jeering and I began to cry - I was only six years old and I truly thought that they would hurt me.

'Look, he's bawling,' said a kid, 'Cry, Baby Bunting, daddy's gone a hunting...' The chant was picked up by the others and I felt even more miserable as they went on. They soon got fed up with the nursery rhyme and a kid shouted,

'Let's drown'ed him!'

I was picked up bodily by my arms and legs and they began carrying me up a steep track; we topped the rise and although all that I could see was the sky and my captors I felt that we were going down hill. I had stopped crying long ago and thinking that they would not really drown me I was resigned to whatever they wanted to do. They halted and the boys carrying my legs dropped them.

When I was pulled upright I saw that we were inside a fence that had long since lost its chain link fencing and consisted simply of a line of iron uprights. The fence posts surrounded an old limestone reservoir tank in which the water level had dropped about two metres exposing the grey moss-coated stone sides, the surface of the water was covered with green weed and a stench rose in the summer heat. Swarms of gnats hung over the water and the buzzing was magnified by the tank's acoustic qualities.

'OK, throw him in,' said the leader and they grabbed my legs again and upended me over the edge of the tank.

I began to yell; harsh incoherent animal yells, cries for help and cries for mercy. My face bumped against the slime of the walls as my hands scrabbled for a grip on the slippery stones, I was not afraid of them drowning me, believing that no kid would do that, but I was afraid that they would drop me, I could not swim and I had no idea of the depth of water beneath that green carpet. I suppose that my struggles placed me in more danger than their antics but thankfully they were strong valley's lads and held me until I was exhausted and hung limp and silent; then they pulled me up, laughing as they did so, and dropped me onto the muddy path .

I sat where they had dropped me, drained of all strength and hoping that they would lose interest in me but that was not the case. They went into a huddle and after a minute or two they burst out laughing and I soon found myself being frog marched along a track leading higher up the mountain, it was now getting late and I knew that I would be in trouble when I got back to the homes.

We reached a small copse and they held me whilst a couple of them searched for a suitable tree, they yelped their success and I was dragged across into the undergrowth where they stripped me of my braces. Using my braces and some pieces of rough cord that every street boy carried with them they tied me to a small tree. They stood back and cheered.

'Now the wolves will get you,' said one kid.

'Yeah, they'll tear you to bits.'

'Soon as it gets dark you're dead.'

They left, jeering and shouting threats of what would become of me and I relaxed against the tree relieved to be rid of my tormentors. As the hours passed my relief turned to worry and then worry to fear as it began to grow dark I asked God to help me, promising to be a good boy for ever and ever (at that age I had a good thing going with God, I knew for certain that he could hear every word of my payers and he never held me to the rash promises that I made to him.)

I was in pain from the tight bonds and as it grew colder I realised that I had peed my trousers from fright. Cramp set in as the tight restraints cut off circulation but my efforts to break free were in vain; the locals had done a good job - maybe from experience.

Night came and with it the nocturnal mountain sounds of small animals. I thought about the wolves; were there wolves on the Welsh Mountains? Worn out with exertion and fright I dozed until I heard voices shouting my name and saw torch light beams bobbing about. It could not have been more than an hour or so since darkness fell but it had seemed to be forever. As they got closer I found my voice and although my cry must have been hoarse they heard it. I was soon being carried back down the mountain by a large policeman, who kept speaking to me as if I were a baby,

'There, there, Bach. It's all right now.'

His gentle Welsh voice must have lulled me back to sleep because the next thing that I heard was Kate Pugh's, 'Where in the name of goodness did you find him?'

Explanations followed, I was told to bathe and go to bed - recriminations followed the next morning after I had confessed to running away. I was called in front of Kate who must have called me every nasty name she knew for the diatribe went on and on. Having exhausted her range of abuse she made me bend over for the dreaded switch laying it on with all the force she could muster.

Although I had learned to accept this abuse quietly it was on this occasion so severe that I kicked backwards like an angry cow, the kick must have caught her on the shin because she stopped beating me and uttered a loud half moan half gasp over and over descending the scale as she did so. I held my breath knowing that I had made a dreadful mistake. Suddenly she burst into a fresh stream of invective, lashing at me again and again. It was my turn to scream and although it did me no good, scream I did. Later that day, still feeling the pain from the switch, I caught her looking at me in a guilty manner and she avoided eye contact with me for some days after that.

Life was not all gloom and pain in the Homes there were happy moments, one being our weekly trip to the Saturday Children's Matinee at the local cinema. Before setting out we were given a small bag of boiled sweets and a three-penny piece for an iced lollipop we were then marched through the park to the cinema.

The cinema's programme usually consisted of several short cartoons followed by the 'cliff-hanger' serial. During my time at the homes the serial was "Captain Marvel" the story of an ordinary young man who had been given extraordinary powers that included superhuman strength and flight. How we followed the plot I cannot say because the racket from several hundred unruly kids shouting abuse at the villains and cheering the hero between fighting each other and hurling boiled sweets was ear-splitting. Despite the mayhem, in which I played my part, I could hardly wait for Saturday to come around and to discover how Captain Marvel escaped from the giant buzz saw or the short fused case of dynamite.

Two things could be counted on in the cliff-hanger films, good always triumphed over evil and the hero respected law and order and protected the weak. How different from today's computer games where youngsters score points for killing people with a car or slaughtering each other with every imaginable type of weapon. Did the moral tone of children's films make us better citizens? I cannot say but at least it slowed our descent into cynicism.

On Sundays we went to church. Despite my lack of christening my mother had taught me about God and read stories from the New Testament to me. Consequently as I , God was as real to me as the man next door and, as I previously mentioned, I talked to him in my silent prayers; truly believing that he listened - I still do. This belief in God was the rule for Britain in the Nineteen-Forties. We were in the main a nation of believers; we believed in God, we believed in Great Britain and we believed in

The British Empire. We also believed in our government and the rule of law. My mother said that God knew all our thoughts and heard every prayer even if he did not always answer them.

I loved the Tredegar church with its incense, its gaily coloured stained glass and the atmosphere that I attributed to being in the presence of God. I also loved the hymn singing and being able to sight read from an early age I joined in as loudly as my young lungs would permit.

My seventh birthday came and went, by now I had learned to scrub floors and tables. There was no visit from my mother, she did however send me a package containing my present; a set of twelve wooden blocks with a printed picture on each face so that you had twelve puzzles where you had to turn the blocks to make a complete picture. I was pleased with my gift but I really wanted to see her; other kids had visitors and I envied them.

The twins not been placed in the homes by officialdom but by their mother who felt that she could not manage with them, she did come to see them every week bringing sweets or comics and kind souls that they were they shared with me. I began to get broody and when I was not working I would sit for hours just staring out over the park and dreaming of happier days.

Soon after my birthday we were told of a special treat, we were to go for a day at the seaside. Although I had been brought up in a seaside town I was as excited as the other kids and when the big morning arrived I fought for a place on the upper deck of the double-decker bus. Off we went armed with a bottle of fizzy mineral water and a small pack of sandwiches for the trip - a mistake because several of the travellers consumed their pop and jam butties before we had left the valley and quickly became bus sick.

The small crises going on amongst my fellow passengers did not concern me as I had, along with Peter and Richard, secured a front row seat on the upper deck and was busy following our progress whilst 'driving the bus' by means of the steel handrail in front of us. The journey took several hours and we were becoming increasingly bored with driving the bus or ridiculing the unwell and had sunk slouched into our seats when a boy shouted,

'The sea, I can see the sea!'

I sat up and I could not only smell the ozone I could taste it. Grasping the front bar I strained my eyes to get a glimpse of the source; it was then that I had the strange feeling of having seen it all before - I had - we were heading down a steep hill towards Barry Island. I was back home.

The bus parked up and we spilled out and lined up. Kate Pugh's assistants went among us and gave a half-a-crown to each child with the admonition,

'If you lose it you won't get any more.'

A half-a-crown or thirty old pennies (twelve-and-a-half-pence in modern coinage) was a small fortune to a child when you consider that you could buy an ice cream for three pennies. A fairground ride cost the same and so did a bag of chips. We were then marched in column to the shops, incurring the amusement of a number of kids who were enjoying that lovely sunny day alone or with their parents.

Most of us chose to spend a whole shilling or twelve pennies on a tin bucket and a wooden spade, essentials for the golden sands. The buckets were brightly decorated with paintings of children building sand castles intended to encourage young designers in their work. Suitably tooled up we were then marched to the beach. I would imagine that few people under sixty years of age have experienced the seaside crowds of our day, this was long before the era of the cheap foreign holiday and a large proportion of British families spent their holidays at the seaside.

Barry Island was the Blackpool of South Wales and hundreds of thousands of holiday makers and day trippers travelled there each year, consequently, during the warm summer months the beach was crowded with thousands of bodies sitting shoulder to shoulder in deck chairs or on their towels; that day was no exception and it seemed to take forever as we marched turning and twisting between the bodies in our search for a good spot. Luckily for us the tide was out and we were able to find a patch of sand down by the water's edge.

As we had been told to put our bathing suits on underneath our clothes before leaving Tredegar, once we had stripped off our top clothes we were ready for the sea. The shallow slope of the beach made it necessary to walk out quite a distance in order to achieve any depth of water and the twins and I waded out until waist deep - quite deep enough for me as a non-swimmer. For a time we happily splashed each other with the warm sea water and then the twins decided to go deeper so that they could swim.

I watched them dive in and splash around cheering them on. Suddenly, I felt myself pushed forward and found myself underwater with a boy's weight on my back. Lacking any warning I had gulped down a large amount of salty water and could not hold my breath; I began to breathe sea water down into my bursting lungs and heard a tremendous roaring in my ears like a thousand waterfalls. I could see a grey mist before my eyes; I was drowning in just over a half a metre of water and could do nothing to save myself.

Because I could not think clearly enough to struggle I must have blacked out because I do not remember being pulled from the sea and I was only aware of someone thumping on my back and shouting my name as I came to. Apparently a local father had spotted what was happening and prevented a harmless prank from becoming a disaster.

My happy day at the beach had been ruined and although I was given lots to drink to get the salt taste from my mouth, my eyes smarted, my back ached from the thumping, my chest and lungs felt as if they were on fire and even a large ice cream cone, courtesy of Kate Pugh, did little to help. I spent the next hour or so sitting on my towel feeling sorry for myself and it was only when Peter and Richard, who had been unaware of my little adventure, returned that I began to take an interest in building a sand castle.

Late afternoon came and we all returned to the bus too tired to chatter. It was dusk when we arrived back at the homes, our buckets and spades disappeared into storage and after a mug of cocoa we were all glad to tumble into our bed. That was the only outing of my stay in the Homes but one such trip was enough.

The summer dragged on with no word from my mother and I became increasingly unhappy my only comfort being my friendship with Peter and Richard. We were playing in the park one day when Peter with no warning said,

'We are going to run away. Would you like to come with us?'

'Where are you going?' I asked. The 'why?' was obvious.

'We are going home. You could come with us and our mum would keep you,' said Peter.

'Yes,' chipped in Richard, 'you can be our brother.'

The thought of a home and a mother figure was inducement enough for me to agree readily and we began to make our plans - or rather Peter began to make our plans. The twins lived in the nearby town of Ebbw Vale and knew the way to their house, it was some distance but Peter said that if we started out as soon as possible after the Saturday midday meal we could get there before dark. We were usually allowed to play unsupervised in the park after the meal and nobody bothered us until supper time.

The big day came and as we played on the green lawns we wandered further and further away from our playmates until were out of their sight. With Peter leading we left the park and began our journey. The South Wales Valleys run parallel to each other divided by steep mountains and - in those days even steeper slag heaps built with the dumping of decades of colliery waste.

Today the valleys are green again but at that time the streets through which we trudged were lined with dirt blackened houses and the roads and paving of the sidewalks were it existed was just as soiled. We eventually left the streets behind and found ourselves on the road that skirted the mountain Traffic was scarce the occasional bus or colliery wagon and nobody paid any attention to a gang of kids.

Although we had planned a direct route we soon began skylarking and ended up chasing sticks down a mountain stream, this came to an end when Richard fell in much to our amusement. So, with a soggy Richard complaining that his wet trousers were rubbing him, we resumed our march and soon we were traipsing our way down fresh streets.

We finally reached the twin's home and were greeted with typical Welsh warmth by their mother, a pretty blonde woman who clasped me to her ample bosom as heartily as she did her sons. The first order of the day was a hot sweet cup of tea and then the twins took me out to see their pigeon-coop. Every other garden in the valleys seemed to have a pigeon-loft or coop and the twins were proud of theirs. The coop stood halfway down a precipitous garden that was tiered in the manner of the ancient Inca City of Machu Picchu.

Great ingenuity had gone into the layout of the twin's garden and the adjoining gardens with tiers varying in colour and content although practical vegetable patches were a feature of each garden. After we had admired the empty coop - Peter explained that the pigeons had flown with his dad and the first thing that he planned to do was buy new birds - we heard the twin's mother calling us to eat. She had prepared a pile of golden chipped potatoes and a dish of fried eggs together with doorstep thick slices of bread and butter. Fresh eggs were unseen in the homes and I tucked in whilst the twins chattered away between mouthfuls of food.

'We can stay home, can't we, Mum?' begged Peter.

'Yes please, Mum?' from his twin.

Their mother looked at them and nodded her head, 'All right, you tykes, I will keep you home - but only if you promise to behave.'

The twins dropped knives and forks and scrambled to hug their mother making promises to be the best behaved boys in the world and so on.

'Cross your heart and spit,' said their mother and they duly obliged.

Then they remembered me. 'And David, Mum. He can stay, can't he?'

Their mother looked at me as I sat silently my heavily loaded fork halfway to my mouth. There was a long silence and then she said, 'I'm sorry, love, but I'm afraid you will have to go back.'

I felt a great lump rising in my chest and lost all interest in my egg and chips.

'Aww come on, Mum,' said Peter, 'you could adopt him and he would be our brother.'

Richard added his pleas but despite their joint whining and cajoling their mother was adamant. 'No David goes back tonight,' she said firmly, 'I'm sorry, David Bach, but I don't want trouble you see.' She then put her overcoat on and went out. We sat there quietly except for Richard's occasional, 'It's not fair,' or, 'Our mum's cruel.'

To which Peter replied, 'It's not her fault.'

I was silent I suppose that I had always known that I would be sent back but I had been enjoying the freedom and put the thought at the back of my mind. When the twin's mother returned she was accompanied by a tall policeman.

'Hello boys,' said the bobby and to me, 'You must be David.' I nodded convinced that I was going to gaol. 'All right, boy,' he said, 'have you got a coat?'

There were no farewell hugs. The twins just sat in silence as my coat was brought and leaving my unfinished meal I was escorted out by the policeman. With one hand on my shoulder gently guiding me he led me through the streets to a bus stop. We waited.

'Run away then, did you?' he asked, 'That was silly now,' again I merely nodded, speechless with guilt and fear.

'Oh well, no harm done really.'

I felt a little better then and that kind man talked away my fear as we waited for the Tredegar bus; when it came he spoke to the driver and then turned back to me. 'Now mind you stay still on this bus,' he said, 'the driver knows where to put you down.' He lifted me up onto the first step of the vehicle and I felt something being pressed into my hand, it was a silver sixpenny-piece.

'Now don't forget to be a good boy mind,' he said and stood back until I had found a seat and the bus pulled away; as it did he waved and smiled and I wished that he was going with me because I knew that I had to face Kate Pugh.

When the bus arrived at Tredegar another tall policeman was waiting for me (I doubt that today's overworked police service could spare such manpower for one young boy.) The new policeman escorted me to the homes and into Kate's office. 'Here he is' he said, 'your escapee.'

Kate gave him her 'special smile for visitors and officials' and enquired if he would like a cup of tea. He declined and after ruffling my hair with a hand like a dinner plate he left. Kate's smile froze into a grimace and I prepared myself mentally for a hard time - I was not wrong but, to avoid needless repetition, I will draw a veil over the beating that followed and the confinement and loss of privileges that followed that. After all one beating is pretty much like another.

Without my twin friends I was even more unhappy with my lot and although the other children included me in their games and chatter I felt totally alone, in all I must have been a miserable and sulky little monster until one afternoon I was called in from my play to report to Kate. Wondering just what I had done wrong and fearing the worst as always I knocked on her door.

'Come in, David,' said Kate and I entered. There was another woman with her and when that woman turned I saw that it was my mother. My shout of joy must have reached falsetto and I threw myself at her. All that I could say was,

'Oh, Mum. Oh, Mum,' over and over again.

'Your mother is here to take you home, David,' said Kate wearing her number one smile.

My mother hugged me tightly, 'Yes, we have a nice home to go to and you'll have a new dad.'

My delight lessened abruptly. The 'new dad' information did not sound good, it had always been me and my Mum but I soon forgot that in the excitement of getting packed up. There were no good-byes to the other kids as they were all outside playing. I did receive a good-bye hug from Kate and a false. 'We'll miss you, darling.' If that woman had chosen an acting career she could have been one of the all-time greats.

Chapter Six

As we sat on the bus enroute to our new home in the town of Blackwood my mother explained just how she had found it (although I was only seven years old she treated me like an adult and took me into her confidence as if I understood everything she said, which was not always the case).

She told me that she had been forced to stay in hospital long after her convalescence because she did not have an address to return to. Once again she had replied to numerous housekeeper advertisements finally receiving a reply from a miner who had advertised for a housekeeper with a view to matrimony. Such advertisements were quite common in the days before dating or matrimonial agencies became popular and I am sure that many happy marriages resulted from them.

She explained that after meeting Jack (Randolph) Williams in a local cafe she had agreed to his offer and I was now on my way to see my new home and meet my future father. The bus passed through Blackwood and on to the outskirts of the town. 'The Bird In Hand,' shouted the conductor and my mother took my hand.

When we alighted I could see that we were outside a public house and we crossed the road to a kissing gate, a small gate swinging in a U shaped enclosure that allowed only one person at a time to pass. After I had tried the novelty gate four or five times we began the walk up a steep path passing an old monastery on the way.

My mother later told me that it was haunted by 'The Black Monk' a piece of information that caused me to avoid the place thereafter. Eventually we crossed a roughly pastured field and reached the rear of a row of council houses, Penllwyn Avenue in the village of Pontllanfraith. My mother who had been living there for some days found the back garden of Randolph's house and we were soon in the small kitchen.

Uncle Randolph, as he told me to call him, was a handsome middle aged man with black curly hair a wide grin and a neat pencil moustache. He was smartly dressed in well-creased trousers, a crisp white shirt and a brightly coloured cravat. I took to him immediately and my fears abated. He showed me to my bedroom that was neatly if sparsely furnished and told me to come down to tea when I was ready. I sat on the bed and looked around me a familiar empty feeling in my stomach, as kind as Randolph appeared to be it was yet another strange bed and another new life.

I felt that something was missing and it was years before I realised that the something in question was a feeling of security. Insecurity underpinned my every breathing moment at that time and for many years to come; strange as it may seem I later felt more secure in a slum where we appeared to be permanently settled than I did in any of the houses large and small in which we lived during that period in my life.

Life in Blackwood soon assumed a pattern; Randolph would go off to work each day the time depending on the shift he was working. Sometimes he would let me carry his 'snap' tin to the bus stop for him; the snap tin was a large oblong tin in which miners carried their mid-shift sandwiches or 'snap.' Each day my mother would carefully line his tin with grease proof paper, place a fresh tomato or spring onions in with his sandwiches together with an apple and top the lot off with a paper napkin.

He would say that his 'butties' (a Welsh term for friend or work mate) thought that he was becoming a Nancy-boy but I think he liked the attention. I liked to go to the bus stop with him and see the long line of miners squatting on their heels in the 'miner's squat' as they waited for the bus to take them to the nearby Oakdale Colliery; many of them were boys not much older than me because a boy went down the mine as young as fourteen years of age. Randolph would come home after his shift and eat his main meal of the day before changing and going down to 'The Bird In Hand' for his pint.

Most miners were steady if not necessarily heavy drinkers; I suppose that they needed to wash the coal dust from their throats and who could begrudge them, working as they did under unbelievably hard conditions to tear the precious coal from the bowels of the earth. There is no doubt that for all his later revealed faults Randolph was a hard worker. Every week on his pay day he would place my mother's housekeeping money on the kitchen table and then he would beckon me over and ask,

'Have you been a good boy?'

Good boy or bad boy I was not a fool and always replied in the affirmative, he would then take my hand and place two shillings in it.

'There's your pocket money then.'

My mother would wait and if I was not quick enough would prompt me,

'What do you say then?'

'Thank you, Uncle Randolph.'

If it was early enough in the day I would then make a sharp exit and head for the local shop. Although my mother bought me comics every week there were always more comics to be had and also toys as the shop served as grocer, news agent and general store to the community. I usually held on to some of my money because I was saving up for a Blow Football game that sat in the shop window. It cost seven shillings and sixpence and the large box featured a vividly coloured illustration of a cup final with a star player shooting a goal past a desperately clutching goalie.

I could not wait to own that game and would check on it every day to make certain that it had not been sold. When the big day came and I carefully placed my seven shillings and sixpence down on the counter I could hardly breathe for the excitement. Once outside the shop I sat down on the kerb and carefully removed the lid of the box, there within lay two small bent wire goals with a flat tin goalie hanging suspended from each, two plastic tubes like drinking straws and a small cork ball. I learned a hard lesson about marketing that day. I think that I attempted to play with that sad game twice before throwing it into the back of a cupboard.

My opponent at the two blow football matches was one of the three boys from next door. I do not recall his name although all four of us played together daily. I do remember his mother's name, Madge Williams, probably because she made and freely dispensed the most mouth-watering custard slices in the world. Sweet firm custard as thick as three fingers sandwiched between feather light puffed pastry and topped with a thick layer of white vanilla icing, her slices would linger on your taste buds for hours and twice a week the boys would bring me two of them in a grease proof paper wrapping.

I often went next door to play with the boys and their collection of Dinky cars that the stored in a large box under the bed, also under one bed was a large white enamel bowl that they used as a urinal in the night. Quite often they would forget to empty it and the smell slightly spoiled my enjoyment of the cars. One afternoon I went next door and found Madge in her kitchen sleeves rolled up.

'Ha,' she said, 'you must have known that I was making custard slices today.' I assured her that I had not.

'Well sit down there and you can watch me make the pastry,' and she called one of the boys down.

'Get me the mixing bowl and don't forget to swill it out.'

'I emptied it last time,' protested her son.

'Well you can bloody well empty it again,' ended the exchange.

I sat and waited watching her dusting her table top with flour and then her son came down carrying the bowl from beneath the bed. There was no mistaking its battered and chipped white enamel. Without pausing to wipe the bowl dry she tipped a large bag of flour into it. I felt ill as memories of countless custard slices came back to haunt and nauseate me. Losing interest in the Dinky cars I made an excuse and got up to leave.

'I'll send you in a couple when they're set,' she said. I thanked her and left hastily. When I told my mother just what I had seen she said, 'You are never to eat anything from that woman again, no matter what she offers you.' I never did and after that day each time Madge sent pastries in they went straight into the bin.

Weeks passed and as my mother made no attempt to register me with the local school I roamed the countryside with my neighbourhood pals, who were usually dodging or 'mitching' school. We went picking blueberries and gorged ourselves with that soft fruit before returning home too bloated to eat our meal. One of Madge's boys would sneak out the lethal looking machete that she used to chop firewood and we would devastate the mountain greenery to build wigwams and dens.

Our lack of respect for living trees and shrubbery was appalling and a kid wandering around today with a long machete stuck through his belt would no doubt be arrested but nobody seemed to care in those days before health and safety awareness. We had never been taught to respect nature or our safety and sallied through our adventures in blissful ignorance.

The big day of my week was Saturday. Every Saturday my mother would take me on the bus to the town of Newport. This ancient town had a history going back some two thousand years but its main attraction for me dated from 1906, the Newport Transporter Bridge. This magnificent engineering feat spans one hundred and eighty-one metres of the River Usk and is one of only eight in the world.

She would pay our toll and we would step aboard the gondola that was suspended from cables attached to the upper span between the seventy-four metre high towers. We would stand at the rail and then as silently as like a well-tuned limousine the gondola would begin its journey across the river, as there was little on the far side but an industrial estate we would return immediately and I would have to wait another week for a treat that never lost its thrill. We would then go to the park to watch

Punch and Judy and on to the indoor market where I was given a shilling to buy second hand comics from a stall.

You could buy a second hand comic in Newport Market for as little as a half penny and following a bust up meal of faggots and peas (for any American reader, a faggot in Britain is a small meat parcel made from offal and bound together with the fat from a sheep's intestines) I would return home clutching my bundle of comics convinced that life wonderful.

If my family had been granted a coat of arms I think our motto would have been 'All Good Things Come To An End' and my good times in Pontllanfraith. I arrived home from pillaging the countryside one day to find my mother sitting at the kitchen table wearing her 'I have got bad news' face.

'What's wrong, Mum?' I asked.

'There's nothing wrong, love,' she said, 'You are going to have a baby brother or sister.'

It was my turn to sit down the thought of sharing her with another kid left me as cold as the idea of a new father had some weeks before.

'Isn't that nice?' she asked. I did not reply, as I had no idea of where babies came from I could only assume that she or Randolph or had gone out and arranged to adopt another kid.

'Isn't that nice, David?' she repeated.

'When?' I enquired what must have been a flat tone of voice.

'Oh, not for a long time yet.'

'Oh.'

107

That was an improvement. I bucked up maybe I could talk them out of it.

'Now when Randolph comes home I want you to stay out of the way while I tell him about it.'

So the baby was her idea. I could not understand why she wanted another child. Just what had I done wrong? When Randolph came home I said hello to him and left them alone. I sat on the top of the stairs trying to hear what they were saying. I heard my mother talking quietly and could not make out what she was saying then I heard Randolph's voice raised as if in anger. I moved down a couple of stairs.

'Aren't you pleased?' I heard her say.

'It's so soon,' said Randolph, 'are you certain?'

'I'm certain,' she replied. 'There's no mistake.'

'Well that is that then.'

'We will have to set a date for the wedding now,' she said.

'Yes. Yes of course. I'll sort it out tomorrow,' said Randolph.

I heard the doorknob rattle and scooted upstairs before I was caught. When I got up the next morning Randolph had already left. My mother seemed happier than she had been yesterday and I quickly forgot my fears and tucked into my corn flakes. Then I went out to play and it was late afternoon before I ambled back. Her happy mood had vanished and she looked really worried.

'What's wrong, Mum?' I asked, although I was as usual more concerned with the impact of her mood on me than I was with her problem.

'It's nothing, love. Go and get washed or tea.'

After my tea I went into the living room to listen to the wireless and read my comics whilst my mother just sat staring into space. The hours went by, I was allowed to stay up as late as I liked and I usually took full advantage of that. It never occurred to me that Randolph had not returned and when she suggested that we go to bed I was still unaware of his absence. The next morning I got down to find Madge Williams with my mother who was agitated.

'What could have happened to him?' I heard her saying. 'Perhaps he has fallen somewhere and nobody has found him.'

'No, No,' replied Madge, 'He'll be OK. He has probably stayed the night with a buttie.'

I sat at the table and my mother automatically served my cereal up as if in a trance. 'Are you all right, Mum?'

'It's Uncle Randolph. He hasn't been home all night.'

She turned away from me choked up and Madge put her arm around her shoulders saying, 'Come on now, I'm sure that he will be OK.' They sat quietly, Madge with her arm around my mother as I ate my breakfast hurriedly.

'I'll see you later, Mum,' I said and headed for the door.

'I think that you had better stay home with your mum today,' said Madge, 'She's got a lot on her mind and she might need you.' I really did not fancy staying at home all day with an unhappy mother but Madge was obviously serious.

'You stay home with me, David, and I'll buy you some comics to amuse you,' said my mother and to Madge, 'Will you wait here, Madge, while I take him down the shop and get some comics?'

We walked down to the nearby shop in silence. I immediately began searching through the comics; I knew when I was on to a good thing and began to assemble a small pile. I heard my mother ask the shopkeeper, 'Are you sure that you haven't seen him?'

'I haven't seen him for days, my dear,' said the shopkeeper. 'Perhaps you should contact his wife.' My mother drew an audible intake of breath, 'His wife!' she exclaimed, 'He hasn't got a wife. He's a widower.'

'You are wrong there, my dear. I don't know what he has told you but he has got a wife and eight kids in Newport.'

I never received my promised comics because my mother grabbed my hand and almost dragged me out of the shop. All the way back to the house she kept muttering over and over again, 'Eight kids, eight kids.'

When we got back home Madge was sitting drinking a cup of tea. My mother was not through the door when she blurted out, 'Oh, Madge, they've just told me that he has a wife and eight kids in Newport!'

'Oh, My God!' 'Oh, Dolly!'

I spent the next few hours watching my mother storm about the house opening and closing cupboards and drawers between muttering and swearing. I was getting hungry and about to ask her for something to eat when she called me from the front bedroom. She was kneeling in front of the airing cupboard. Its door was open, 'Look at this,' she cried, 'Just look at this.' She then threw a handful of slips of paper to me. They scattered and I began to pick them up.

'Do you know what they are?' she shouted. I did not. 'They are postal order receipts for maintenance payments!' she yelled, 'Maintenance payments!' I was no wiser but realising that the papers were something bad I kept my mouth shut.

'He has been sending money to his wife all this time. The rotten swine.'

I was shocked; I had seldom heard her swear, the exception being when she lost her temper completely. She went charging down the stairs clutching a handful of papers. I followed her through to Madge's house where she began to wave the papers about.

'He has been sending them money ever week,' she cried, 'Every bloody week while I thought he was a widower.'

Madge tutted sympathetically and led her to a chair, 'They are all the bloody same, Doll,' she said (my mother later told me that Madge had divorced her husband).

Madge waved me upstairs to play with her boys. I had a terrible feeling that my world was about to crumble around me again and when Madge brought me up a cup of tea with a couple of custard slices I ate them without even thinking of their source. The day finally ended and I was glad to escape to my bed. I was surprised to be woken by my mother the next morning. She usually allowed me to lie in. 'Come on,' she said, 'we've got a lot to do today.'

Once downstairs she threw my breakfast onto the table and disappeared up the stairs again; when she came down she had her outdoor coat on and she was carrying my school mackintosh. I pushed my cereal down my throat and as she dressed me asked,

'Where are we going, Mum?'

She answered with one word,

'Newport!'

Less than a half-an-hour later we were on a double-decker bus heading for Newport. There was no question of treats on that occasion we went straight to the small terraced house of Randolph's wife. A strong pungent unidentifiable smell hung over the street and seemed to reach down into your stomach like a nasty tasting medicine. My mother knocked on the door and it was soon opened by a small red haired girl who stood there looking at us without saying a word.

'Is your mum in, love?' enquired my mother.

The waif turned,

'Mammy!' she shrieked in a piercingly loud voice.

A woman came shuffling down the narrow passageway accompanied by several kids - all girls. The woman who wore a pinafore dress and carpet slippers was middle-aged, plump and pleasant looking. She folded her arms across her chest and looked at my mother.

'Yes?' she asked in a tone that really said, 'Are you looking for trouble?'

'Are you Mrs. Randolph Williams?'

'Who wants to know?'

'My name is Dorothy. I've been housekeeping for Randolph.'

The woman looked to one side and then the other as if to prepare herself for what was coming, 'What has that old goat done now?' she asked in a tired voice.

'May we come in?' asked my mother.

The woman turned without a word and walked back down the passageway accompanied by her brood. My mother took this as an invitation and we followed her into a small warm kitchen. Randolph's wife, as she turned out to be, sat in an armchair by the fire and indicated for my mother to sit which she did whilst I stood alongside her chair.

'Well what has he been up to?' she asked.

'You are his wife?'

'Oh yes I am his wife and I've got eight girls to prove it in addition to my marriage lines.'

My mother paused and looked down at her hands, when she was nervous or concentrating on something she would interlock her fingers and twiddle her thumbs.

'It's difficult.' she said

'You're pregnant.'

'Yes. How did you know?'

'Oh you are not the first one, my dear,' said Mrs. Williams, 'and you won't be the last.'

There was a long silence. Mrs. Williams turned to the eldest girl who appeared to be a couple of years older than me.

'Put the kettle on.' 'There's a good girl.'

'What do you mean I'm not the first?' asked my mother.

'Oh he's done it before, love. That's why I left him. Since then he has had at least two more housekeepers,' she said curling her lip on the word housekeepers, 'and you are the second one that he's put in the family way.' She went on to catalogue Randolph's crimes against the female of the species until the tea arrived and as we were sipping it my mother asked.

'Do you know where he might be?'

'Oh, he could be anywhere, dear. He's got a couple of fancy women that he shacks up with when he is in trouble.'

After tea and biscuits my mother got up to leave but Mrs. Williams seemed reluctant to let her go. 'Take your time, dear,' she said, 'David can go out and play with my girls for a bit. You'd like that, wouldn't you, love?' I said that I would and the eldest girl led us out into the back garden. The garden ran down to the river bank and the smell seemed even stronger there. I asked what it was and a girl said,

'It's the glue factory.'

'Yes,' said another, 'that's where they turn dead dogs and cats and things into glue.'

'They boils them down.'

As horrible as the thought was at least it accounted for the smell. When we went back indoors my mother told me that we were going to stay with the Williams family for a few days. I was once more to sleep on a combination of two armchairs whilst my mother occupied the settee. On the second day I went out to play with the girls and this time they climbed over the fence that divided the gardens from the river bank and onto the rough grass land by the river. Very soon one of the girls began taking her frock off shouting,

'Mud bath!'

There was a chorus of agreement and they were all soon stripped down to their knickers. I turned away in embarrassment.

'Come on,' said the eldest, 'you're not scared are you?'

A chorus of jeers and shouts of, 'Scaredy cat! Scaredy cat!' shamed me into stripping and I tentatively followed the Williams clan down onto the river mud. Slowly at first and then more confidently as I saw that they were safe I waded into the thick grey mud. The mud gave forth a sulphurous stench and here and there it was streaked with black but it was quite warm once you got used to it; the stench seemed to blot out the smell of the glue factory and I completely forgot about it as I scooped up handfuls of mud and flung them at my companions with enthusiasm.

Time passed quickly and when we heard their mother calling us indoors I realised that I was covered toe to chin in mud. Following the girls I allowed myself to be rubbed down with grass until I was almost clean although I still smelled strongly of mud. We got dressed and the number one girl said,

'Don't tell them. They won't notice if you don't tell them.'

I was sceptical but said nothing to my mother and it was not until we were in our make-do beds that she said,

'What is that funny smell?'

I sniffed dramatically (are all kids natural liars?) and enquired,

'What smell, Mum? I can't smell anything.'

She looked at me with that 'Oh yes?' look she used when she knew that I was lying but she let the matter drop. We returned to the empty house in Pontllanfraith the next day and the first thing she did was drag in the tin bath from the shed and begin boiling pans of water. I hated that bath placed in front of the fire the side nearest to the heat soon became too hot to touch and the opposite side was ice cold. The worst thing was her habit of inviting callers in with me sitting in the soapy suds covering my embarrassment with the flannel.

'Mum,' I would complain, 'you shouldn't ask people in when I'm bathing.'

'Don't be silly. You haven't got anything that they haven't seen before,' she would answer.

Having removed the scent of the River Usk from my person I spent the next few days alone with my comics whilst my mother enquired about Randolph among the neighbours and went about arranging National Assistance for us. National Assistance was a feature of the new Welfare State, and is amazingly still a part of the British Welfare System provided financial and other support for the destitute and Randolph had left us destitute. Her coming and going went on for about a week and one morning I awoke to find her packing one of Randolph's suitcases.

'Get your breakfast and then you can pack any things that you can carry,' she said. I stood for a few minutes watching her pack and then asked, 'Where are we going, Mum?'

'I don't know,' she replied, 'we'll find somewhere.' I could only think of one thing and I must have spoken in a small voice when I said, 'I won't have to go back to the homes will I?' She gathered me into her arms and held me close saying, 'You'll never have to go anywhere without me again, my love. I promise you that.'

That was the end of my brief period of security and life in Pontllanfraith. We never saw Randolph again but when a number of years later we had found a permanent home my mother got in touch with him and he began to send a weekly maintenance postal order for his son my brother. He continued this without fail every week until my brother's sixteenth birthday and then the payments ceased without communication of any kind.

We left the small council house, waved off by Madge and kids, on a wet autumn day and began our travels once more. This time, however, there was a difference; I was a year older, several years sharper and much more afraid of the unknown.

Chapter Seven

For a change my mother did have an idea of where we were going, she planned to contact an aunt who lived in Buckinghamshire but Pontllanfraith was a long way from Buckinghamshire and we had very little cash. Not to be daunted she decided to make the journey in easy stages beginning with a walk of about nine miles or fourteen kilometres to the town of Abercynon where she had an old friend. Although my legs had been toughened up in the Sunlight Homes they began to ache after the first couple of miles and I complained as only a young child can - loudly.

'I'm tired, Mum. My legs hurt.'

'Yes, yes,' she said, 'it's not much further.

'Mum, my legs hurt.'

I continued whining, the intervals between grumbles getting shorter and shorter until I must have sounded like a damaged vinyl record finally I threw myself down on the grass verge and when she turned to look back I stared at her defiantly. Amazingly she resisted the urge that she must have had to shake me or smack me around the head and sat down beside me. She then began to tell me the story of John Rees and the Devil's Field illustrating it with demonic facial expressions and wild gesticulation.

Thankfully passing motorists were rare because any such would have seen a wild woman grimacing and waving her hands sitting next to a vacant faced boy and concluded that they had escaped from some institution. After the story and a short rest we began our walk once more. It was not long before I was once again complaining; my mother put up with it in silence for a few dozen yards and then she halted, 'I know, we'll sing like the soldiers do when they are marching,' she said and we marched off like soldiers singing loudly.

So began a pattern that was to carry us over many long miles during the next year or so. She would tell me stories or sing her favourite old songs and teach me the words as we went along. I soon knew most of the Old Time Music Hall numbers verse and chorus and the songs of Al Jolson, one of her favourites, became as familiar to me as any nursery rhyme. When I was too tired to walk another step she would say, 'Let's count the telegraph poles. I bet that by the time we have counted one hundred we will find a town,' and on we would go.

The miles went by and we reached Abercynon only to discover that my mother's friend had moved away. The woman who now occupied the house was unable to offer us lodgings but she knew of a widow who had a vacancy. 'You might find her a bit strange,' she said, 'but her son was murdered a couple of years ago and she has not been the same since.'

She then went into the gory details of the crime, the woman's ten year old son had been found on the mountainside with his throat cut, 'From ear to ear,' she said with relish. She then related that he had been assaulted 'physically' and she allowed the Welsh lilt in her voice to linger on the word 'phys-ic-ally.' The authorities had taken photographs of the retinas of the dead child's eyes in case they had retained the image of his killer (a popular myth of the times) but nothing had been found and the killer had not been caught.

After listening to the murder story I was not eager to visit the odd woman but my mother told me not to be silly and off we went. The house was a typical terraced miner's house with a facing of grey limestone. In answer to our knock the door opened slightly and a woman's face appeared in the gap.

'Yes?' she asked.

Once you had made it through the door and broken the ice there were none more generous or warm than the people of the Welsh Valleys but until you had established your credentials they could be suspicious and hostile treating you as if you were a wild Englishman intent on rape and pillage.

'Is that your boy?' the face enquired.

My mother said that I was and explained that we were looking for lodgings. The woman opened the door wide and stepped back,

'Come in then,' she said impatiently.

We entered and were led through to the ever dominant kitchen, after we were seated my mother explained that we were on our way to England but needed lodgings until she heard from her aunt. The details were settled over a cup of tea and Mrs. Evans who had explained that she was a widow and alone in the world since her only son had been killed several years before rose to her feet,

'I will show you to your bedroom,' she said and carrying our luggage we followed her up the narrow staircase. At the top of the stairs was a door immediately on the right and a corridor to the left. She stood back against the wall and we squeezed past her into the corridor. She indicated the door at the top of the stairs and looking right into my eyes said,

'You must never go in there; never.'

We looked at her in silence.

'That was my Derek's room,' she said,' and it is just the way that he left it on the day that he was murdered.'

I am certain that my mother must have felt the same chill that ran down my back because all that she did was look at me without a word.

'Nothing has been moved,' said Mrs. Evans, 'and nothing ever will be until the day he returns or the day that I die.'

I was bewildered by the thought of her dead son returning but politeness kept me from commenting.

'I am so sorry,' said my mother and that seemed to close the conversation because Mrs. Evans promptly conducted us to a small neat rear bedroom and having shown us the large white chamber pot beneath the bed (for night use, she explained) she left us. I put my arms around my mother, 'I don't like it here, Mum,' I said.

'Don't be silly,' she said, 'It's the living that hurt you not the dead.'

We sat on the bed and I learned about my mother's aunt in Buckinghamshire. She had been cook to a titled family for many years so many years that, according to my mother, she was like part of their family. Time passed and Mrs. Evans called us down to our tea. After tea my mother related the circumstances that had brought us to her door, leaving out the bit about her pregnancy and then we heard more about her son's murder. She told us what a lovely boy he was,

'Not much older than you,' she said to me, 'but better looking.' She went on to tell how he had gone out one afternoon to play on the mountainside as usual and how worried she had been when darkness fell and he had not returned home. 'I was worried,' she said, 'but only because I thought that he might have had a fall you see.'

She had waited until late evening and then gone next door to seek help from her neighbours. The man next door and his sons had gone out to search for Derek without success. Finally she had called in the police and after listening to her story they had agreed to launch a search at first light.

The hours must have seemed like eternity to that poor woman as she waited comforted by her neighbours and then a solemn faced policeman had knocked the door. He came in and stood looking at her for several moments as if he wanted to give her the terrible news without speaking.

'It was then that I broke down,' she said. 'I knew something awful had happened to my boy.'

The policeman told her that they had found Derek's body deep in the ferns. She made an attempt to leave the room, wanting to see her son but they restrained her. When they had finally got her to bed the policeman told the neighbour that the boy was naked, he had been brutally assaulted and his throat had been cut. The neighbour later told Mrs. Evans that, as he told the details, the great tall police officer had been shaking as if on the verge of breaking down and had said that he never wanted to see anything like that again.

Although the woman had said that our new landlady was strange I found her kind-hearted and felt sorry for her. She did have a strange habit of pausing in mid-speech and gazing into space for a moment or two but as her conversations were with my mother, apart from her remark about my lack of good looks, that did not bother me greatly.

The day after our taking up lodgings my mother wrote to her aunt asking her for help. My days over the next couple of weeks were spent getting to know the local kids although my mother strictly forbade any play on the mountainside.

'Remember what happened to Mrs. Evans's poor boy,' she said.

The ban did not cause me any problems as there was a great play area nearby. Ours was one of four streets the backs of which formed a sort of large quadrangle, in the middle of this quadrangle bounded on each side by a back lane was a steep sided depression about ten feet deep and the area of a football pitch. Nothing grew there because the dirt sides and floor were constantly trodden by dozens of kids and for us it was a perfect play area. Football, cricket, rounders were all played and there was never any risk of losing the ball or breaking a window because the steep embankments acted as natural fencing.

Epic marble marathons took place on a daily basis played in different forms the most popular games being "In The Pit" and "The Square." The first was played by standing on a mark and attempting to pitch your marbles into a shallow depression dug by someone's heel, a sort of kid's marble golf. The first one to get all of their marbles - the number having been agreed - into the hole won the lot. The second game consisted of 'knuckling' your marbles at a square in which players had placed a number of marbles; any that you knocked out of the square were yours. I loved to watch these games but could not join in because I lacked a bag of marbles; when I was not out playing I mooched around the house listening to the radio or reading.

My mother always said that the Devil made work for idle hands and there were none idler than mine. Mrs. Evans supplemented her income by working as a charlady and every day she would disappear for several hours. One day when she was out working and my mother was out seeking government help I had an urge to look inside the front bedroom.

Climbing the stairs quietly, why quietly I do not know, perhaps because although I was alone in the house in some way I felt that I was not; standing in front of the forbidden door I was both scared and excited and I could feel my heart thumping in my chest. I finally summoned up the courage to try the doorknob and finding it to be unlocked I opened the door; the first thing that I noticed was the atmosphere, smell would not be the right word, odour might come closer but atmosphere is best.

If there was any smell it was that of decay, of a room that had not known fresh air for years. I stood there taking everything in and realised that I was not alone. There was no apparition, no ghostly noise or any other paranormal sign but I knew that he was there with me. I resisted the desire to leave and shut the door on whatever or whoever existed in that room and looked around.

In the far corner was a small bed the bedclothes thrown back and hanging down to the floor. On the bed lay an open comic book and a football sock. Clothing was scattered about the floor waiting for a cleaner who would never arrive. On a wooden chest that stood against one wall were a number of toy cars and tin soldiers. A dressing table with a tall mirror stood in the window blocking the light and making the room gloomy; at the foot of the bed was a large pile of comic books. A thin film of dust coated the surfaces of the furniture.

I remembered what my mother had said about the dead not hurting you but it was of little comfort because I knew that Derek Evans was beside me watching me and resenting my presence in his room. 'I won't hurt anything, Derek,' I said out loud, 'Honest I won't,' but I felt no easier for that.

I moved further into the room and up to the heap of comic books. They were yellowing with age. Carefully lifting the top one I laid it open on the floor and began to read. After a few pages I would pause aware of that sad boy looking over my shoulder but such was my hunger for reading material that I would soon resume reading feeling that he had every right to read his own comics. When I had finished the comic I replaced it carefully and left the room. Before closing the door something prompted me to say, 'Thank you, Derek.' I knew that he had heard me and hoped that he had forgiven me.

Over the following days I visited the bedroom many times gradually working my way through the comic heap but never staying too long and always replacing everything exactly as I had found it. One day I opened the top drawer of the dressing table, amongst the usual boyish bits and pieces was a square biscuit tin. As soon as I lifted it I knew its contents, marbles, there were dozens of coloured marbles together with several large plain glass Taws or Tolleys.

When I next went to the play area I put Derek's marbles to good use, consoling myself with the thought that I was only borrowing them and might win a few more for him. Unfortunately I failed to win him extra marbles, I lost the lot. Neither Mrs. Evans nor my mother ever discovered my misdeed; my punishment was to have both that room and its unseen presence imprinted on my memory for years to come.

We lodged with Mrs. Evans for a couple of weeks and then my mother received a reply from her aunt together with a postal order to help with the train fare. We would be welcome to come down and her mistress would give my mother a job on the kitchen staff. It was pleasant to be travelling by train rather than walking and to watch the countryside flashing past whilst trying to imagine who lived in the countless houses and cottages.

It was early evening when we arrived in High Wycombe having made the last stage of our journey by bus. My mother's aunt was at the bus stop to greet us, a short plump woman with neat grey hair and a happy face. Another short bus trip took us to her house, although a full-time cook she lived out and commuted the short distance to her work each day. After supper she and my mother chatted in front of the fire whilst I listened to the radio and then she led us up to a cosy bedroom filled mainly by a large brass knobbed bed. I was soon asleep in the deepest feather mattress that I had ever been buried in.

The next morning she took us on the bus to her place of employment, she had explained that her mistress's young son was home from boarding school and that if I was very well behaved I would be allowed to play with him and take meals with him but she added,

'You must be good, mark you, because he is a Right Honourable.'

She must have assumed that I knew what a 'Right Honourable' was and I had learned not to show ignorance.

The home of the young Right Honourable was a large house set in its own grounds, we entered through the rear garden into a kitchen that compared in size with that of the Sunlight Homes kitchen but there any resemblance ended. Gleaming copper pans and utensils hung from hooks and sat on racks, a large scrubbed table dominated the centre of the room and a fire glowed in the open fireplace.

Upon our entrance the handful of young women who had been seated at the table rose to their feet, I later realised that this was in deference to my mother's aunt who was absolute ruler of that domain. After a few brief exchanges of 'good mornings' and introductions my mother and her aunt left the room and I was left in the care of the kitchen staff.

I soon found myself seated at the table with a glass of milk and a slice of cake before me then, as the women busied themselves with their duties I gazed around me. They had opened a large walk-in larder and I saw hanging from a hook in the ceiling a dead bird. I was shocked and could not take my eyes of the poor thing; thankfully they soon closed the door.

I resumed my examination of the kitchen and was studying the gleaming white cooker with its chimney pipe running up through the ceiling when my mother returned. She was not only accompanied by her aunt but also by a tall handsome lady - the word woman would not suffice for that person whose appearance and bearing shouted 'lady.' The lady crossed to my chair and said,

'So you are David. How do you do, David. I am...'

'Hello,' I said.

'Say, How do you do, My Lady,' said my mother's aunt. I dutifully complied and received a warm smile from the lady,

'I think you should meet Philip,' she said 'Come along,' and she took my hand. I recall how cool her fingers were as if she had just washed in cold water.

My mother and her aunt remained in the kitchen. I was led along corridors and up staircases until I had lost all sense of direction. Our progress was marked by a steady improvement in decor and furnishing and then at the end of a short corridor we came to a white door. The door opened into a large bright room and I saw a fair-haired young boy a little older than I sat on a bed reading a book. He jumped up when he saw the lady and rushed to hug her with a cry of,

'Mummy!'

She eased herself from his grasp and said, 'This is David, my darling. He is going to spend some time with us and you must make him welcome.' Philip and I looked at each other for a moment and then he extended his hand and said,

'Hello.'

'Hello,' I said and shook his hand.

'Where is Nanny?' asked the lady.

'I believe she is next door,' replied Philip.

'I must leave you now, my darling, mind that you are kind to David,' said the lady and left the room closing the door quietly behind her. We stood and looked at each other in that awkward way that boys will upon meeting a stranger. It was Philip who broke the silence,

'Do you like soldiers?' he asked.

I nodded and he crossed to a chest whose brass drop handled drawers were long and narrow. I followed him and watched as he opened a drawer I do not know if I gasped but I am certain that I drew a deep breath when I saw the contents, there lying on green baize was an army of brilliantly coloured lead soldiers. The dangers of lead were not recognised at the time and although model soldiers were beginning to be cast from safer metal a great many of the lead variety were still in circulation.

Philip picked up a model lancer mounted on an upwardly rearing charger and handed it to me. I found that although it appeared fully three dimensional it was in fact quite flat, one of the variety known to collectors as 'lead flats.' I later discovered in the course of our play that each drawer - and there were at least eight of them- held a complete regiment of soldiers; cavalry, infantry, artillery, there were even bands-men with bright gold instruments and waving banners.

I helped him lay out his army on the highly polished floor of the nursery and we were kneeling deeply engaged in a battle when the door opened and a woman entered. Philip rose to his feet,

'Hello, Nanny,' he said, 'this is David.'

Nanny a pleasant young woman wearing what looked like a nurse's uniform without the cap gazed at me for a long moment and finally said,

'Yes.'

'We've to make him welcome,' said Philip.

'Yes,' said Nanny.

I was still on my knees but I decided it would be a good idea to stand up and did so.

'I am Nanny Hicks but you may call me Nanny,' she said.

I could think of nothing to say but, 'Thank you.'

She turned to Philip, 'Hands,' and he held out his hands for inspection. I was not to escape,

'Hands.' I held my hands out palms up and Nanny took hold of them and turned the palms down,

'You bite your nails, David.'

She pursed her lips. I had been biting my nails for as long as I could remember but never until that moment had I felt guilty about the habit. I looked down at my feet in shame.

'We do not bite our nails,' she said.

I waited for a long lecture but that was it Nanny Hicks did not believe in wasting words and she did not need to, one word from her was sufficient to reduce you to instant obedience, guilt or joy as she wished.

Later that day I sat at the nursery table with Nanny and Philip and enjoyed my first luncheon in his home - I had never heard the word luncheon before the midday meal being dinner in my vocabulary. I also began my education in the etiquette of an English dining room and the manners of a young gentleman. My chameleon like nature took over and within a couple of weeks I was using 'one does this' or 'one does that' as if I had never known any other form of speech. Nanny kindly arranged for breakfast to be served after my early morning arrival each day and supper before my evening departure.

Philip was a kind generous child the juvenile personification of noblesse oblige and I soon grew to regard him with affection. With the exception of the twins in the Sunlight Homes I had never known a true friend but Philip by his patience, his polite consideration, his great sense of fun and his generosity with all that was his taught me very quickly what the word friend meant.

Nanny Hicks was all that was good about the British Nanny, firm but gentle, patient but persistent and a mistress of child psychology able to bend us to her will without our realising that we were being bent. Philip adored her, understandably so perhaps because I only saw his lady mother in the nursery once or twice in all the weeks I was a guest in their house. I should not, however, imply criticism of a lady who gave succour to a stranger and her child.

We had been in Buckinghamshire several weeks when my mother paused in the middle of dressing for work and said, 'We will be leaving here tomorrow, love. We have to go back home.' She did not realise that the word 'home' had little meaning for me. I had long since ceased to feel that any place was home, in truth our present situation felt more like home than any place that I had known. I think that the knowledge that I would not see Philip or Nanny Hicks again was a sharper blow than that I had felt when we left Barry Town.

On my last day in the nursery Nanny handed me a neatly packaged bundle of comics saying, 'You can read these on the train,' and for the first and only time she kissed me on my cheek with 'God Bless you, my dear.'

When my mother came to collect me the lady was with her and in what was again an only instance she hugged me saying, 'Take care of your mother, David,' then she turned to Philip and said, 'Philip has something to say.'

Philip looked sad as he held out his hand, 'I am sorry that you are going, David,' he said. I shook his hand awkwardly. Then he looked at Nanny who held out a mid-sized leather suitcase. He took it in two hands (it was obviously heavy by the way he lifted it) and placed it on the floor in front of me.

'Philip wants you to have these to remember us by,' said the lady.

I looked at them and then at my mother.

'Say thank you,' she said.

I said my thank you and went to pick up the case. It was indeed surprisingly heavy and it was as much as I could do to lift it; seeing me struggle my mother took it from me. When we were back at my mother's aunt's house we opened the suitcase, inside, individually wrapped in newsprint, were scores of Philip's lead soldiers. There must have been well over a hundred of them and I would have unwrapped them all and played with them immediately but my mother told me to wait until I could do it properly and packed them up again. That kind boy had given me a complete drawer-full of his precious soldiers and I believe that the idea to do so was his alone.

Excluding the ill-bred nouveau riche who dominate today's upper circles I believe that breeding is apparent where it truly exists and I hold inside of me the image of a fair-headed young Right Honourable gentleman whose identity must remain shrouded in the mists of time because I never knew his family name or title and never will; his gift was wasted because I never got to play with those brave soldiers. Like my gallant cowboy and my Grampie's promised gifts they were destined to disappear.

Chapter Eight

Following my mother's tearful goodbye to her aunt on the next day we took the bus to the nearest railway station and were soon en-route to South Wales. My mother had decided to return to Pontllanfraith in the hope of pinning down the errant Randolph.

We arrived at Cardiff station early evening and it was getting dark so she decided to spend the night on the station. Main line railway stations were a lot different then and were not the inhospitable wind tunnels that they are today. Cardiff boasted two large waiting rooms on every platform each complete with roaring fires that were kept alight day and night by smiling porters. There were separate cloakrooms on each platform for ladies and gentlemen and the buffet restaurant was open twenty-four hours a day. When I think of the way in which people would then joke about British Rail buffets I think of how warm and hospitable they seem now.

My mother tucked me up on one of the long leather upholstered benches and went to buy tea and a sandwich, when she returned we ate and then settled down for the night. Providing you had a valid train ticket no one bothered you and I spent the rest of the evening reading or studying the many travellers who passed through the waiting rooms.

Occasionally I would go and sit on a bench on the platform in the hope of seeing an express train thunder through the station. This was the age of the steam engine and these monsters would hurtle through the station shaking the platform and deafening any waiting passengers. It was as if the very earth shook and the vortex of their passing was both terrifying and thrilling making you feel an urge to surrender to it and fall under their wheels.

The hour grew late so my mother made me lie down and get some sleep. I obeyed but it was a fitful sleep interrupted by whistles, train announcements and thundering locomotives. The next morning being a Sunday and trains being few we once again enjoyed British Rail buffet hospitality whilst we awaited our train.

When we arrived at the Pontllanfraith station my mother deposited my case of soldiers in the left luggage office saying that it was far too heavy to lug about; I never saw it again and for all I know it may still be sitting on a luggage office shelf awaiting its young owner but I doubt it. Having shed the weight of my soldiers she decided that we could walk the four miles to Oakdale where she planned to visit Randolph's sister in the hope of tracking him down. I had long since ceased to protest at her appetite for long marches and off we went with me carrying my package of comics; I was not ready to give that portion of Philip's gift up easily.

We reached Oakdale a couple of hours later after counting dozens of telegraph poles and singing a lengthy selection of old time songs. Randolph's sister made us welcome and as usual I was sent out to the garden to play with the kids. Randolph's nieces and nephews together with several neighbour's kids were rehearsing a popular song. One of the older girls who obviously knew the words was reciting them line by line and after each line the kids would sing as far as they had learned. The song was called "Who Were You With Last Night?" and the kids all thought they were being daring by singing lines like, "... It wasn't your sister. It wasn't your ma. Oh, Oh, Oh, what a liar you are." When it came to the part that went, "... Are you gonna tell your missus when you get home?" We all fell about laughing and rolling our eyes. Oh how innocent we were in those happy childhood days.

When my mother eventually called me indoors she told me that Randolph's sister knew of a housekeeping vacancy nearby and we were soon tramping back along the road that we had walked earlier in the day but not all the way. About a mile down the road we came to a public house boasting the title, "The Prince of Wales" on a swinging sign adorned with a painting of the Three Feathered Crest of that prince.

The pub was closed so we went around to the back of the building and found ourselves in a large flag stoned yard. To the rear of this yard were a number of low-walled enclosures each with its own small building. The area smelled strongly of some sharp odour that stung my nose and a grunting and scuffling sound came from the enclosures. My mother knocked loudly on the rear door of the pub and getting no response shouted,

'Hello.'

'Hello,' the answer came in a disembodied voice.

I looked towards the voice and saw a large red faced man straightening up behind the gate of an enclosure. 'Wait a bit,' he said and turning he swore and appeared to kick out at some other inhabitant of the space. The man opened the gate, once again turning back and uttering loud threats, and then having closed it firmly he crossed the yard. He was wearing wellington boots that were covered in what I took to be mud but later discovered was pig dung and a flat cap several sizes too large for him that would have covered his eyes had it not been held up by his large ears.

My mother spoke first, 'Mr. James?' She enquired.

'Yes that's me.'

'I was told that you were looking for a housekeeper,' she said.

'Are you a housekeeper?'

'I am and I have references.'

He looked at me, 'This your boy?'

'Yes,' she answered, 'and he comes with me.'

'You'd best come in,' he said and led us into the dark interior of the pub.

The building must have been centuries old and the kitchen into which he led us had an enormous inglenook fireplace and dark oak beams running across the ceiling. From these beams suspended by hooks were joints of meat covered in a thick brown crystalline crust. It was the total opposite of the light airy Buckinghamshire kitchen and I was fascinated by its dark smoky atmosphere.

'I'm Billy James,' said the man, 'and I am looking for a housekeeper.'

My mother introduced herself and me and asked, 'Do you live on the premises?'

'Ay,' said Billy, 'I lives, sleeps, eats and breaths here. This is a free house. I'm not a tenant landlord.' He offered her a drink and when she declined he proceeded to make us a cup of tea. During the process they chatted.

'I keeps pigs,' he said, 'I breeds them. Billy out there is three times champion.'

I wondered idly why he had named a pig after himself and then went back to studying the room. We were seated on a hard cushioned high backed settle that together with another of the same opposite ours made an extension to the chimney corner. A long scrubbed table ran down the centre of the room and a bench together with a couple of wooden wheel back chairs provide seating, a large gas stove with a number of shelves above it holding or providing hanging space for pans and utensils served for cooking. A butcher's chopping block stood alongside a large dresser. I had noticed in front of the window by the door a square white sink or bosh standing on brick supports. The window was apart from the fire the only source of light and although it was early afternoon the room was dark. It was my first experience of an old fashioned country kitchen.

Billy James and my mother must have reached an agreement whilst I was studying the room because I found myself following them through into a long passageway and from there into the public bar area; like the kitchen it was dark and cool with a smoke stained ceiling and panelled walls. This was another first for me and I sniffed in the smell of stale beer and old tobacco smoke, I found it quite pleasant and sat down happily on a large settle as Billy took my mother behind the bar.

'You'll be wanted to help out behind the bar when needed,' he said,' Think you can do that?'

She assured him that she could. He then lifted a box from behind the bar and said,

'Come here, boy.'

I crossed to the bar that was at the height of my chin. He tilted the box towards me and I saw that it was filled with brightly coloured metal discs with serrated edges. I later discovered that these were crown bottle tops from the beer bottles.

'Help yourself,' said Billy, 'Go on fill your pockets.'

I obeyed and my jacket pockets soon bulged with bottle tops complete with their beer smell.

'You can play games with them,' he said, 'Soldiers, pirate treasure. My boys used to play for hours with them.'

Possessing a vivid imagination fed by comic books and children's film matinees I found no problem with his suggestion and spent the remainder of the afternoon fighting battles on the large scrubbed table. I would have preferred my lead flats but the variety of bottle tops gave plenty of scope for military units of all types.

After supper that my mother had prepared from the stock in Billy's larder he beckoned me to accompany him through into the public bar. I looked at my mother, 'Go on,' she said, 'Go with Mr. James.'

We both followed him through. The bar room was not much lighter with the dim electric lamps switched on. He crossed to the bar. 'There's a lot of valuable stuff in here, boy,' he said, 'and a lot of thieves would like to get their hands on it.'

I was a little puzzled by his words. He continued,

'But we won't let them, will we?'

I shook my head.

'No. We won't let them because we can see them at it.'

With those words he laid his flat cap on the bar turned away and bent over. When he straightened up still with his back to us he beckoned us towards the bar. We went across and as we reached the bar he turned stepping back and indicating his cap said,

'Because we keeps an eye on things.'

There lying on his cap was a large glass eyeball staring blindly at us. I do not know if I yelped but I recall my mother gasping and I am not sure if that was from shock or the way in which I gripped her arm in both hands. Billy roared with laughter and when he calmed down said, 'Got you there, that's my glass eye that is; look,' and he showed the empty eye socket.

I felt sick and leaned on my mother. 'Oh, Mr. James,' she said.

'That always gets them,' he said and nudging me, 'I don't really keep it there; it goes in a glass of water by the bed.'

That night my dreams were filled with giant bloodshot eyeballs chasing me down dimly lit corridors and I have never felt comfortable with prosthetic body parts.

The next morning after splashing cold water on my face from the jug that stood in a large china bowl on the bedroom's washstand I went down to the wonderful aroma of frying bacon. Billy James was seated at the large table wiping his plate with a thick slice of buttered bread and when I was seated my mother put a plate before me on which were two fried eggs and two thick slices of bacon. I looked at it this was unlike any bacon I had ever seen; as thick as a man's finger it appeared to be nothing but fat edged with brown crust and showing thin streaks of meat in one or two places.

'That will do you good, boy,' said Billy, 'That's my own bacon, cured in that chimney.'

I was about to experience that which locals called 'Rusty Bacon.' I cut a piece and tasted it. The bacon was the saltiest thing that I had ever had in my mouth but surprisingly tasty and the crust was satisfyingly chewy. I soon put eggs and bacon away along with several slices of farmhouse bread spread thickly with butter. It must have been one of the unhealthiest meals on record but I loved it and became a life long convert to home cured bacon.

Our days at the "Prince of Wales" were happy ones. Every morning after a breakfast of rusty bacon and farm eggs I went into the bar and collected my treasure trove of bottle caps after that I was free to wander the valley behind the pub and Billy allowed me to help him prepare the pig swill that he cooked up in an old washing boiler from potato peelings and other vegetable off cuts donated by friends and customers. We would then carry buckets filled with the swill to the pig pens and fill the troughs.

I grew fond of the two old sows and their litters and learned from Billy that pigs were highly intelligent creatures ranking with domestic dogs in the animal IQ tables. Billy allowed me to help him muck out and change the bedding of the beasts explaining that pigs were also clean animals and preferred clean dry living quarters. I was soon taking a large part of the work off his hands the exception being duties involving Billy the boar. I was never allowed to enter his pen, not even in the company of his owner. 'Never ever go in with that boar,' said Billy, 'He'd kill you as soon as look at you.'

This of course would have been a challenge to any boy and I was desperate to prove him wrong; after all he went in with the animal. I began to court Billy the boar taking him tit bits and treats in the shape of bits of cake or biscuits. I would cautiously approach the low gate of his pen the top of which came level with my nose and standing on tiptoe I would call his name and throw in the tit bit.

If I was a little slow between the calling and the throwing he would hurl his weight at the gate and it appeared as if the whole pen shook. He was, as Billy James had said, a quick tempered beast. About six feet in length from snout to curly tail his girth was that of a young bullock. He had a big wet snout, sharp tusks and tiny malevolent eyes.

There is no doubt that his kind had good reason to hate humanity and it was as if generations of hate had come together in one vengeful pig but I persevered and continued feeding him until one day when I called there was no response in the shape of a hurtling mass of pig. I peered over the gate. Billy stood in the far corner of his pen pawing the concrete and grunting in a deep low way. I threw the biscuit and he ignored it. I called his name and he grunted louder and pawed the ground harder.

I was puzzled. I had never seen him behave this way. I hooked my elbows over the top of the gate and heaved myself up until I was hanging suspended with my top half in the pen and my bottom half dangling against the gate. I called his name again and held out a biscuit struggling to maintain my balance and not fall into the pen. Suddenly the monster moved, so quickly that I did not even see the beginning of his charge. I saw a great open sharply tusked mouth approaching, heard a grunt that was more like a bellow and felt myself flying through the air backwards. I fell onto my hands and knees as the boar hit the gate cracking the timber in his rage.

'You stupid stupid boy. What did I tell you?' roared Billy James, because it was he who had spotted my peril and dragged me back from it by the scruff of my pants.

He led me back into the house leaving Billy the boar charging around his pen screaming with frustration. My mother was busy in the kitchen ignorant of how close I had come to becoming pig food. He sat me down and told her what had happened.

'Do you know how close you came to being killed' he asked, 'Do you realise how dangerous a pig like that is?' He then went on to tell the story of a fellow pig breeder who had been crushed against the wall of a pig pen by an angry boar, 'No one heard his cries for help,' he said, 'and the beast gored him to death. When they found him the boar had eaten his face away and was sitting beside the body crunching the man's jawbone in his bloody teeth.' The message went home and I never went near the mad boar again.

Christmas came and with it my first taste of goose and my first glass of "Stone's Ginger Wine." 'A glass won't hurt the boy and it is Christmas,' said Uncle Billy. My mother had the curious habit of insisting that I call her friends or even acquaintances Auntie or Uncle, I may have been poor in possessions but I was rich in uncles and aunties. Thankfully I did not have too many true aunts and uncles or I might have been a very confused child.

It was about this time that my mother began eating aspirin. She was about four months into her time but it did not show and I was bound to secrecy. Twice a week she would take me to the take me to the cinema in Blackwood. I loved 'the pictures' as we called them and being devoid of any critical faculty believed everything that I saw on the screen. The romanticism that the films instilled in me was to remain for decades and cause me a great deal of trouble. One film that left a lasting impression was "The Wizard of Oz" and I recall clearly the thrill that I felt when the screen changed from monochrome to Technicolor; my heart jumped in my chest and I ceased to be an onlooker, becoming an inhabitant of that magical kingdom.

Before going into the cinema she would buy me a bag of sweets and once inside she would produce a bottle of aspirin from her handbag. As I munched sweets she would crunch aspirin tablets. She never appeared to be affected by her consumption of the drug and the habit continued up until the birth of my brother ceasing thereafter, so I assume that it must have been some kind of pregnant woman's fancy.

Early in the New Year Uncle Billy announced that he was closing the "Prince of Wales" due to a family crisis and so we were to part company with that character of a man his glass eye and his pigs. My mother set about finding us a lodging place but before we left the pigs were taken away and it took six men with ropes and chains to drag Billy the boar into the slaughterer's truck. I can close my eyes today and hear his screams ringing in my ears. I am sure that he fought hard for his life at the other end of his journey and not being fond of slaughter men I hope that he made them suffer.

We moved to a lodging place in Pontllanfraith and the search for a housekeeping job began anew. One morning soon after the move my mother opened a letter and became excited. It was news of an interview for a job in Merthyr Tydfil. On the morning of the interview I wished her luck at the bus stop and went back to my books. It was late afternoon when she returned and she was not in through the door before she burst out with the news. She had been given the job living in with me included and could start as soon as she liked.

'You'll never guess who it's with' she said and before I could attempt to guess, 'It's with the Ex-Lord Mayor of Merthyr,' she said, 'and you should see the house.'

I should point out that there were no ordinary town mayors for my mother there were only Lord Mayors. I of course had no idea what or who a mayor of any description was but it sounded grand and she was happy. There was, as always, a down side: our money had almost run out, by the time we paid the landlady we did not have bus fare to Merthyr Tydfil.

'Never mind,' said my mother, 'it is not far away.' It was fifteen miles.

We set off the next day and by the time that we had reached the first small hamlet on our route I was tired irritable and hungry.

'We'll have something to eat,' said my mother.

We found a small cafe with red chequered table cloths and bent wood chairs typical of hundreds that served the communities of the Valleys. I was glad to sit down and the smell of fried food coming from a back room made me even hungrier. My mother leaned across to me, 'You know that we haven't much money so don't ask for anything,' she said, 'just leave it to me.'

When the waitress came to us pencil poised over a little pad my mother ordered, 'A pot of tea for two, bread and butter for four and might we please have a pot of English mustard.'

The waitress looked at her over the pad but said nothing scribbled away and left. I was waiting for my mother to order egg and chips or sausage and beans but she just sat there smiling at me.

When the waitress returned with our order my mother thanked her and asked her for a knife.

'One or two?' asked the woman in a sarcastic tone.

'Just one please and an extra plate.'

When she had her knife and the extra plate my mother opened the pot of mustard sniffed it suspiciously (mustard was always made in-house from mustard powder and water or milk and could become stale or sour). Satisfied she gave it a stir with the tip of the knife and proceeded to spread a generous layer on the bread.

A child of today would undoubtedly make some comment if offered bread and mustard but I accepted my allotted portion folded a piece in half and ate away. I was very hungry and it was not too bad, something like a ham sandwich without the ham. We finished our meal and when we were back outside my mother turned to me and said, 'Now we can say that we have had a hot square meal.' We laughed at that and set off again. It was late afternoon when we reached the town of Quakers Yard and we had both had enough of walking having covered about eight miles.

'Now then, let's find a house with friendly curtains,' suggested my mother.

She was a great believer in friendly curtains friendly front doors and friendly lights in windows; there were never unfriendly ones those not classed as friendly were deemed to be sad. She was oddly enough seldom wrong and to this day I often go down a street thinking of friendly curtains. We walked up a small street and halfway up and she said, 'That's a friendly pair of curtains.'

All curtains looked the same to me at that age, ninety-nine per cent of Valleys houses having faded white lace ones. She knocked on the front door of the friendly house and an elderly woman opened it.

'I am sorry to bother you, my dear,' said my mother, 'but my little boy and I have nowhere to sleep tonight and I wondered if you had a settee that we could sleep on.'

If fortune favours the brave kindness must favour the cheeky because the dear old lady asked us in and within minutes we were sitting in front of a glowing fire while she brewed a pot of tea. The tea came with buttered bread and jam and as she sat watching me eat she muttered, 'Poor dab. Poor dab.'

We slept in her spare bedroom that night, in a feather bed warmed by several stone hot water bottles. I was an imaginative child and when sleeping in those strange rooms I would try to picture the former inhabitants and think of them sleeping in that bed. On that particular night I was so worn out that I did little imagining and was fast asleep before my mother climbed into bed.

When we set off the next morning it was cold and raining as it can only rain in Wales. Before we had gone far the rain was running into my coat collar and down my back (we never did own an umbrella although my mother was always talking of buying one). We sheltered as best we could under an overhanging tree and she opened the suitcase and found a towel. With the towel tucked around my neck and into my collar I was leak proof and we began again. As usual she chattered away distracting me from my discomfort with tales of our family or her life. She never seemed to regard me as a child telling me in the most respectable terms the most lurid or chilling stories; as I knew no better I took it in my stride storing it all away in my fertile young imagination.

The town of Merthyr Tydfil had grown during the industrial revolution as a great centre of iron production and the mountainous slag heaps and industrial scars on the landscape became more and more evident as we approached. Here and there a scrawny sheep struggled to survive on the little vegetation left to it, bleating for sympathy as we passed.

By the time we reached the town centre the rain had stopped and my mother took me into a public toilet (Ladies) to clean me up. I hated being dragged into a ladies cloakroom because it usually meant some degree of undressing and I was only too aware of critical looks and muttered remarks of any women using the place. My mother seemed oblivious to any criticism and I was soon changed into dry clothes, face washed and hair combed.

We made our way through to the other side of the town and turned up a driveway between two gate portals surmounted by crouching stone lions. I saw the house for the first time: 'The House" is the only title that fits it. I was awe-struck at first sight of a large red brick and bath stone building that appeared to be the size of a small castle to an impressionable young boy except that where one would expect towers there appeared to be a forest of ornate chimneys.

At the end of the curving drive a wide flight of stone steps led up between two more lions to a tall double glass panelled front door the lintel of which was held up by two Greek columns. This door, however, was not for us and my mother led me up the steps and around to the back of the house following the gravelled veranda that surrounded the house.

We passed a number of mythical beasts carved or cast from stone and several French windows through which glimpses of dark interiors could be seen. When we reached the rear I saw a set of steps identical to the front steps leading down to a large garden area overgrown but clearly marked by its gravel paths and stone borders. A small glass windowed door was set deeply in an entranceway. My mother pressed the brass bell push for several seconds and then we waited.

After a little while the door was opened by an elderly man: I immediately thought of my grandfather because the man was neat, white haired and of similar build and features: he was wearing a white shirt with collar and tie, black trousers and what I would now recognise as a smoking jacket. He gave us a welcoming smile and said,

'Ha, there you are, my dear,' whereupon he beckoned us into a large kitchen.

I was fast becoming quite blasé where kitchens were concerned and not unduly impressed.

'This is my son David,' said my mother

The man extended his hand, 'How do you do, David,' he said 'I am Mr...' and regrettably I cannot recall his name perhaps because my mother referred to him as 'the mayor' or it could be because I always addressed him as 'Sir.'

I held out my hand, I don't think that any grown up had offered me such a courtesy before and I was embarrassed. His handshake was gentle like a child's. 'Please come through,' he said and led the way down a short passage through a door and into the entrance hall of the house. He walked slowly bent over and pausing now and then to take a breath.

Where the kitchen failed to impress the hall succeeded fully having a high ceiling and being as large as any two household rooms of my experience with dark panelled walls on which hung oil paintings in elaborate frames. A multi-coloured tiled floor led to the front door and I could see that the door panels were formed from vividly coloured glass. To one side of the hallway a wide staircase with a dark wood bannister of substantial proportions led up to a gallery. Several doors beside the one through which we had entered led off the hallway.

'I'll show you to your room,' said the man. He slowly led the way up the stairs pulling himself up each step by use of the handrail. The upper gallery of the house was as elegant as the lower floor the passageway lined with warm brown wood panelling and hung with paintings. He led us along to a room at the far end, 'Here we are,' he said, 'there is a bathroom just down the hall. Come down when you are ready and we'll have some tea.' He left us and my mother laid our suitcase on the counterpane of the brass knobbed double bed and looked around her, 'This is nice,' she said.

It was indeed a most pleasant room, there were no panelled walls but wallpaper with a pattern of large blue and grey flowers did the job quite tastefully. There were a number of pictures including a large landscape that hung above the tiled Victorian fireplace. In addition to the high bed (I usually resorted to stepping on a chair to climb into it) a dressing table, wardrobe, washstand, bedside tables and several chairs completed the furnishings of the large airy room. Heavy floor length curtains were drawn back to reveal a view of the rear garden through the tall windows.

`It was the finest bedroom that I had ever seen and a little intimidating. My mother took it all in her stride and set about unpacking whilst I examined the room opening wardrobe doors and drawers. The drawers of dressing table and wardrobe were lined with tissue paper and smelled of mothballs. I looked underneath the bed and saw the usual large china chamber pot but this one was decorated with a print of large flowers and possessed a white china lid.

We later went down to the kitchen for tea; my mother and I would always eat our meals in the kitchen whilst the mayor took his in the dining room. It was at the mayor's kitchen table that I first tasted venison; my mother explained what it was and thankfully for a highly impressionable child I had not yet seen Walt Disney's film "Bambi." That was my first and only experience of the taste of game, I have not eaten venison since that day but I recall clearly the strong sweet taste and the texture of the meat.

Apart from the other bedrooms I was given the run of the house and enjoyed roaming from room to room touching and feeling the numerous collectable objects that sat upon every square inch of display space. There were china figurines of shepherds and their ladies, milk maids, mythical figures, European and Oriental animals, bronze statuettes of heroes fighting mythical beasts and many other fascinating objet d'art. My favourite was a large bronze of Perseus standing with one foot on The Gorgon's head. I was careful never to move them from their resting place and handled them with such care as would have done credit to a museum curator.

On our first morning in the house it snowed and the overgrown rundown gardens were transformed into exhibitions of delicate ice sculptures. Stark bare bushes and shrubs became beautiful crystal traceries. Broken down greenhouses became ice palaces. The pitted paths were rivers of shining glass and the whole area was a wonderland of sparkle and dazzle. I was entranced and spent the entire morning wandering and wondering. When I returned to the house I wanted to tell my mother of my experience and the thrill of it but I lacked the words and my pathetic attempt to paint a picture for her failed to convey my wonder.

I seldom saw the mayor as he would spend most of his day in the study. When we did meet he was always kind and polite in his brief conversations with me. As he went about the house he would pom-pom tunelessly in the manner of "Winnie the Pooh"; Pom, pom, pom, tiddle, om, pom, pom. On one occasion he paused in mid pom as we passed each other and he asked me if I was reading anything interesting. I made some polite reply and he then said, 'Your mother tells me that you enjoy reading. Is that so?'

'Yes, sir,' I replied, 'more than anything.'

He studied me for a moment, 'And you know how to take care of books.'

I nodded and after a further brief pause he indicated for me to follow him and led the way to the library. As he beckoned I noticed not for the first time that his fingers were bent and hooked, and I could not know that this was a symptom of the crippling disease of arthritis. His condition was far advanced and he must have been in constant pain but his only indication of that was an occasional deep sigh.

We entered the library, I had been in that room with its floor to ceiling wall to wall bookshelves before but although sorely tempted I had never dared remove a book from the shelves. 'Well?' he asked, 'What do you think of my library?'

My command of the superlative was non existent and I was truly lost for words. He indicated an upholstered armchair and I sat. 'Now then,' he muttered and began circling the room examining the books. After a while he pulled a book from a shelf and using both hands to carry it he placed it on the leather covered table next to me. I leaned forward but he indicated that I should sit back and went on to select five or six more books each of which he laid on the table. 'Would you fetch that chair, David?' he asked and I carried a small library chair across to the table. 'Thank you,' he said, 'Now I think that you will enjoy these.'

He had selected a number of classics for me including: "Oliver Twist" and "Great Expectations." 'Have you heard of Charles Dickens?' he asked. I revealed that the name was unknown to me. 'You will learn to respect Charles Dickens,' he said, 'He was the greatest of English authors.'

To assist me in my reading he dragged a large dictionary down and spent some time explaining its use. Unfortunately, he did not take the time to explain the pronunciation key and as a result I spent many years knowing the correct word but loath to use it in case I pronounced it incorrectly - one example is the word 'misled,' I pronounced it 'mizzled' until my late teens and suffered some embarrassment as a result. Regardless of that slight problem I soon became a lover the works of Dickens and would spend every spare moment in the library devouring his wonderful words.

Many years later during my university days I was accused of plagiarism by a new lecturer who insisted that my essay was 'Mandarin English' and must have be a consequence of poaching. It was only when I explained my self education by means of the works of Charles Dickens and submitted further essays that he accepted the work as mine. I hope that I have gone some way towards correcting my failings in that direction. You must be the judge.

We had been several weeks with the mayor when he became ill. The doctor was called and advised bed rest. I missed the mayor and his pom, poms. I also missed his visits to the library and the interest he took in my literary education. My mother said that the mayor was suffering from old age and needed peace and quiet. I was therefore curious when she called me from the library one day and told me that mayor wished to see me. His bedroom was much larger than ours and to my eyes very grand. He was lying propped up by large white pillows in the middle of great bed with a tall wooden post at each corner. He looked very small and very old; my mother took me across to him.

'Hello, my boy,' he said,' I have missed our talks.'

'And me, Sir.'

To my mother he said, 'Please bring that chair across, Dorothy.' My mother carried a tall back bedroom chair to the side of the bed. 'We will need cushions.' he said and she obliged.

He motioned me to sit and I climbed up onto the chair. 'Have you heard of chess?' he asked. I had heard of chests and thought that he must be talking about a chest of drawers or suchlike but being uncertain I simply shook my head. 'You'll find a board and chessmen in that cabinet, Dorothy. Would you bring them over?' Again she complied and laid a heavy chess board and a wooden box on the bed between us. 'Thank you,' he said 'I think we can manage now,' and dismissed her with a smile. He then slid open the lid of the box and tipped hardwood chessmen onto the board.

Over the next few weeks he patiently taught me the rudiments of the greatest of board games; explaining the moves of each piece and correcting me when I made a wrong move. On most afternoons after that I would join him at his bedside and I soon began to enjoy our games. My kind opponent coached me through each move until the games lasted for an increasing number of moves. He never let me win and for that I am grateful but he did let me survive through the games and imbued me with a fondness for chess that has never left me.

The time spent in Merthyr Tydfil was one of the happier periods of my childhood; my mother was contented having only light duties thanks to the help of a cleaning woman who came in daily and I had regular meals, access to countless books and the companionship of a highly intelligent grandfather figure. It was too good to be true.

We had never heard the mayor speak of his family and my mother must have assumed that he had none; such matters did not enter my head. Then some weeks after our chess lessons had begun a couple appeared at the house, I believe that it was his son and daughter-in-law and they had come to take him to live with them.

I have often wondered if he was happy to go with them but nevertheless after spending a lengthy time with him the woman came downstairs and told my mother to seek new employment meanwhile she would herself be taking up temporary residence. We were given a week's notice and once again my mother began scouring the situations vacant columns of the newspapers. By the end of the week she had failed to find anything and we were about to become homeless.

On our last day my mother took me up to say goodbye to the mayor. He looked very old and tired and his voice had lost its resonance. I do not know what I expected but he simply said, 'Goodbye, David, look after yourself and keep up your reading,' and that was that.

Chapter Nine

We left the Mayor's house that same day and moved into a bed sitting room or what they now grandly call a one room apartment. The room was in a poor part of town and a shock after the mayor's house. Beneath the dirty curtainless window was an equally unclean sink with its wooden draining board. Adjacent to the sink was a small grey gas stove that would have looked at home in a child's Wendy house. A wooden table, two chairs, an old sofa and an iron framed bedstead completed the furnishings. The floor was covered in linoleum that had once boasted a pattern long since removed by countless feet; my mother detected my sadness at sight of our new home, 'Never mind.' she said, 'it won't be for long.'

When we went to bed on the first night she lit a candle because of my fear of the dark and switched off the single electric light whose lamp hung nakedly from the cracked ceiling. I snuggled into her side and was soon fast asleep. I could not have been asleep for any length of time when I was awakened by her suddenly sitting upright. It was pitch dark in the room she had obviously waited until I was asleep and blown the candle out; we sat there silently in the darkness after a moment or two and then she said, 'Listen. Can you hear a noise?'

I held my breath and listened I could hear something, a faint sound like the dripping of hundreds of tiny water taps. My mother jumped out of bed and switched the light on a second or two later she gasped as if in pain and backed towards the bed. I followed her stare and saw on the wall facing us countless numbers of red spots moving around the surface aimlessly. They were bugs; she sank onto the bed, 'Oh, My God,' she muttered and again, 'Oh, My God.'

Her reaction scared me more than the presence of the vermin and I had little sleep that night as she prowled the room burning the bugs in the candle flame; she had tried squashing them with a piece of paper but quickly became disgusted at the red smears left on the wallpaper. She confronted the landlady the next morning to be told that you must expect infestation in old houses and what did she want for the rent she was paying.

We endured life in that hovel for several weeks whilst my mother searched desperately for work, spending our daylight hours in public buildings and our night time hours fighting the bug army. Eventually she found a job as a cook housekeeper with a poultry farmer in the hamlet of Severn Tunnel Junction a place so small that it does not appear on most maps. After scrubbing ourselves with red carbolic soap we left the filth and the bugs behind us.

I cannot recall much of the farmer but I quickly fell in love with his farm and his stock. It was a large free range farm with a duck pond the size of a tennis court and several acres of much pecked bare land studded with apple trees and clumps of shrubbery. I was given the job of helping to collect eggs and this was great fun, like an Easter egg hunt twice a day. The chickens and ducks were cunning in the extreme and would lay their eggs or thrust deep in the roots of plants, under earth overhangs, in old rat holes anywhere but the nesting boxes scattered about the farm. It was here that I tasted my first duck egg, an experience that left me ill for a whole day.

When I was not collecting eggs or helping to feed the birds I would sit on the bank of the duck pond listening to the ducks arguing and bickering; their arguments often ending in violent confrontations. I later learned that some of the fights and ducking each other under the water stunts were part of the mating game but that was above my young head in those days.

One sunny afternoon I was lying by the pond allowing the gentle clucking of my feathered friends to lull me to sleep when I heard shouts from the nearby lane; climbing the bank of the hedge I forced myself into a gap between two bushes and looked down into the lane. I say looked down because the bank was much higher on the lane side over two metres whereas my side was less than a metre. The lane itself must have been hundreds of years old and could be likened to a mud floored hedge walled tunnel that ran twisting away into the countryside in one direction and equally twisting down into the hamlet in the other. Several men were standing on the hamlet side talking loudly whilst pointing and waving their arms.

As I watched two of them left the group and passed beneath me heading towards the countryside. They were scarcely out of sight before I heard them shouting loudly, 'Look out!' 'He's coming!' and other such warnings. They appeared again, running now, and soon rejoined their fellows. The whole group then hurried off in the direction of the hamlet and it went very quiet so that I could hear the ducks and hens muttering to my rear.

Suddenly I heard a drumming sound something like a distant train, it grew louder and louder and then an enormous bull careered around the bend of the lane all several tons of him crashing into the bank as he hammered his way down the lane. He halted, beating the ground with his hooves. I could see steam rising from his broad back and clouds of hot breath spraying from his nostrils, his flanks were coated in mud from contact with the bank and that same bank with its sharp protruding roots and stones must have caused him injury and pain. So quickly did he appear and so surprised was I at his appearance that I could do nothing but lean back and clutch at the bushes on each side at sight of him. I was terrified and filled with admiration at one and the same time. He was truly a magnificent animal his bulk almost filling the narrow lane and his head on a level with my feet.

My movement must have caught his attention because he looked up into my eyes his own white walled brown eyes rolling wildly. I froze and for a brief moment, during which I experienced a strange empathy with the beast, we stared at each other then he retreated a little way and throwing back his massive head gave forth a great cry that was a mixture of pain, fear and rage. He pawed the ground again shook his head and with a bellow took off down the lane.

I felt the bank shudder as he went and watched as he disappeared in the direction of the men. As young as I was I felt sorry for them if they were about to meet up with the beast who had just passed me. The bull vanished from sight and the sound of his drumming hooves faded. I waited but nothing else happened and eventually I climbed down

I went in to tell my mother of my adventure and I believe she thought it an exaggeration but she later told me that the bull had lost its mind; a brainstorm is how she put it, and escaped from a nearby farm. 'Thankfully,' she said, 'they cornered it and shot it.' I did not feel thankful I felt sad and filled with pity for such a beautiful but demented animal killed through no fault of his own.

The bull episode stayed with me for some time and is one of the most vivid of my childhood memories. For days I found myself imagining scenarios where I had found some way to placate the great creature and save his life but as time passed I returned to my domestic idyll with 'my poultry' as I now thought of them. Not for long; my mother's pregnancy was becoming advanced and she was finding the work of cleaning, cooking and preparing large vats of poultry mix too hard for her. She announced to me that we were moving on. I was sorry to leave the duck pond and promised myself that I would have a pond of my own one day - I am still waiting for one.

I cannot recall any farewells when we took the train to the town of Newport and although I would like to think that the birds missed me I somehow doubt that they did; them being too busy arguing, mating and laying their eggs. By now I was becoming quite laid back where train journeys were concerned and the view of some of England's finest scenery with its rolling hills verdant forestry and multi-patterned fields on the run from Newport to Hereford failed to impress or register on my memory's eye.

We stayed overnight in a bed and breakfast of unmemorable status and the next morning my mother took me sightseeing. Hereford was and still is a most attractive historic city with many unforgettable sights. We visited the Norman cathedral and she pointed out the wonders of its architecture but I was more interested in the mediaeval tombs. We saw the ancient castle but all that I could see was a mind's eye picture of Hollywood star Errol Flynn swashbuckling his way along the battlements clad in Lincoln green.

After our tour she bought sandwiches and we sat by the River Wye for a picnic lunch, then she broke the news. We did not have sufficient money for bus tickets to Evesham, her next target town, and we would have to walk. Why she had chosen to head for the ancient market town of Evesham I do not know and she never told me. Perhaps she had some grand plan to head north and seek out some obscure relative – my mother had an inner library of undiscovered relatives. I was also ignorant of the distance (over forty miles) but at the age of seven I was a walking bundle of trusting ignorance and would have followed her anywhere.

So we set off yet again. We had lost the suitcase somewhere on our travels and ended up with a couple of canvas hold-alls these were lighter and I could get my arm through the handles of one of them and take the weight on my shoulder, a great improvement on carrier bags. We were now into early spring the days were long and the weather mild so walking was a pleasure when compared to our slogs of the former winter.

We made good progress on the first day and slept that night in an old air raid shelter. The place must have been an emergency public convenience for the locals as it smelled strongly of stale urine. My mother found a reasonably clean area and laid down a rough bed of our coats. Once we had become accustomed to the local atmosphere we slept quite well, my rest being broken once or twice by the cry of animals a sound that my mother told me was Mrs. Fox calling her babies home. In this way we continued and the days and the miles passed.

On the first day after leaving Hereford my mother persuaded a shopkeeper to provide us with food in exchange for a number of the coupons from our Emergency Ration Book. It was a good deal for the shopkeeper as the coupons he received would have allowed him to ignore rationing for some time and although highly illegal it provided sustenance for a mother and child.

When we were back in the country we found a grassy bank and ate; although sixty years have gone by I do not believe that I have enjoyed a meal more than I enjoyed that picnic with my mother in the Malvern Hills. Lacking a knife she tore apart on of the two the fresh crusty loaves and spread the chunks with farmhouse butter from the small packet included.

Butter in those days was both a luxury and a rarity and I can only assume that the shopkeeper's conscience at having made such a good deal pricked him into providing it. I believe that my mother used the back of her nail file as a spreader and I am certain she would have wiped it first. The bread was accompanied by chunks of farmhouse cheddar cheese and we finished with sweet crisp local apples so juicy that the juice ran down one's chin at every bite. What a feast, what tastes, what flavours, all complemented by crystal clear Malvern air.

Full and happy I lay back on the grassy bed and stared up into a cloudless blue sky. I imagined what would happen if the world was suddenly turned upside down and I fell up - or down - into that sky. I would certainly come to no harm as there was no hard surface to fall on and I would probably fall for ever and ever. I was still pondering my ultimate fate when I fell asleep to the cawing of crows from a nearby copse.

My mother must have let me sleep for some time because when she awakened me the sun was overhead and shining directly into my eyes. If I fell now I would fall straight into its fiery eye. 'Come on, sleepy head,' she said 'there is another hill to climb.' I was discovering just how many steep hills there were in the English Midlands the only good news was that having gone up they went down on the other side.

Despite the countless hills we reached the county town of Worcester on the third day and there we went to the local National Assistance office to obtain emergency money; something much easier done in those days of easy bureaucracy. Having been given a small payment we found a cafe and had our first hot meal for some days. My mother then sought out the bus station and we were soon on the bus to Evesham. It was so pleasant to lie back in the padded seat with no bag to carry and no hills to climb.

Evesham is an ancient market town famous as the site of one of the great battles in English history. It lies on the River Avon and in 1948 was growing into the modern town of today. I recall that on one side of the river was the old town including the 8th century abbey and on the other bank was the more modern part of the town.

The first thing we did on reaching Evesham was to look for a cup of tea. Halfway down Vine Street, a wide and ancient thoroughfare of the town, we found The Vine Cafe, housed in a tall narrow building that was - as we discovered - three hundred years old. The interior was dark and cool with parchment shaded wall lamps to aid the little light that felt its way in through the tiny Tudor windows. Circular topped tables were draped with crisp linen tablecloths each table held a silver and glass cruet set, a glass filled with linen napkins and a folded menu card. Cutlery was carefully set out for a meal. At each table were four unoccupied bent wood chairs.

We found a table away from the other diners and when the young waitress appeared my mother ordered tea and toast. The waitress repeated the order in a querying tone, 'Tea and toast you said, love?' She gave us a curious look.

'Yes please.'

After the girl had left my mother leaned over to me and whispered, 'I hope they are not all as odd as her.'

At that moment the waitress returned with an older woman; I was about to meet Mrs. Berry, one of the sweetest, kindest women that ever entered my childhood life. She stopped at our table and in a gentle but firm tone said, 'We are serving lunch at the moment. I am afraid that toast is not on.' My mother looked at me and pushed her chair back. 'Come on,' she said stiffly, 'we'll find somewhere else.'

'You won't find anywhere else around here.' The woman said. 'Only the Horse and Groom and they'll be on lunches at this time of day.' My mother leaned back and sighed. I had a premonition of another bout of hunger. I chipped in with a whispered, 'I'm hungry, Mum.'

'Well you will have to wait a while.' She replied.

The woman sat on a spare chair and leaned over to my mother, 'What's wrong, my love?' she asked. I could see that my mother was on the verge of tears - she had previously explained to me that her condition made a woman weep without reason at times; there was no gooseberry bush with my mother and I knew the facts of life from an early age.

'Come on now,' said Mrs Berry, 'tell me what's troubling you.' My mother poured out the bones of her story to that patient lady and explained that we could not afford a lunch. When she had finished Mrs. Berry rose and handed her the menu. 'The beef is very good.' she said and whispered, 'You order a good meal and don't worry about money.' Then she left us.

I could see that my mother was choked up and wondered why. We had just been offered a free meal and I was already tasting roast beef, something I had enjoyed on too few occasions. Just then the waitress returned and politely asked for our order.

The meal that we enjoyed was first rate and I could not remember having felt more satisfied.

We were enjoying the pot of tea that followed the lunch when Mrs. Berry returned. 'May I join you?' She asked. Upon receiving an affirmative she sat down. Turning to me she said, 'You don't want to be stuck indoors on a lovely day like this.' and indicating a door, 'Ask the lady in that room and she will show you where the garden is.' 'You can play out there.'

I did as I was told and the waitress directed me through a door with a sign that read 'Toilet This Way' on it to the long narrow garden. It was as old as the building with tall limestone walls, a narrow cobbled path and many ancient fruit trees interspersed with thick clumps of herbs. I made my way to the far end of the long path and saw that an ancient vine grew along width of the rear wall. It was begging to be climbed by a small boy.

When I reached the top of the wall I found that it was two courses thick and easily sat upon. On the other side were allotments, that particularly British custom where small plots of public land are let to residents for cultivation. Conceived in the Eighteenth Century to ease the burden of displaced farm workers the allotment scheme had been a life saver during The Second World War and must have been thriving in Evesham because a number of people including several children were digging and delving, chattering happily as they worked.

It occurred to me that these people lived in real houses and did not have to move around from place to place; I pictured a cosy living room with a family gathered around the radio, such as I had seen in magazine illustrations, and I felt inexplicably sad. How long I sat there watching these happy folk and trying to make out what they were saying I do not know but it only seemed like minutes before I heard a woman calling my name. Twisting around I saw the young waitress standing on the pathway, 'Your mother wants you.' she said without any particular intonation and went back down the path. When I got back to our table, wondering if I was in trouble for climbing the wall, my mother and Mrs. Berry were chatting away over the tea cups. I sat down.

'I've got wonderful news,' said my mother, 'we are going to live here.' Had I then known the word nonplussed I could have applied to my reaction. How could you live in a cafe? 'This lady is giving me a job,' she said indicating Mrs. Berry, 'and we are going to have rooms here.'

Mrs. Berry waited until the lunch time rush was over and then showed us to our bedrooms. Mine was at the top of the building directly beneath the heavy oak rafters. A tiny garret with a small square paned window to provide light it had no electric lighting and a wax night light sat in a saucer of water to provide illumination after dark. I had grown used to sharing a bedroom with my mother and the thought of sleeping alone in that ancient attic combined with my fear of darkness made my stomach sink but I had learned to keep my mouth shut and accept what came.

My fears regarding the darkness were unfounded because directly across the square from the Vine Cafe was an inn whose owners had installed a bright red and blue neon sign on the roof. When darkness fell, this sign, flashing alternately red and blue, reflected on my ceiling and filled my room with coloured light and I fell asleep that first night and each subsequent night lulled by the light display above my head. I still have a fondness for neon and cannot see a neon sign without recalling Evesham and the friendly inn sign. The next morning I was awoken by the sound of bells pealing from the nearby Abbey. I felt at peace and at home.

I was not mistaken; the weeks spent at Mrs. Berry's were amongst the most contented of my childhood. That kind lady, who with her tight black iron flecked curls and walnut tanned face resembled a Romany Queen, made it her business to make me feel at home. For my amusement she made a lasso from a long length of string with a large round rubber jar seal tied to one end and showed me how to hook tree branches. I spent many hours sitting atop the ancient wall lassoing branches and other objects in the allotment and I never bored of the sport.

One day she told me that I should have a job. I had visions of boot cleaning and scrubbing as in the Sunlight Homes but Mrs. Berry had another idea of work. She had her handyman install a square box with a slot cut in a sliding lid on the outside lavatory door; on the front of the box "Toilet One Penny" was printed in large letters. She then told me that my job was to watch and make sure that customers using the lavatory paid a penny for the privilege; in return all money so earned was mine. I grew six inches taller with pride in my new status. When I told my mother about the box she said that she would open a Post Office Savings Account for me and that I would one day have a great deal of money.

I began work that very same day lurking around the lavatory door like a diminutive pervert. Pretending to be occupied with my lasso I would peer with mistrusting eyes at anyone using the facility but people were surprisingly honest and my collection of pennies quickly mounted. My mother would take me to the Post Office each week to buy savings stamps although I was reluctant to do so having a miser's dislike of banks and preferring to gloat over a hoard of copper coins.

Such was my avarice that I began to seek excuses for not leaving the confines of the cafe fearing that someone would rob my box. Then one day it happened that a woman, obviously in distress, threw the door open and entered my domain without depositing a penny. I was incensed, how dare she? Throwing down my lasso I pounded on the closed door with clenched fists. 'Excuse me,' I cried; my mother had taught me to be polite even when being rude, 'you haven't paid your penny.'

'Go away,' cried the poor woman.

I continued my pounding, driven by my greed for copper, 'You have to pay a penny!' I heard what sounded like sobbing from inside.

'Bugger off!' she cried.

'You have to pay!' I retorted.

Eventually after about five minutes of shouting and banging the door opened and a red faced female emerged looking for her persecutor, she caught sight of me and glared at me with a look of hatred, 'You disgusting brat!' she snarled.

I stood my ground. 'One penny please.' The woman snorted and rummaged in her handbag; finding a penny she threw it at me saying, 'I'm going to report you, boy.'

She stormed back into the cafe and I followed her, my bravado draining away as we went. Mrs. Berry listened to the customer's angry complaint making consoling sounds and nodding frequently. She then went across to my mother who was waiting on her table and spoke a few words. Whatever was said appeared to mollify the woman who left with air of a victor. When the woman was gone Mrs. Berry looked at me winked and then burst into a gale of laughter. 'That's my boy,' she said and disappeared into the kitchen still chuckling.

The weeks in Evesham passed happily but all too quickly as spring grew towards early summer. Among the best days of those swift weeks were the Sundays when my mother and I spent the mornings on the banks of The Avon listening to the abbey bells as I sailed a small toy canoe bought from my lavatorial earnings.

The time arrived when my mother's pregnancy could no longer be disguised. Mrs. Berry was eager to help and told her that as she herself had no family she would adopt her and make her the sole beneficiary of her estate; my mother was, however, determined to move on. It was almost as if she was afraid of settling down and was pursuing some secret dream; whatever her motive, on a bright summer day we packed our few belongings and bade farewell to Mrs. Berry and The Vine Cafe; once again I felt empty and sad at leaving what had become home to me.

Chapter Ten

My mother would not tell me where we were heading - I do not believe she knew herself. When the bus stopped at the town of Ludlow she said that she needed to stretch her legs and we alighted. The town is another ancient township with a medieval castle famed as the place where the unfortunate fifteenth century Princes Edward and Richard were housed before being taken to meet their unknown fate in The Tower of London. After a pot of tea and a snack in the local cafe we went for a walk in the castle grounds, My mother walked slowly in obvious discomfort and when we got to a bench in a tree shrouded alcove beneath the castle walls she stopped, 'I've got to rest, David,' she said and sank back onto the bench.

By now it was late evening and it was pleasant to sit there in silence listening to the first notes of evensong and watching flights of swifts darting back and forth to catch the evening insect swarms. However, as it grew dark I began to get worried and asked her where we were going to sleep. 'I think we'll sleep here,' she said, 'it's nice weather and we're sheltered in this alcove.'

I was not happy at this prospect, enroute to Ludlow she had filled my head with stories of murdered princes and the castle ghosts and I did not like the idea of encountering either but there was no arguing and we settled down on the wooden bench as darkness fell. By now I was accustomed to the sounds of the countryside at night and not put out by scurrying little feet or rustling bushes; this did not prevent my fertile imagination from turning the sounds into those of the feet of dead children or other phantoms and I slept fitfully and was glad to see dawn breaking

We sat there for some time listening to the world awakening and sipping the cold remains of yesterday's flask of tea. Finally my mother rose to her feet groaning in pain, 'We'll cut across to those houses,' she said indicating an estate that lay across the fields. We crossed several fields and passed through a kissing gate into what looked like a football field. During our short journey made longer by her halting every few yards to gasp and softly groan. Day became night as the sky turned from bright blue to inky black and the sounds of a rapidly approaching thunder storm grew louder.

As we made our slow way across the football field the storm broke; a storm that challenges description. The black clouds appeared to descend upon our heads like solid objects and swords of forked lightning stabbed down with a crackle that chilled my blood, each stab almost instantly followed by a crash of thunder loud enough to make my head ring and then another streak of lightning until lightning and thunder became one. Sheets of rain obscured vision and within seconds we were soaked to the skin; I cried out as the stinging rain filled my eyes and burned my face.

Halfway across the field was a small wooden hut with a veranda surrounding it; I began to run toward it slipping in the mud. I had not run far when I realised that my mother was not with me, turning I peered through the solid curtain of water and saw her standing motionless a few yards behind. I went back to her, 'Come on, Mum,' I shouted over the storm's fury, 'there's a hut over there.'

'I can't move, David,' she cried, 'I think the baby is coming.' I did not know what to say or do; I just wanted this to end. We stood there the storm forgotten and I stared up into her eyes praying for a sign of the mum I knew, refusing to believe that she had given up. She was my rock my world she could not fail me.

We must have been a ludicrous sight as we stood there in the midst of heaven's wrath gazing at each other through rain filled eyes. She put a hand on my shoulder, 'Help me across to the hut,' she said. I dropped the bags and putting her arm across my shoulder began to drag her across the mud. How we reached what was the old changing rooms of the football field I do not know but thankfully when we did we found that the entrance door had long since fallen off its hinges.

My mother collapsed onto a wooden training bed that had survived the abandonment of the building and lay back panting loudly. The storm slammed the door behind us and screamed spitefully through the broken window panes as if frustrated by our escape but at least we were out of that merciless rain. My mother clutched at my jacket pulling me closer to her, 'Go across to those houses and tell somebody that your mother is having a baby and needs help,' she whispered.

I looked at her and wondered if she was serious. She was; she really wanted me to go back out into that storm. She pulled me closer, 'Please, run, there's a good boy,' I hesitated. 'Please, David,' she gasped, 'if I don't get help I will die.'

That did it, pulling free of her grasp I hurled the door open and panic stricken rushed out of the hut. I halted to get my bearings and then began to run and slide towards the house. When I drew closer I could see that a man was working in a greenhouse close to his garden's low wire fence. I leaned over the fence waving and shouting but he could hear nothing over the storm's noise. I thought about throwing a stone through the glass but decided against it. Somehow I managed to half climb half fall over the fence. I opened the greenhouse door and the man noticed me for the first time, 'Good God!' he cried at sight of this rain soaked mud streaked child.

I repeated my mother's words to him and had to repeat them again before he grasped their meaning. He uttered a blasphemy and leaving me in the greenhouse he ran back into his house. It seemed like hours before he appeared again but when he did he was accompanied by two other men and a boy, 'You get in the house, boy' he shouted and led his team in the direction of the hut.

A woman was standing in the doorway of the house and taking my hand led me into a warm kitchen, 'Oh, you poor mite,' she said, 'Just look at you.'

'He's soaking wet, Mam.'

For the first time I noticed the children. The girl who had spoken was a few years older than me, a pretty child with long blonde hair and a freckled face; her brother must have been a year or two younger than me and just stood there staring at the apparition that his mother had let into the house.

Mrs. Swift, as I later discovered, was as fast as her name and no sooner had she shooed the children from the kitchen than she peeled my wet clothes from me dried me with a warm towel from a pile of ironing and dressed me in a pair of striped man's pyjamas. She was turning the sleeves and trouser ends back when there was a banging on the door. She opened it and her excited daughter burst in crying, 'They're here! They're here!'

Down the small hallway I could see the open front door and two men carrying my mother who sat on their linked arms in what

Boy

used to be called a fireman's seat; she was groaning loudly and I made a move towards her but Mrs. Swift grabbed me, 'No, love,' she said, 'not now.'

The men turned sideways and began to take the stairs one at a time. They disappeared from view a moment or so later I heard my mother begin to shout and Mr. Swift came almost tumbling down the stairs. 'Towels!' He cried 'Towels!' and grabbed a pile of laundry from the table.

This time nothing could stop me from following him. I reached the bottom of the stairs and looking up saw my mother lying on a small half landing with a bright pink baby between her knees. 'Mum!' I cried and again, 'Mum!' she did not appear to hear me but lay there breathing deeply. I lost sight of her as Mr. Swift began to busy himself with the towels and I began to cry. All the pent up fear and emotion of the past hour caught up with me and I heaved great sobs that left me gasping for breath.

Mrs. Swift led me into their living room and sat me down on the settee. 'Go and make him a nice sweet cup of tea,' she instructed her daughter. I do not know for how many minutes I sat there; the cup of tea arrived, it was weak and pale but hot and sweet and I was sipping it gratefully when Mr. Swift entered with two ambulance men said that my mother wanted to see me. I nearly knocked the poor men over as I forced past them in my haste. The first bedroom door was open and I saw my mother lying in bed propped up with pillows; she looked tired and pale. I rushed over to her and threw myself upon her; she hugged me and whispered, 'I have to go into hospital for a while.'

With the selfishness of childhood I immediately thought of another spell in a children's home but her next whisper dispelled my fears, 'You're going to stay here with these nice people until

175

I'm back home,' she said. In my relief I hugged her even tighter and she cried out, 'don't squeeze me, love, I'm very sore.' I released her and it was then that I noticed a chest of drawers with the bottom drawer pulled out. Lying in the drawer wrapped tightly in towels was a tiny red faced creature.

My mother smiled weakly, 'Say hello to your brother.' I studied the wrinkled face and decided it was the ugliest that I had ever seen. 'His name is Peter,' she said, 'isn't he lovely?'

I looked at her, thought about it, disagreed but nodded. I did not want to upset her and after a quick peck on the cheek accompanied by a 'Be a good boy' from my mother I was ushered from the room. Although he was named Peter my brother was referred to simply as 'the baby' for the first few years of his life.

I didn't see my mother and brother leave in the ambulance. I had a meal with the Swifts and a bath then I was packed off to bed with their son. Their daughter, Lily, came in to tuck us up and kiss us goodnight. I thought her kiss was sweet and kind and the experience of my first kiss on the lips a pleasant one. Within a few days I had ceased to think about my mother. It was summertime and under the guidance of my new friends I explored the countryside around Ludlow. When we were not out chasing and playing we played in Lily's bedroom and her favourite game was mothers and fathers.

This involved a great deal of scolding followed by kissing and making up and Lily's brother, whose name I cannot recall, played the child of the family. I soon discovered that Lily's kissing and caressing aroused an odd but pleasing feeling in me and this grew as she encouraged me to explore her warm young person giving instructions in a whisper.

A few days after my mother had left for hospital, Lily took our game a step further; we were in the old football hut and she had sent her brother home. The air in the wooden building was sultry to the point of being non-existent and we were playing 'making up' after Lily had been scolding me for staying out late in the pub. Seated beside her on the planks of the old first aid table I could smell the soapy flowery scent of her and feel the heat of her body, separated from mine by a thin cotton dress and an equally thin shirt.

Without a word Lily stood me up, pushed my braces down from my shoulders and pulled my shirt off over my head. Then she undid my trouser buttons and pulled both trousers and underwear down and off. Taken by surprise I was embarrassed and covered my nakedness with my hands but she gently pulled them aside and making soft unintelligible cooing noises she caressed me. I had occasionally awoken in the condition to which she soon roused me but never experienced it during the day.

After a few minutes Lily stopped caressing me stepped back and in a hasty matter of fact way removed her knickers. Lying back on the bench she gestured me towards her and completely under her spell I found myself kneeling as she indicated, conscious of the grit on the bench hurting my knees; I soon, however, forgot my discomfort as she pulled me towards her and guided me to the consummation of her desires.

Afterwards I lay in her arms for some time as she stroked my hair and held me close; I had never felt so safe and so loved. Then she rose dressed herself and as practical as a busy housewife helped me to dress making sure that all was in order before we returned home; not a word had been spoken since the moment she began to undress me it was only when we were once again out in the sunshine that she began to chatter as if nothing had happened. It was four days after my eighth birthday.

My mother must have remained in hospital for six to eight weeks during which time Lily furthered my education in the act of love (the art of love came many years later). I use the word love because I dislike the word sex to describe an act that was and should always be a demonstration of mutual affection and consideration. During those soft summer days filled with the scent of fields, the drying creosoted timber of our football shed and the just scrubbed lilac soap scent of Lily I grew truly fond of that dear young girl and was deeply saddened when my mother appeared one day with my new brother in her arms. I realised that my life was about to change again; we were now three.

The next day I parted company with my first love never to see her again, I hope that eventually she found a man to appreciate and respond to her gentle and generous nature. With my mother carrying my new brother because we could neither afford nor deal with a pram we set off back to Wales.

Chapter Eleven

As we left the town of Ludlow with my new baby brother I learned that my mother had hopes of introducing Peter to his father and after several days on the road we reached Blackwood. There she obtained tenancy of a basement flat, a dark dank hole where the walls and our belongings were always damp and the only light seeped in through a glass cobbled grating. I loathed that basement and sought every excuse to get out into the daylight and stay there as long as possible.

One escape was school – my mother actually enrolled me at the local school and as luck would have it I was just in time for the annual school treat, on this occasion a day trip to the ruined medieval Abbey of Tintern. It was a bright sunny day when the coach rolled into the Abbey car park and having disembarked buzzing with excitement I followed our teacher through the ruins clutching my brown paper packet of jam sandwiches and a bottle of yellow lemonade, listening in awe as she vividly told the Abbey's tale.

Tintern Abbey had been one of the many monastic victims of King Henry the Eighth's reformation and all that remained of the great building were the arch pierced walls defiantly proclaiming the glory that had once been. I fell under its spell within seconds of entering the structure and as I later lay in the shade its walls eating and drinking I knew that I was in a magic place. I have never lost that conviction and I have returned many times to the Vale of Tintern to refresh my soul – try as I may I have never rekindled that first wondrous spark. I accept now that one can never relive the wonder of youth's awakening emotions and must be grateful for the shades of the past expressed in memory.

Soon after that happy day an outbreak of poliomyelitis or infantile paralysis as it was called occurred in the area. An epidemic of that crippling disease would break out every summer striking swiftly and indiscriminately but chiefly, or so it seemed, targeting children and mass immunisation was a thing of the future. My mother immediately withdrew me from school and isolated me in the dungeon of our flat. I had probably received two weeks of schooling; hardly a major addition to my education but my romantic nature had been stimulated by the trip to Tintern. As the epidemic peaked the local grapevine became heavy with fresh horror stories of deaths and then as quietly as it had begun it faded away.

Although the polio epidemic was over my mother decided not to send me back to school; attendance control was lax in those easy going days. I spent the rest of the year playing on the mountainside, reading voraciously thanks to the local lending library and watching my baby brother grow. Christmas arrived and departed uneventfully as usual and with the New Year a cruel January wind whistled through the valleys. The cellar was so cold that you could see your breath like a mist and a layer of ice formed on the condensation of the walls. That was enough for my mother who lived with a perpetual fear of pneumonia and she began to pack our few belongings.

We headed down the valley reaching the small town of Cwmfelinfach (or Valley of The Little Mill in the Welsh tongue) towards evening. Down deep into the valley bottom we found a small street near the river. My mother began looking for one of her friendly windows and halfway along the street she found one. A small neat grey-haired woman answered the door and having listened patiently to Mother's brief telling of our story she led us across the street to her sister's house, explaining as we went that her sister had a bed sitting room looking for a good tenant.

The front door was not locked (no Welsh Valleys doors were ever locked in those happy days) and our new friend walked in calling her sister's name. A handsome woman in her mid-thirties with neat dark hair appeared at the end of the passageway; she ushered us in, sat us down and immediately put the kettle on.

Tea was a ritual in Welsh homes and visitors of any kind were always greeted with a cup of what was then the national beverage. To decline was unthinkable, that would have implied that there was something wrong with the household brew. Negotiations of tenancy were quick and pleasant and we were shown into a front parlour that had been converted to a bed sitting room by the addition of a three-quarter size bedstead complete with bedding.

It was the beginning of another brief period of normality in my life. Auntie Eileen as I came to know her was that rarest of creatures, a Christian who believed in and lived for her faith. The Lord God was as real to her as a next door neighbour and she lived her life in strict obedience to his commandments; the Sabbath day was observed fully and devoutly and playing cards - the Devil's picture book - were banned from the house. Her husband was a quiet man who kept himself to himself as far as we were was concerned.

Every Sunday I accompanied Auntie Eileen and her family to worship at the local Pentecostal Church where she was the organist and I reconnected to the God that I had found in Tredegar's Sunday school during the spirited singing of the hymns. The concept of God appealed strongly to my burgeoning romanticism. I can say without doubt that (apart from my mother's recounting of stories from the Bible) any faith that has existed in my life came from my Auntie Eileen, her teachings and her example and it is thanks to her that I remain a Christian, if not one of the best, to this day.

The couple had three children, Royston, Tony and Sandra and they easily adopted me as a playmate although it was Tony with whom I formed the closest bond. He was a natural leader and as such instigated most of our games. My favourite being the launching of roughly made wooden boats with paper sails upon the nearby river. I would watch these rude craft bobbing away in the swift current and imagine that I was embarking on some epic voyage of discovery, sometimes becoming so lost in my dream that I would come to sharply when one of my companions shoved me onto my back and burst out laughing at me.

Another favourite game was sliding down the coal tip on sheets of rusting corrugated tin. The nearby colliery of Nine Mile Point was one of the major coal producers in Wales and its spoil tips were of the proportion of mountains. The tip in use at that time was thirty metres high and a track way ran along its summit carrying the buckets of waste coal or slag to the end of the tip where they would be tipped out to add to the man made mountain, hence the name tip.

We would drag our tin slides up the steep face of the tip until we reached a suitably high point and then wriggle aboard and then, holding onto the upturned front of the tin, we would hurtle down to end in a heap amongst the scattered lumps of waste. A large part of the fun was dodging the off loaded bucket waste that often contained lumps of slag or stone as big as your head. These missiles would bounce down the side of the tip with great force and although I never heard of a child being injured by one the risk must have been considerable.

The tips were also a source of fuel because visible to the educated eye amongst the waste could be found coal that had slipped through the selection process. Mother was grateful for this supply and once I had learned what to look for I was kept busy collecting it in a tin bucket, once again dodging the bouncing lumps of slag.

Of all our diversions my favourite was The Dingle swimming pond or more appropriately The Dingle mud hole. The Dingle was a small valley halfway up a mountainside, a stream ran through it and local youngsters would build a dam across this stream at the beginning of each summer (you could depend on nature to give you a summer in those days). The construction of stones, sods of turf and mud was a credit to the junior structural engineers who built it and held back the stream forming a pond about five meters wide with sloping sides. Although I could not swim I could safely slide into the pond and immerse myself in its cool muddy water joining in the splashing and shouting that was a part of the game.

Life was not all play because - wonder of wonders – my mother had once again enrolled me at the local school (this was becoming a habit). In preparation for my first day I received a haircut. Ianto Thomas a retired miner performed this service for the sum of three pennies. He would sit you on a kitchen chair in the backyard and go to work with comb, clippers and scissors breathing heavily and smacking his lips as he concentrated. The end result left you with a shorn head from neck to above the ears topped with an all round fringe that resembled a hair skull cap.

There were one or two incidents during those days that left an impression on my child's mind; the most significant being the day that I broke my baby brother's nose. Tony had a small bicycle and I was racing him along the pavement pushing Peter ahead of me in his pushchair. Seeing that Tony was charging ahead and determined to win I put a spurt of speed on but, unfortunately, at that moment the pushchair hit a gutter running across the pavement. The pushchair and I stopped abruptly but Peter, who was not strapped in to the chair, kept going; as I watched helplessly he sailed through the air in slow motion and landed with an audible thud face first on the stone pavement.

There was a long silence. Tony and I looked at each other and then at Peter who was lying motionless face down. After what seemed like minutes but could only have been seconds. I ran around the wreck of a pushchair and turned him face up - he was not breathing, his face was purple and a trickle of blood ran from his rapidly swelling nose. In panic I picked him up and shook him; as I did he drew in a mighty gasp of air and expelled it in the most piercing scream that I had ever heard; by now his nose was turning blue black and so was the flesh beneath his eyes.

I carried the screaming child back to our house with neighbours rushing to their doors to see what the noise was. I arrived home as my mother rushed from the front gate and her scream when she saw what I was carrying was almost as loud as my brother's. She went into a fit of hysteria as I stood there holding the baby and repeating, 'I'm sorry, Mum, I'm sorry,' over and over again.

By now Auntie Eileen had arrived and taking the baby from me she rushed him indoors to administer first aid. My mother was still sobbing uncontrollably as she leaned against the garden wall and I carried on apologising knowing full well that no apology could protect me from the wrath to come.

Suddenly my mother stopped sobbing and glared at me with bulging eyes then, without warning, she grabbed by the neck of my shirt and dragged me choking through into our small room. Her strength was amazing and she threw me onto our bed as if I were a rag doll. She locked the door and turned to face me; I was looking at a mad woman and I was frozen with terror. There followed the worst beating of my life as screaming the most obscene of curses at me she punched me and slapped me in an uncontrollable rage.

Not being a child to suffer in silence, I yelled, I begged and I called on God and my dead grandfather to help me, all to no avail; finally when I was convinced that my mother was going to kill me God sent help in the person of Auntie Eileen. That saintly woman banged on the door and shouted for my mother to stop until gasping for breath she ceased her attack on me and collapsed on the bed in a fresh flood of tears.

I opened the door and threw myself into the comforting arms of my Auntie. Every part of me felt broken and I was in shock. Auntie Eileen took me through into her parlour and sitting me in a soft armchair proceeded to make me a sweet cup of tea. As I drank it I looked at my baby brother lying wrapped in a shawl on the settee, he was asleep and every few seconds would give out a sob followed by a deep sigh. Later examination revealed that I had broken his nose and I was wracked with guilt and filled with contrition for years to come.

My mother's temper outbursts were, thankfully, rare and normally she was gentle and caring. She never went anywhere alone without bringing me back some small surprise on one occasion it was the first issue of the Eagle comic. Nothing like this glossy well illustrated and written comic paper had been seen by British children before. It was a revolution in the British comic world and sent my imagination soaring to new heights fuelled by the brilliantly coloured illustrations fascinating true life articles and adventurous stories. Admittedly it was, like most of the comic papers, written for boys but within a year a companion paper for girls was published - called imaginatively 'Girl'.

There were other noteworthy events such as the arrival of sliced bread, although this had its drawbacks. One day in mid 1950 a neighbour came running in with the announcement that the local baker was selling bread ready sliced; not only sliced but sliced into wafer thin slices, something almost impossible to achieve with a bread knife. Nothing like this had been heard of before and I was sent to the baker's shop to buy one of these amazing loaves.

I watched with interest as the baker laid a loaf of bread in the machine (obviously placed in the front shop to impress) stepped back to study his audience for effect and with a little flourish pressed a button. Within minutes a score of circular blades had converted the loaf to thin slices. So far so good but when it came to handing it over, rather than wrap it, the maestro of the loaf simply snapped a large rubber band around the slices to hold them in place.

Disaster was guaranteed and halfway down the back lane the band slipped and scattered slices of bread everywhere. I managed to retain my grip on the end crusts and two or three slices but this did not save me from a clip around the ear. Nevertheless, I was still sent to buy bread but on future occasions I insisted on being given a carrier bag to hold the wobbly loaf.

The outbreak of The Korean War took everyone by surprise. The Second World War was fresh in the memories of everyone and the thought of another world wide conflagration with the use of the atomic bomb was uppermost in their minds. As it turned out the war (officially termed a 'Police Action') affected only those unfortunate soldiers and civilians directly involved and, of course, the many British families who lost loved ones in the war that never was (even today it is listed as a 'police action'). My generation were selfishly engrossed in local events and adventures and took little notice of a conflict that cost so many lives.

During my time in Cwmfelinfach my growing romanticism was further fed by the discovery of a ruined cottage at the Ynsddu end of the old railway line; it was said to be the cottage of Islwyn the nineteenth century poet. I would stand alone in that ruin for long lengths of time attempting to evoke the spirit of that Welsh genius whom I later came to regard as our own Omar Khayyam.

As much as I loved the place and people I was still dependent on my mother and when her wanderlust came upon her our bags were packed. She had been corresponding with a widowed businessman of her own age in the port of Milford Haven - as this was the birthplace of my grandfather she hoped to find those longed for relations there. When he offered her a housekeeping job with matrimony in mind she accepted and in late December 1950 we climbed aboard a west bound train at Cardiff.

Chapter Twelve

After about one hour of travel we left the comfortable corridor train with its washrooms and buffet car at the Welsh market town of Carmarthen and took up sole occupancy of a non-corridor compartment in a rail car that must have dated back to the Victorian era.

A long high backed seat stuffed with horsehair ran across each side of the compartment from window to window. I know it was stuffed with horsehair because stuffing was escaping from a tear in one seat and, in typical juvenile constructive/destructive style, I began to help its escape. My mother promptly told me that it was filthy horsehair probably full of fleas and I just as promptly changed seats and began to study the pictures, three each side above the seat.

The two end pictures one each side of the larger central one were sepia tinted photographs of piers and promenades with grim boarding houses. The middle larger ones were much more interesting and occupied my attention for some considerable time.

The first brightly coloured poster - for such they were - featured a green promenade complete with the obligatory palm trees. Two young men dressed in white oxford bag trousers with long sleeved white shirts Fair Isle knitted pullovers, neckties and floppy flat caps were striding manfully down a path chatting and laughing. One held a briar pipe and the other a cigarette - one could not stride manfully without a pipe or cigarette in the Nineteen-Thirties and that would obviously have been the date of the posters had I been old enough to appreciate the fact.

The second poster was from the same era but featured two rosy-cheeked white smiled young women. Standing on a grassy bank above a golden beach both had straight bobbed hair topped by a cloche hat. They each held one hand up to shield their eyes from the glaring sun (was this truly an English resort) as they gazed out across an unseen ocean? The breeze whipped their gaily coloured neck scarves away behind them and pulled their skirts teasingly tight against shapely legs.

After I had spent some time enjoying the posters I wiped the condensation off the window and turned my attention to the landscape but it had grown dark outside and all that could be seen was falling snow; a blizzard had begun and it was so heavy that it obscured everything.

I sat back in my seat and began to read my Beano comic but not for long because the train was slowing as it rattled over a series of points. I returned to the window in time to catch sight of a brightly lit junction box and as that disappeared from view the train slowed even further. Within minutes we were drawing into a small station and my mother was tucking Peter into his pushchair.

Leaning out of the open carriage window I could see a long platform lit by flickering gas lamps and heard a porter shouting, 'Milford Haven, end of the line.' There were only two other passengers and they quickly disappeared into the falling snow leaving my mother, my brother and me alone on the platform with the exception of the porter, a dark figure overcoated from ears to ankles who was chatting to the engine driver.

My mother approached him gave him our tickets and asked if anyone had been waiting for the train as we were being met. His reply was negative and he then said that we would have to leave because he was about to lock up the station.

We left the shelter of the station and found ourselves on the long approach road to the station this was walled and lit by weak lamps every fifty metres; lamps that struggled unsuccessfully to penetrate the snowstorm. With me pushing Peter and my mother struggling with our luggage we headed into the unknown; by now the time was approaching eleven o'clock and although she must have been panicking she did not show it.

We had reached the second lamp post when the porter passed us giving us a goodnight as he went; obviously in a hurry to get home he was almost out of sight when a stooped figure appeared shuffling towards us. As the figure grew closer it was apparent that he was elderly and infirm. I looked at my mother.

'Mr James must have sent his father,' she said.

The man drew close, 'Hello, my dear,' he said, 'you must be Dorothy.'

'Yes,' she replied, 'who are you?'

'I'm Billy, my dear.'

There was a long silence and we all stood there turning white with the falling snow. Thankfully Peter was tucked up asleep and dry. Finally my mother broke the spell,

'I think that there has been some mistake.'

'No mistake, my dear. I told you I would meet you and I've got supper all ready for us.'

His speech was broad, almost English West Country - I soon discovered that there was little of the Welsh in the Pembrokeshire dialect and that the county was known as 'Little

England Beyond Wales.' Another silence; by now we had stood on that spot for several minutes.

My mother was standing homeless in a strange town in the middle of a blizzard late at night with two young children. She later told me that she had been close to breaking down but she did not show that at the time. Pushing past the old man she told him that they would discuss the situation when we were indoors. She did not speak another word in the long walk to his house.

Catching up with us he almost bowed and in an ingratiating manner offered to carry my mother's luggage. She ignored him and we continued the trudge through the snow up one of the steepest hills that I had encountered outside of the Welsh Valleys; I had expected hills there but had not realised how hilly a seaside town could be. With me slipping and slithering as I pushed the wheelchair we continued our walk through the town, made eerie by the silence engendered by the sound muffling snowstorm and the absence of any living creature. It was as if the town had gone into hibernation; finally we reached Billy James's house.

In his letters he had described a fine spacious house; the reality was a tiny terraced cottage. He opened the front door with a key that he fished through the letter box where it hang on a length of string, this was not unusual as a great many working class people (we still had classes of society) hung their key so that family and friends could gain easy access.

As we removed our frozen coats Billy enquired if we would like a nice cup of tea.

'No thank you,' said my mother, 'I would just like to get to bed.'

'Yes. Yes. Follow me my dear.' Came the response and he opened a small door in one wall. With difficulty we followed him up a cramped staircase leading to a bedroom so small that there was just room for a narrow washstand alongside the brass framed double bed that filled it almost wall to wall.

'There you are, my dear. This is where we sleep. The children can sleep on the settee.'

Without a word my mother swept him aside with one arm, sending him staggering and she dragged me with her as she crashed down the stairs. Pushing me down on the settee she was putting her coat on as she left the house leaving me instructions to look after my brother. She slammed the front door behind her and I was left alone with my baby brother and a weird old man.

A few minutes passed and the stairway door that my mother had slammed shut creaked open. In the manner of a comic opera comedian Billy James peered around the door frame checking if the coast was clear and then emerged into the room. We stared at each other. I looked around the room for some weapon of defence but saw nothing. After exchanging stares in silence he gave a grunt and turning abruptly disappeared into the back scullery, I wondered if he had gone to get a knife and my always dramatic imagination pictured him bursting in screaming and waving a butcher's cleaver.

Time passed and although it could have been no longer than fifteen minutes it seemed like a lifetime. I was plucking up courage to take the baby and follow my mother when there was a loud knocking on the front door. Billy opened it and stepped back to admit the tallest police sergeant that I had ever seen followed by my mother.

'Up to your old tricks are you, Billy' said the policeman.

'I don't know what you mean, Sergeant Gough.'

'You know very well what I mean you old rogue. You've brought this young woman here on false pretences.'

My mother chipped in, 'And you expected me to sleep with you. You dirty old man.'

The policeman pointed the large white gauntlets that he carried at the old man, 'You,' he said in a no arguments tone of voice, 'are going to sleep on that settee and this good woman and her children will sleep in your bed.' he paused, 'and let me hear that you have attempted to join them or offended her in any way and I will come down on you like a ton of bricks.'

Billy James shuffled his feet, 'I can't be expected to give up my bed at my age.'

The policeman took a step towards him and emphasising his point by poking the old man with his gauntlets said, 'You will do as you are told, laddie. Do you understand me?' Turning to my mother he said, 'You know where I am, my dear. If you have the slightest trouble with him you come and fetch me and he will sleep in the cells for the night.

When the policeman had left Billy James escaped back into his scullery and my mother wasted no time in getting my baby brother and me up to bed. The bed was clean warm and soft and I was asleep in no time; my mother later told me that she did not sleep a wink for fear of the old rogue attempting to climb in with us.

The next morning we were awakened by a hesitant knock on the door it was Billy James.

'I've made breakfast for you and the children, Dorothy.'

As I washed my face and hands in water from the large jug I asked Mother if we were going to stay with Mr. James. 'We'll see.' she replied and proceeded to change the baby, not a pleasant task to observe before breakfast.

Once downstairs I could see that the fire was lit and the table laid for breakfast with cups, dishes and a pot of tea; also laid out was a loaf of bread, a jar of marmalade and dish of butter, a box of corn flakes a bottle of milk and a bowl of sugar. I was ravenous not having eaten since Cardiff station on the previous day and gratefully tucked into a large bowl of milky corn flakes.

My mother without asking permission went out into the scullery and prepared the baby's feed. Returning she poured herself a cup of tea and cut a slice from the loaf as she ate the old man attempted conversation but all that she would give him in response was a series of grunts; finally he gave up and we ate in silence.

Following breakfast Billy lit his pipe and sat puffing away for (passive smoking was unheard of and no-one objected as he filled the small room with aromatic smoke). My mother switched on the radio relay box that stood on the deep window ledge and the sound of Christmas music killed the uncomfortable silence (appropriately a choir was singing 'Silent Night'). Billy knocked out his pipe and interrupted the carol,

'Do you think that the boy would like to see the docks?' he asked.

I looked at my mother hopefully and she saw that I was eager to accept. 'Would you like to see the docks?'

'Yes please, Mum.'

Wrapped up in overcoat and the obligatory woollen scarf I followed the Billy James down the steep steps of the cottage. It had stopped snowing and a thick crust of frozen slush made walking difficult. The street was extremely long by small town standards the nearer end stopped at a tall stone wall whist the other end was almost invisible in the distance.

The town of Milford Haven takes its name from the great natural harbour on which it lies and one of its founders in the late eighteenth century was Sir William Hamilton, husband of Emma and friend to Lord Nelson. Nelson visited the town several occasions and called the harbour '...the second greatest natural harbour in the world after Trincomalee.' Laid out on the American grid pattern the street in which Billy lived was one of the three long main streets. Oddly enough I later discovered that my maternal grandfather had been born in that same street, possibly in the cottage that we had slept in.

A few yards up the street we turned downhill into one of several steep streets that traversed the three main ones. The incline was so steep that I was forced to hold on to the walls of buildings to prevent myself falling. The old man appeared quite at home on the glassy slope but reduced his pace to mine. We crossed the main street of the town through throngs of people buying their last minute Christmas shopping and continued our downward progress. By now I could hear the loud screams of seagulls and see that the sky towards the docks was whitened with thousands of the fish maddened birds swooping and diving in a great feathered circus; all the while screaming like fiends from Hell.

At the top of the final gradient was a small news agency and taking me into this shop, which scarcely had headroom for an adult and was crammed with every possible book and publication, the old man bought me the Christmas editions of The Dandy and The Beano, these were not only my second favourite comic papers after The Eagle but they were the Christmas issues. I loved the snow capped lettering and the illustrations of slap up festive feasts, bulging Christmas stockings and all the things that I had never known outside of their pages and I would dream that these things would be mine someday.

With me feeling more kindly disposed to the old man (I was anybody's for a comic paper) we continued downwards and crossed the last of the main streets. A chest-high stone wall ran down the dockward side and he lifted me up to lean over it. I was immediately gripped by vertigo as I looked down a sheer eighty foot cliff face to Milford Docks laid out beneath me. A massive retaining wall was built against the cliff and a steep wooden stairway ran down the side of that wall. Everywhere I looked I saw the tiny figures of dock workers bustling about.

He pointed downwards,

'That is the longest fish market in Europe,' he said and I politely responded with, 'Gosh.'

Below me I saw a long pitched roofed building stretching almost the entire length of the dock and it did look as if he spoke the truth. I was more impressed by the forest of masts and tall black smokestacks belonging to the trawling fleet, there were more than a boy could count and I wondered how they managed to fit so many ships in so tightly. Years later when I worked as a dock labourer on that docks I discovered at first hand how, when they did not have steam up, they were pulled around the docks by hand and packed in like sardines in a can. Once started two or three men could easily move a vessel weighing hundreds of tons.

As I watched the scene below I felt a breath of wind on my cheek and glancing to my left I found myself face to face with an enormous seagull, a member of that species called The Great Black-backed Gull. Many Milford locals believed that the gulls were the souls of drowned seamen and as a consequence they were never harmed; if that is so then this must have been a particularly malevolent sailor because I was staring into the most evil eyes that I had ever seen. As I looked the bird spread its wings to their full stretch of almost six feet and dancing a step or to towards me opened its beak in a hideous laughing scream; if the old man had not been supporting me I believe I would have fallen off the wall. Removing his flat cap he shook it at the bird shouting loudly and the creature beat its wings and swooped away.

That was my first encounter with the monarch of the gull species, I later saw one of them swallow a fish as long and as thick as a wrestler's arm by distending its beak and throwing its head back as it jumped up and down to let gravity force the fish down; as it was swallowed so it was digested the sea gull having one of the strongest digestive acids in the animal world.

The encounter with the gull shook me and seeing that the old man lifted me down and took me back to the cottage. The remainder of the day passed uneventfully with me listening to the radio and my mother pottering with the baby. There were no 'good nights' exchanged as we went to bed, there was just an icy silence.

I awoke the next morning - Christmas Eve - to the crying of my baby brother as my mother changed him. There was no breakfast call and when we went down the cottage was silent. A note lay on the table,

"I will be spending Christmas with my family. I expect you to be gone when I return. W. James."

The old man had done a bunk as they used to say. My mother sat down and read the note over again, 'The rotten old monster,' she said, 'how could he run off like that?'

I tried to comfort by telling her that we were better off on our own but she was furious. She became even more incensed when she discovered that he had locked up the pantry and the cupboard that held the prepayment meters for gas and electricity.

When she had calmed down she sat me beside her and explained that there would be no Christmas for us because she was broke and had no way of buying food or gifts, I hadn't thought about it until then and I never expected more than my comic annuals and a few sweets but the thought of nothing at all depressed me. To take my mind of things my mother gave me the small fire shovel and told me to clean the ice off the front steps.

After scraping away listlessly for a while I sat on the top step and thought about all that I was missing; I soon began to enjoy my excursion into self pity and became lost to reality only to be brought back by a gentle voice,

'Cheer up, love. Father Christmas is coming tomorrow.'

I looked up to see a pleasant faced woman carrying several shopping bags.

'Come on give me a smile.'

The gentle tone of her voice touched my chord of self pity, already stretched to snapping, and I began to cry; she put down her bags and sitting beside me put her arms around me, 'There, there. Nothing is that bad,' she whispered.

I poured out my heart telling her that we were not going to have a visit from Father Christmas because Mr. James had locked everything up. She listened quietly and then said, 'Let me see your mother.'

When I took her indoors my mother told me to go back and finish clearing the steps, I had been scraping away for some minutes when the woman came out, as she passed me she patted me on the head and said, 'Everything is going to be alright.'

I half heartedly completed my work and went back indoors; my mother was busy as usual playing with the baby and so I turned on the radio. The popular song that year was "Rudolph the Red Nosed Reindeer" and I never tired of listening to it.

It must have been about a half-an-hour later that there came a knock at the front door, it was the friendly woman and she was accompanied by her husband. They each carried a large cardboard box. Laying the boxes down on the settee without a word they began unpacking them; out came half a Christmas cake, half a large Christmas pudding, mince pies, fruit, nuts a small chicken and every possible Christmas treat that I could imagine.

As they unpacked, the woman, - whose name we never knew - explained that when she had told her husband of our situation he had insisted that they divide every item of their Christmas fare in two halves and give one half to us. My mother was speechless as she saw the food appearing from the boxes; eventually she managed a 'thank you' and repeated it over and over as each item was brought forth.

When all was unpacked, the couple who would take no thanks saying that it was their Christian duty and that they could they could not have enjoyed the holiday knowing of our plight, left quietly wishing us 'A Merry Christmas' as they went. My mother sat down and began to cry. I could not understand why she cried when she should have been happy but by then I was examining our gifts uttering 'hums' as I did so.

Having cried herself dry my mother looked me straight in the eye and said, 'You must never forget this, David, and if ever you find someone in need you must do all that you can to help them.' (to my shame I have failed far too many times to act on that advice.) Then gathering herself together she stood up as straight as a guardsman and in a determined tone of voice said, 'Right, we've got the food now we need the gas and electricity.'

Donning her overcoat she told me to look after the baby and not to touch the food and disappeared out of the door. When she had left I examined each item of food again imagining how it would taste and wishing that it was tomorrow, time passed and I heard the door open, it was my mother with the police sergeant from the first night. He crossed to the meter cupboard and grasping the lock in his gloved hand wrenched hasp, staple and lock away from the door.

'Oh dear,' he said, 'I seem to have broken it.'

The pantry padlock received the same careful attention and telling us to enjoy our Christmas he left. Repeating her instructions regarding baby and food my mother followed him. Left alone once more I switched on the radio and to the sound of Christmas songs and carols sat down to read my comic books. It was growing dark when my mother returned clutching several brown paper parcels. Opening the meter cupboard she laid the parcels in side and closed the door on them.

I went to bed that night still ignorant of the contents of or the reason for the packages. Christmas Day dawned with that special glow that only a Christmas sky can give. My mother was already up and as I went down the narrow stairs I heard her talking to the baby, a surprise awaited me; as I entered the room I saw several parcels wrapped not in brown paper but in bright red gift paper and laying on the table a large Christmas stocking.

I looked at my mother,

'Happy Christmas, love,' she said, 'Go on they are yours.'

I needed no second instruction and began tearing open the parcels. In the first I discovered a collapsible wooden fortress complete with turrets and a drawbridge. In the second was a large boxed set of "Britain's" toy soldiers in bright red uniforms with tall bearskin hats armed with rifles and posed in various fighting or marching attitudes. I thought that my heart would burst with excitement and immediately began assembling the fort whilst she told me the story.

On Christmas Eve she had received an emergency payment of a few shillings welfare allowance but had said nothing planning to buy food with it. When our kind neighbours filled our Christmas pantry she decided that I deserved something special, so she took the money to the local toy shop and having told our story to the owner managed to buy toys and stocking for a total of ten shillings. What had begun as a miserable Christmas turned out to be the happiest of my childhood and the one that I remember most vividly.

Chapter Thirteen

The New Year came and as 1951 aired its baby clothes in a flurry of snowflakes there was no sign of Billy James, then in mid January Mother received a letter from him stating that he would not come back until we were gone. It was not pleasant knowing that we were living where we were not wanted and my mother spent her days searching for alternative accommodation.

One day towards the end of January she came home filled with excitement and told me that she had found lodgings with a nice Irish family, the O'Sheas. 'They've got three children so you will not be lonely,' she said, 'and we can move in today.'

Move in we did and I met Sheila O'Shea and her children - Mr. O'Shea was at sea on a fishing trawler. We were given the downstairs front room as a bed sitting room, furnished with a bed a table and two chairs and two wall cupboards for storage; kitchen and bathroom facilities were shared.

Although I had shared a house with other children before they were nothing like the O'Shea kids who were untamed and free spirited in the extreme, their behaviour alternating between fighting and squabbling and fierce loyalty towards each other. There were four of them; Shaun the eldest, then there came Eileen, Patrick and Kathleen in turn.

Shaun was an introversive bespectacled lad about a year older than me but quick tempered and a fierce fighter, Eileen was the mother-surrogate of the brood and Kathleen the baby. Patrick or Paddy as he was commonly called was an obsessive and would sit on the broken down old sofa rocking ferociously backward and forward from the waist doing further damage to the poor springs that twanged loudly with every backward bounce and singing the first two lines of "Gaily The Troubadour" - a song made popular by Tennessee Ernie Ford - over and over again in a tuneless tone; after a few score of repetitions Shaun would pull the settee over backwards banging Paddy's head on the floor and bringing the concert to an abrupt end; the fight that followed was much more interesting.

Sheila O'Shea was a local born red haired woman in her early thirties attractive and passionate natured given to fierce outbursts of temper that usually resulted in her hurling any object that came to hand at her chosen target. She juggled her love life carefully between her husband and her South African lover known to one and all as Big Chris.

Life was not easy in the O'Shea household; money was scarce and enforced minimalism the order of the day. Our small bed-sitting room was the most heavily furnished room in the house. The main living room contained only an ancient three piece suite missing several castors and extruding its springs but beloved by Patrick. Bedrooms held only a bed and the odd chair and the kitchen a table, a brightly painted kitchen cabinet and five creaky chairs.

For those who are dirt-poor treats are rare but welcomed, appreciated and remembered; one treat was the once weekly evening meal of fish and chips, these were bought at a tiny lock up fish and chip shop known locally as Revver Door's. The shop was owned by a Belgian named Redvers D'or and the interior measured about nine feet square, this allowed nine feet by five feet for the frying range and preparation area and the narrow remainder for customers who queued in a horseshoe formation shoulder to shoulder. The size of the shop combined with a low ceiling the heat from the range and the body heat of the customers resulted in a Turkish bath atmosphere that left everyone perspiring, not least the proprietor who would frequently wipe the streaming sweat from his face with a grubby once white rag; no one seemed concerned that he gripped the fish portions with the same rag when dipping them into the batter and plunging them into the boiling fat.

Hygiene aside the food was superb, freshly caught fish in rich batter and local potato chips both fried in beef dripping and served up wrapped in newsprint. I would queue with mouth watering knowing that I could tear open a corner of the newsprint wrapping on the way home and sample the food.

One attraction of the shop for me was the multitude of local characters that frequented it. I would stand silently drinking in titbits of local gossip, many salacious or colourful and not meant for a child's ears. My favourite character was Big Tex, a giant of a trawler man famed locally for having been the stunt double who dived from the mast in Gregory Peck's film of "Moby Dick". The dive had cost him his hearing as his eardrums had been permanently damaged by water pressure but this did not appear to diminish his exuberance for life; whilst waiting for chips to fry he would buy one or two large pieces of hake in batter and eat them in the queue, joking with his fellow customers and roaring loudly at his own jokes.

The only drawback to fish and chip night was the need to walk the mile and a half both ways often in the rain and the passage through a long dark lane lacking any form of lighting and inhabited by countless shadows and night shapes. I was terrified of the dark and at the beginning of this lane I would stop, screw my courage to the sticking point and walk through as fast as I could singing a song then popular entitled "Sugar Bush". Once through I would breathe a sigh of relief and relax until the return journey.

Doing the weekly shop at Slough's shop was also a treat, the shop was perched precariously atop another of the several steep embankments that fell away down to the beach and the supporting walls beneath it formed a storage cellar. Slough's was not much larger than the fish and chip shop but, with the exception of clothing and footwear, it sold everything that a household could need. From hammers and nails to sugar and tea the groaning shelves held all manner of necessary goods.

There were two big attractions at Slough's for a kid: broken biscuits and penny lollies. Biscuits were sold loose from large square glass topped tins displayed along the floor in front of the counter. Every time you bought biscuits Mr. Slough would dig his hands into the tin and shovel the biscuits into a brown paper bag, this would result in a number of broken biscuits being left in each tin and these could be bought at one penny a bag - one bag per customer. He also sold home made penny iced lollies, strawberry or orange that were really fruity and lasted for quite a time.

Yet another treat was Winnie The Pasty's baking. A little way down the hill from our new home was a row of lime washed houses sitting at the top of another steep embankment; from the front they appeared to be two storied but at the rear they descended down the embankment a further storey. To reach the rear a customer descended through a narrow tunnel beneath the houses called a 'gully' by the locals. Once through the gully one house was seen to open onto a stone patio crammed with potted plants and herbs this was the house of Winnie the Pasty Woman and from this house would issue the most delicious baking smells.

Winnie, a woman of Eastern European origin, earned a living baking and selling Cornish pasties, meat pies and cream filled pastries that would have secured her a job as pastry chef on Mount Olympus; all achieved in a domestic gas oven. Her pastry truly melted in the mouth and the generosity of her fillings both sweet and savoury made one doubt that she could make a profit. Twice a week I would be sent down to buy pasties and cream horns from Winnie and I would wait in her small kitchen my mouth watering as she bagged my purchases eager to be home and tasting her creations.

The embankment on which Winnie lived formed the top of a steep hill running down towards the sea and I was curious about what lay at the bottom. As spring approached and the weather improved I took advantage of a fine sunny day to explore and found that the hill ended in a small cove on the edge of the docks, this triangular shingle cove was formed by the retaining wall of the dock on one side a long stone jetty on the second and the sea on the third. That day of exploration must have been a Sunday because the docks were silent and there was not a soul in sight.

To reach the beach I climbed down a steep set of stone steps set into the dock wall and as they had no handrail I could imagine my mother warning me to be careful. I stepped down upon the shingle carpet and felt a deeper silence close around me, interrupted only by the soft whisper of the sea as it lapped against the beach. The high stone walls created a world within a world and trapped the smell of ozone intensifying it so that it left me light-headed. I stood for a while intoxicated by the atmosphere and then began to explore.

Near the top of the sloping beach was a broad band of jetsam made up of seaweed and dried sticks free of the hideous plastic and cans of today's tidal leavings. I crunched my way across this and saw a brightly coloured band of similar width near the edge of the receding tide.

When I reached this second band I saw that it consisted of hundreds of thousands of seashells. I sat down in the middle this treasure trove of nature and began to examine my discovery. In addition to the bright cockle shells there were horn shaped Marlin, strangely patterned Cowrie, Strawberry Trochas, Spotted Literatus, Silvery Trochus, Screwshells that reminded me of a unicorn's horn, Frogsheels and Cowries and countless other brilliantly coloured sea offerings all laying in a brilliant mixture of pebbles and beach gem stones; crystal quartz, rose quartz, tiger's eye, pebbles of many hues and shapes each highly polished by the action of the sea and glistening wet from the tide.

I sat down among my finds and became lost in their beauty. Maybe it was the warmth of that suntrap of a beach coupled with the scent of a thousand sea smells from its composite parts that intoxicated me or the repetitious, 'shush shush,' of the waves on the shingle, whatever the narcotic was I very soon lost touch with reality; I was alone in a world of my own. A hitherto unknown sense of what I now recognise as peace descended upon me. No-one could touch me, hurt me or disturb me and, although I could not put it into words or conscious thought at the time, I had found Shangri-La on a small West Wales beach. I do not know how many hours passed as I sat there but a cold breeze blowing from the rising tide brought me back to reality and I realised that evening was near.

Filling my pockets with as many shells and pebbles as they would hold I made my way slowly home. I cannot say exactly how but I was a different child from the one that had walked down the hill that day. On reaching home I emptied my treasure out upon the bed to examine it again but to my dismay all that I saw was a pile of lifeless shells and pebbles, the magic was not in the finds but in the beach and in the moment. I was deeply disappointed having thought that I could bring the wonder home with me. I did, however, rediscover it albeit to a lesser intensity on the many occasions that I returned to that beach and I like to believe that should I return there today, sixty years on, I would still find it.

Every one of the O'Shea children was teeming with lice and accepted them as a part of life, scratching vigorously and vying with each other for the size and condition of their parasites. I discovered that they ran louse races on the bare striped ticking of their pillows, cheering on the winner only to crush it on the back of a dessert spoon at the end and - once I had become infested - I joined in enthusiastically. We lived with the O'Sheas for several months and I became like one of their family joining in the fights and games and acquiring and breeding my own stable of racing head lice and body lice. Despite my mother's hard work with a fine toothed nit comb along with shampoos and soap that burned as if to remove my skin nothing would prevail against these pernicious vermin.

Sheila and Big Chris were constantly falling out and on one occasion I remember him coming into our room late at night crying. He lowered his giant frame onto a small kitchen chair causing its joints to complain loudly, 'She hates me, Dolly,' he cried.

'Don't be silly she doesn't hate you.'

'She does and I love her madly from her angel blue eyes to her sweet corn coloured ...'

If my mother was shocked she didn't show it but simply steered the conversation away from things corn coloured. I sat there quietly trying to imagine what a corn coloured... looked like, I could not think of Sheila in the terms by which I remembered Lily and I cannot say that I pondered the matter for long because one has more important things to think about at nine years of age. My mother eventually calmed the big man down and he left. Such visits were quite frequent and always ended in his expressing undying gratitude for my mother's understanding heart.

The happy ménage à trois of Chris, Sheila and Sheila's husband worked well largely due to the fact that when one man was at sea the other was at home and vice versa. I cannot recall one occasion when they were both home together although I suppose that must have occurred but I am sure that she would have dealt with that in her happy go lucky way.

Amongst the more important things in my young life was the acquisition of spending money; too young to work we kids resorted to begging. A "Wesley" was the local term for a gift of money and The O'Shea kids quickly taught me how to raise cash for the cinema or other treats by obtaining one. We would lurk at the top of the steep steps that Billy James had shown me on my first day in the town and as the trawlermen came up carrying their heavy kit bags having just received their pay and poundage (poundage was the cash bonus paid for the size of the catch and could amount to a sizeable sum in those days when the fishing grounds were well stocked) we would accost them.

They were almost foolishly generous particularly with kids and in response to our cry of, 'Gi'us a Wesley mister?' they would drop their kit bags dig into their pockets and bring forth handfuls of silver coins. These they would distribute amongst the kids with no kid ending up clutching less than half-a-crown. A half-a-crown was a large silver* coin worth two shillings and sixpence a relic of the days when it was half of the old British Crown of five shillings. *Those coins that predated the year 1910 were solid silver.

If we had been greedy and possessed the stamina for a long stint of begging we could have ended up with several pockets full of money but we were content with ten to fifteen shillings and went home happy leaving the territory to a fresh gang of young beggars. We visited the dock's steps about once every ten days or sooner if we ran out of spending money and, as the cost of a cinema ticket plus a lollie and bag of potato crisps only came to two shillings, we could entertain ourselves cheaply and frequently.

There were three cinemas in town and in those pre-television days there was usually a long queue for admission. They ranged in class from the Astoria, a true local picture palace with Greek column flanked entrance and spacious refreshment room through the midstream plain but clean Empire to The Plaza - known deservedly as The Flea Pit. I always returned home from The Plaza scratching at the bites of several fleas and I suffered because the bites would result in large blisters resembling a nettle sting. Despite this I continued to patronise that dingy picture palace.

The cinemas changed their programme three times a week so a kid with fifteen shillings could see a different show every night except Sunday and as the show consisted of an 'A' film, a 'B' film, a cartoon, trailers of forthcoming films and a newsreel you had value for money; you also had "God Save The Queen" to close but we kids, running the gauntlet of patriotic abuse, would make a beeline for the exit on the opening drum roll because standing for the National Anthem could mean missing the last bus and an hour long walk home.

As an added bonus you could go to the first showing and, if could escape the eagle eye of the usherette, sit through the main feature twice; if she spotted us and asked for our ticket we would produce one that we had chewed so as to destroy the serial number and she was helpless. We loved the cinema in particular the cowboy films and would replay the plots in our games after fighting over which of us should play the hero.

The O'Shea house was usually filled with people but on the few occasions when I was left totally alone my mother would employ the services of a girl named Ruby as a child minder. Ruby was a statuesque young woman about eighteen years old who, with her long raven curls and shapely figure, would have found ready employment as a model in a later generation bore a striking resemblance to Hollywood's Jane Russell. She would sometimes be accompanied by her boyfriend who was a local rugby star and he often gave me the price of a cinema ticket as a gift.

On one particular night Ruby told me that we were going to play a new game, I would hide behind the settee whilst she and her boyfriend sat on it. The aim of the game was to see how long I could stay out of sight. I was allowed my comics and Ruby would hold my hand over the back of the settee to make certain that I did not cheat. The game got under way and I could hear them murmuring to each other then as time went by Ruby's grip on my hand grew tighter and I heard her moan. I asked if she was all right and was told that she had cramp.

Despite my experience in Ludlow I was quite naive. I thought nothing of it as the murmurs and moans increased but when Ruby began scratching the middle of my palm with a long fingernail I found that I was becoming affected; it was not an unpleasant sensation and similar to the pleasure of being tickled. Despite my naivety, as the scratching continued and Ruby's moans became louder I slowly comprehended what was happening and realised as my feeling of pleasure deepened that she was consciously or unconsciously including me in her game. There are many shades of child abuse and I suppose that I was a victim of several - incidentally I won the game and received a shilling piece and a kiss from Ruby for my victory.

I was settled with the O'Sheas and would happily have remained there but one day my mother told me that she had heard of a place that locals knew simply as 'The Camp', a former American army camp that was home to a number of displaced families; apparently once you inhabited a hut there you were guaranteed a council house in due course.

On a warm summer day in my tenth year the bus dropped us off on a quiet road at the northern edge of the town and I looked down upon the place that would be home to me for the next two years. I saw, sitting in a depression in the land, row upon row of light grey shallow pitched rooftops. A concrete road curved from where we stood running out of sight around the edge of the area. The camp was an irregular rectangle measuring about one by one and-a-half miles. It was bordered on the South by a tall hedge and a concrete road that ran around the entire camp, on the North by the portion of the concrete road on which we stood, on the West - a short side - by the back gardens of a housing estate, on the East by the back gardens of another estate. The Camp was a world apart from the world, a ghetto that forbade the interference of outsiders.

As I soon discovered, the huts were built of concrete and grey asbestos and I believe worth describing in detail; each hut was about sixty feet long by fifteen feet wide with a shallow pitched double skinned asbestos sheet roof and external walls formed by a double skin of the same material slotted between concrete post uprights. The cavity in walls and roof was filled with more asbestos packing made of straw soaked in a liquid asbestos packed between the sheets and left to dry out. Dividing walls were made of concrete blocks and ended at the base of the roof leaving a gap between walls and roof the length of the hut. There were no internal doors simply apertures in the concrete walls. Heating and cooking was by means of cast iron stoves whose pipes ran up through the roof. A single electric light hung from the roof in the main rooms. The construction would cause a modern health officer to pale but we were not as health and safety conscious as the present generation and, or so it appeared, little the worse off for it.

Because this had been an American army base the huts were laid out on the American grid plan with concrete paths between them, each path being protected from the rain by a tall veranda that ran the length of the path. These verandas were roofed by sheets of corrugated asbestos and I soon found out that those roofs were great to run along although, as they were worn in places, you never knew when a loud crack would signal that sheet of roofing was about to collapse; despite the danger and frequent falls we somehow survived. Another risk was being caught by an angry resident whose veranda space was threatened with destruction, such people did not complain to one's parent they simply gave the offender a good beating and there was no point in telling your mum that Alfred Khan gave you the bruise on your face because you would simply be told that you must have deserved it.

One performer of note on the verandas was a young man known as 'Circus' due to his claim to have been a performer in the renowned Chipperfield's Circus. He would perform the most daring swings and acrobatic manoeuvres and was admired by all the kids. Although I did not know it at the time this man was to later play a major part in my life.

We followed the road around and with my mother pushing the baby in a wheelchair made ramshackle by my frequent use of it as a racing buggy (I had not learned from the Cwmfelinfach episode) we entered one of the tunnels formed by the veranda, I say tunnels because the roof and the close proximity of huts on each side gave the impression of entering a subterranean world.

It was like a regimented maze with paths leading in four directions and it was quite easy to lose one's way. One or two screaming children went haring past and then we came to a place where the veranda roof had been destroyed allowing the sunlight to bathe the path. There in the brilliant patch of light a small blonde boy was crouched with shorts down around his ankles answering the call of nature in the middle of the path. We stopped at this strange obstruction and he turned his face up to us gave us the most angelic of smiles before returning to the task in hand.

As we watched in stunned silence we heard a woman's harsh voice yelling a boy's name, it was the child's mother and she appeared at the door of a nearby hut. Pulling up his shorts as he went, the child ran to her. My mother steered around the product of his labours and we approached the woman who stood with arms folded perhaps anticipating some criticism of her son.

'Excuse me,' said my mother, 'can you tell me where I will find number 76a?'

The woman stood with chin up and continued to stare without replying. My mother's polite and educated mode of speech was to earn her the derisory title of "The Lady" amongst the majority of camp dwellers who communicated in loud voices peppering their conversation with obscenities.

'Mr. and Mrs. Thomas,' my mother expanded.

'I know...' began the child but his mother cut him off.

'Go right down to the road and turn left,' and turning on her heel she dragged the child inside and slammed the door shut.

My mother thanked her and we continued heading south. 'I hope there aren't too many like her,' she said.

Huts that had been divided into sublets had the hut number at one end and the main entrance and the same number suffixed by the letter 'a' at the opposite sublet entrance. We soon found 76a and standing on an old fish box that was part of an interesting selection of rubbish surrounding that end of the hut I peered through a dirty window. Fly tipping was not a problem in the camp as most of the inhabitants threw their non perishable rubbish out into the area between the huts. Some would take the trouble to carry it down to The Wilderness but more about that area later.

76a consisted of one room about twenty feet square, in the centre of this empty concrete floored barn stood a black cast iron ship's stove with its pipe running up through the roof. The door aperture in the concrete dividing wall and the roof space above the wall was filled with various coloured sheets of cardboard. There was no sign of an electric light and we discovered that our portion of hut did not boast an electricity supply.

I was thrilled at the first sight of this cavern. I could only vaguely remember when we had last had a home of our own with our own key and the ship's stove with its brass taps and handles looked promising from the point of view of a young pyromaniac. Most kids of my acquaintance loved fire; give us a box of matches and something flammable and we were away. We never to my knowledge burned down anything of value like a house but during my days in the camp we managed a few spectacular blazes. Some of the more delinquent among the gang even boasted of a haystack or two but thankfully I was never tempted in that direction.

Going around to the other end of the hut we met our new landlords a young couple with several small children who welcomed the extra ten shillings a week that we were to pay in rent. When we had been given the key we quickly inspected our new home more closely. It smelled strongly of damp concrete but it had been kept clean and there were no panes of glass missing from the windows.

I examined the stove and discovered that it had a large water tank at the rear fed by a loose iron cover and piped to a large brass tap. Hot water on tap! (it turned out to be rusty brown in colour and taste but it was hot.) My mother greeted this stove with the smile of pleasure that a modern housewife would give at sight of her new designer kitchen.

We returned to the O'Sheas because it was several days before we could move into 76a Picton Place (the local council had renamed site after the famous Welsh general but it was known to one and all as The Camp). In the meantime my mother had obtained help from the local Red Cross and we moved in with two folding iron camp beds a kitchen table, two chairs and a selection of army surplus bedding (no sheets but one became accustomed to the rough grey blankets and they were plentiful - a half a dozen for each bed - and warm).

In addition to the absence of electricity the hut lacked two major amenities, a lavatory and running water. There had been a sufficient number of communal lavatory blocks when the camp had been a military base and the first squatters had secured a unit by placing a padlock on the door, the communal showers had been swiftly wrecked by the young Camp hooligans but the padlocks had enabled each hut to have access to the basics. Unfortunately if a family moved out and rather than hand its lavatory on simply removed its padlock the young demolition artists moved in with bricks and iron pipes and destroyed the unit leaving the overhead cistern laying on the floor gushing water until a council plumber arrived to disconnect it.

For latecomers the only solution to waste disposal was a bucket and a trip to The Wilderness; the area called The Wilderness by camp dwellers lay on the far side of the lower concrete road that ran the length of the southern edge of the camp. About one and one half miles long it varied in depth from thirty yards to one hundred yards, the first ten to fifteen yards being waist high wild grass interspersed with bracken the remainder an impassable mixture of bramble and blackthorn. A maze of narrow paths had been worn through the area and these together with tunnels made through the woodland by camp kids made a great adventure playground - there was one drawback, the stench.

The disposal of sewage was accomplished by digging a pit within the grassy parameters of The Wilderness dumping your bucketful into that pit and covering it; the snag being the fact that lazy persons or those who lacked a spade did not bother to or could not cover it (fortunately for us the Thomas family allowed us use of their spade and left it behind when they moved.) In the hot summer months these uncovered deposits could be pinpointed by the thick swarms of blow flies that hung above them and so avoided, in the winter you just had to pick your way carefully.

I do not know how we survived without an outbreak of some deadly disease but living in dirt must have made us resistant to harmful germs. I hated s*** patrol as the kids called it, the chief difficulty being finding a fresh undug patch but as the man of the hut the duty fell to me; so armed with a spade borrowed from our landlord I would trudge reluctantly to my task.

Another little problem was the lack of plumbing; water was obtained from one of a number of stand pipes located on the fringe of The Wilderness and carried home in buckets or jugs. We acquired two large white enamel farm jugs that each held about one gallon and with the exception of bath day (accomplished by standing in a bucket of hot water and dipping it over you with a tin mug) one trip a day usually provided sufficient water for drinking and cooking.

In the winter it was necessary to take along newspaper and matches to light a fire around the pipe and unfreeze it having first turned on the tap to prevent a burst. Heating was by means of coke, that by product of coal that resembles volcanic pumice in lightness and texture. Coke was cheaper than coal and burned well in the cast iron stove giving a clean and fierce heat.

Chapter Fourteen

On our first morning in the hut I set out to explore the surrounding area, having been warned by my mother to take care – haven't all mothers since the beginning of time cast a protective spell over their children with those words? The community was stirring; women beat mats against the walls of their hut, a few small children ran up and down the paths screaming excitedly, a man was kneeling chopping firewood to add to the smoke that curled up from the many stove pipe chimneys, a mother could be heard yelling at her child to get out of bed. All the sights and sounds of a close knit community, sights and sounds that were to become familiar to me over the next two years because; although my mother had been told that we would be re-housed within weeks we were among the last few families to leave Picton Place.

I wandered along the network of paths, here and there a hut had been demolished leaving only the concrete floor (as the huts became vacant the council demolished them to prevent squatters moving in, often merely completing the work of the juvenile demolition teams). I was some distance from our hut when turning a corner I found myself face to face with a group of scruffy kids about my own age or slightly older blocking the pathway. For a few moments we stood staring at each other and then they moved towards me.

A tall kid whose face was disfigured by a hair lip that gave him a permanent sneer stepped up to me and shoved me in my chest. Unprepared I staggered back and almost fell. A mixture of fear and anger flooded over me and I pushed him back - a mistake. He shoved me again and began punching and kicking me. I had never encountered such violence in another kid and I had not recovered my wits when he grabbed me and twisted me to the ground. He then sat on my chest and began punching my face. Recovering I tried to punch back or throw him off but he was kneeling on my arms. The other kids were cheering him on with cries of "Get him, Dai. Go on kill him" and the like.

Thankfully his punches, although painful, were not intended to injure but to humiliate. I shouted loudly calling him the few swear words that I knew over and over again and eventually he stopped - whether it was from my shouting or because his arms grew tired I do not know. He leaned back, 'Have you had enough?' he asked and I nodded.

Suddenly he leaned forward and kissed me wetly on the lips. In addition to being astounded I was nauseated and horrified and, pushing him off, I began to punch him in a blind fury. Anger and disgust must have increased my strength because he began to give ground. The kids began to cheer again but this time for me. I threw my arms around his neck and attempted to throw him down but he was prepared and we wrestled back and forth with me cursing him, then he began to laugh. At this my rage subsided and I loosened my grip on his neck. We backed away from each other and he ended his laugh in a snort and a question,

'What's your name, kid?' he asked. I told him.

'Do you want to join our gang?'

There was only one sensible answer to this and I found myself a member of The Dai Griffiths Gang. Dai was one of four brothers and three sisters belonging to the roughest family in the community and, although I did not know it at that moment he and his gang of scruffs - of which I was now one - ruled the younger inhabitants in a reign of fear that would have made Al Capone proud; they were also not above intimidating adults if they could get away with it. Such was my introduction to juvenile thuggery and petty crime. There were five other kids in the gang, two brothers from Scotland, a dark North Welsh kid known as Taffy, an Anglo-Indian kid who boasted the odd combination name of Albert Khan and Dai's cousin Mad Tony.

Tony, fourteen years of age, was in the politically incorrect idiom of the day "slow-witted". He once tried to swallow a mixture of crushed sheet asbestos mixed with some of the asbestos soaked straw that served as insulation between the building sheets; he failed and was violently sick. We didn't know then that asbestos was dangerous and we kids used it in our games in all shapes. As the council demolished each hut as soon as it became vacant there was never a shortage of debris. Sometimes flat pieces of it passed as a toy currency. At other times it was crockery, cutlery, food or writing materials. We crushed it, frequently accidentally inhaled it, tasted it and - with the exception of Mad Tony - did everything short of actually eating it.

Tony being sick was commonplace, but invariably interesting. Sometimes we would dare him to eat the most bizarre items simply to watch how far he could throw up, cheering on his projectile output and commenting on colour and content. In hindsight we were truly obnoxious kids and Tony was dangerously psychopathic; although the fact that this hulking great youth had the brain of a violent and capricious four-year old and the strength of an ox it did not bother us kids, he was simply an entertainment and perhaps he derived some pleasure from the notoriety that his eating tricks gave him.

Now that I was one of the gang I was told that I must prove my worth. They took me to a veranda at the edge of the camp and pointed to a thick bare wire protruding from the woodwork at a height of about six feet. Dai told me that if I could grab the wire I would be in the gang. It looked easy and I jumped and grabbed at it. An excruciating pain shot through my body and I felt as if I was being pulled apart, I could not breathe and could not open my grasp on the wire. Thankfully, gravity acting upon my dead weight tore me away from the live high voltage cable and I collapsed semi-conscious unaware of my surroundings until the laughter of the gang members slowly penetrated my benumbed brain. They thought this great sport and would entrap any gullible kid that fell into their hands by promising not to beat them up if they passed the wire test.

Through my mother's friendship with his parents I made one friend who was not in the gang; his name was Henry and he lived an isolated existence because his parents, with the exception of his school hours, would not permit him to play outdoors. I enjoyed my visits to Henry because he owned a collection of impressive toys; his family had relations living in America who would send him all sorts of electrical and mechanical toys the like of which would not be seen in Britain for decades; he also received regular delivery of bundles of American comic papers that, once read, he passed on to me.

I was soon hooked on the favourite characters and could not wait to read the next episode of The Katzenjammer Kids or Little Orphan Annie; I still retain fond memories of those brightly coloured pages. Those of you who have seen the film "Giant" may recall the scene where Rock Hudson is sitting up in bed reading the comic pages; when I first saw I felt a pang of nostalgia for my childhood comic pages and despite the sweeping story line and

Boy

fine acting the memorable moment in the film for me is the bedtime comic reading.

Henry was a kind generous friend and I missed him when he and his parents emigrated to America; 'To give him a better chance in life,' said his mother. We never heard from the family again but years later as I watched newsreel of The Viet Nam War I realised that my friend Henry would have been amongst the many young Americans inducted and I have often wondered since if he survived.

Entertainment in the camp was, with the exception of the radio and the cinema, home made and pocket money was something that posh kids received. We were forced to obtain spending money by whatever means we could. A popular means was extortion, several housing estates bordered on the camp and the respectable youngsters from these would occasionally make the mistake of taking a shortcut through our gang's territory; if caught they paid with whatever money or trinkets they were carrying and usually went off bawling following a smack in the face to teach them respect.

We felt no guilt about our activities and it occurs to me that social workers and reformers would do well to learn the lesson that a person only regrets an action or fears its consequences when they have developed a social conscience and an empathy with their victims or when a tomorrow exists. We lacked a conscience and for us there was no tomorrow, we lived for the moment and only thought as far ahead as the next misadventure. I later found this to be the case in my association with petty gangsters in London; whilst they dreamed of the big hit that would put them on easy street their lives consisted of reaction to or taking advantage of the day's events with little thought of the consequences.

Any money or goods obtained by our criminal acts was distributed in a the Dai Griffiths democratic manner; Dai took what he wanted and allowed the gang to fight over what was left. We accepted this as part of the natural way of things. There was never any retribution following the incidents of extortion, either the kids were afraid to tell their parents or the parents did not wish to tangle with camp dwellers. Another lucrative activity was collecting and selling scrap-metal. We knew the going rate for every type of non-ferrous metal and were not particular from where we collected it. There is no doubt, however, that our behaviour was disgusting.

When not extorting money or electrocuting kids we would hang out in our den, a dugout about six feet square by five feet deep roofed with corrugated iron sheets and sods of grass. Here we would plan our next exploit, boast about our successes and smoke hand rolled cigarettes made from shiny toilet paper and the contents of cigarette ends collected from the gutter; at least some of us would. I tried smoking once and the resulting bout of nausea put me off for several years, although I still inhaled a great deal of smoke because the den had very little ventilation.

I did not realise that the tobacco from the cigarette ends contained much of the nicotine filtered through from the smoked portion making it three or more times stronger and causing my violent reaction. I told my mother of the cigarettes and she warned me that a person could catch lip cancer from someone else's cigarette end but Dai laughed at this saying that we were not using the paper of the butt.

We had not been living in our new environment for many weeks when Dai Griffiths told the gang that his elder brother had made a discovery, it appeared that the Americans, being electricity hungry, had laid down miles of underground copper cables throughout the camp; these were buried about two feet deep protected only by a layer of sand.

Our devious little brains quickly worked out that if we dug and discovered a bundle of wires then traced the probable route and dug again some yards away we could cut the wires at both ends and pull long lengths of copper wire from one hole. The fact that it was buried in sand made it easy to pull and within days holes two feet in depth began appearing all over the camp area.

Regrettably it never occurred to us to backfill our diggings with the result that unfortunate hut occupants would open their door and step out into a hole. Many and varied were the threats heaped upon our heads but we led a charmed life and escaped the consequences of our misdeeds - thankfully no one was seriously injured by our copper pits.

Once dug the copper wire was burned on a bonfire to remove the rubber covering, a smoky and smelly operation that did not endear us to our neighbours. Reputable scrap dealers would not buy from young scruffs so we sold it to Dai's older brother, Bill, who paid us about half the value and then sold it on at a profit - or so he thought. The rewards were beyond our dreams; there could be as many as fifty or more thick copper cables in one hole and within days we were earning more than a full grown working man. We strutted around like undersized Chicago gangsters; kids who had smoked cigarette butts now sported tins of small cigars known as "Whiffs" and local toy shops sold out of top of the range cap guns and luxury toys.

Once the operation, that lasted for many weeks, was under way Dai told us that Bill stored the scrap in their shed until he had a bulk lot; so we simply sold it to Bill then stole an unnoticeable proportion of it back and sold it to Bill again. The poor man never caught on and must have wondered why he failed to make the anticipated profit, despite that he did very nicely from our activities and never complained.

We were victims of "Copper Fever" (our juvenile equivalent of gold fever and just as deadly) and there is no telling where our lust for the wire may have led had it not been for Dai's older brother, Johnny. Johnny was digging at the edge of the camp area when he struck the mother lode; a bitumen coated wire the thickness of a baby's arm. Having excitedly widened his excavation to the size of a small quarry he made the first cut by swinging a large woodman's axe at the wire; the wire exploded, the axe head melted, Johnny was thrown back several yards and a large area of the town lost its electricity supply. The ensuing investigation and dire threats from those in authority brought "The Great Copper Mining Rush" to an abrupt halt and we were back to scrounging for old brass taps, bits of lead and other meagre scrap finds.

We did not devote our entire time to pecuniary pursuits we also found time to re-enact our films, boarding pirate ships, conquering castles and the number one favourite winning the Wild West. Completely under the spell of Hollywood we were quite uncompromising in our attitude towards the Native American regarding all "redskins" as baddies along with any cowboy who wore a black hat and any mediaeval authority figure. There were also seasons for games and although no one officially announced the start and end of a season, like homing pigeons we instinctively knew when to start collecting conkers or when to take our pocket knives and cut bows and arrows.

Then there was the catapult (slingshot.) Every working class boy knew how to make a catapult and most owned one of these potentially lethal weapons. A "Y" shaped tree branch the thickness of a man's thumb was cut to size, and a leather end from a pair of braces nailed to each prong. You could buy a yard of thick rubber "Catty" elastic for sixpence and the tongue cut from a shoe held the missile (we never considered the cost to our parents of replacing a pair of braces and a pair of shoes and accepted the consequential beating as part of the process).

The local bird population suffered severely from boys with a catapult and a hunting instinct; thankfully I was content with knocking cans off walls. My mother detested my catapult calling it 'that horrible thing,' and I was obliged to smuggle it in and out of our hut.

Another favourite but less deadly weapon was the pea shooter; when in season we would cut straight lengths of the stalk of the cow parsley plant that were often nearly two feet in length and the stalks with their hollow stem made an ideal pea shooter, particularly when loaded with an unripened berry or haw from a hawthorn tree. Propelled by a young pair of lungs these projectiles of which there was an endless supply could reach a velocity that would knock a tin can off a wall.

It remains one of childhood's mysteries that no kid (in my experience) lost an eye but bloody punctures on faces were common because we were unmerciful in our use of the weapon and we hunted one another through woodland and field, in particular "Foster's Field" with its chest high grain crop. There is little doubt that we caused a great deal of damage to that poor man's crop but as we were ignorant of the harm we caused we felt no remorse.

This brings to mind an incident where the physical nature of male to female intruded once more into my young life. Since meeting them I had been puzzled by the fact that an old and ugly couple like Ma and Pa Griffiths could produce two very attractive daughters; like most children I could not conceive that the old couple had once been young attractive and virile seeing only their present condition. The youngest of these girls, Jenny, who was about fourteen years of age, was a slim being with corn flower blue eyes moist lips and short curly blonde hair. I was fascinated by what I saw as her beauty and would become terribly embarrassed whenever she discovered me staring at her and returned my stare with a contemptuous grin.

On the day of the incident we were playing in Fosters Field and I had caught Jenny Griffiths. Although slimly built she was taller than me and we fought fiercely for several minutes until I climbed on top of her pinning her wrists above her head, I also found my leg between her thighs pressing against her mons pubis. She ceased struggling and lay there looking me questioningly. We lay quietly breathing heavily from our exertions and I felt her body heat flowing into me. Still she said nothing. In her experience, that was no doubt greater than mine, she realised that I did not know what to do next and shoved me away from her; still without saying a word.

I looked down at her as she lay there with her arms above her head knees bent and legs wide apart. I could see the vee of her navy blue knickers so popular with mothers of that era and I saw a patch of wetness; concluding that my attack and her struggle had caused her to pee her knickers I felt guilty and pretended that I had not noticed. After a few minute's silence Jenny stood, straightened her clothing and walked away without a word.

That first summer in the camp was an education in many ways. On a bright Sunday morning Dai knocked on our door to tell me that we were going to play cricket - an unusually gentlemanly occupation for us scruffs. I followed him to Albert Khan's hut and waited. A group of about eight or ten urchins had gathered when the door opened and Albert's father, Alfred, emerged. He was a vision in gleaming white, complete cricket whites, cap, pads and gloves, he also carried a cricket bat and a bright new cricket ball.

Without a word he swung the bat under one arm and in the manner of a gentleman player at the famous Lords ground strode away in the direction of The Wilderness followed by Albert, carrying stumps and bails, and a motley collection of scruffy kids of which I was one. I was excited at the prospect of being a player in a real cricket match and could not wait for my turn to bat - it never came.

We filed down one of the narrow paths through the bracken and onto the school playing field that adjoined the area. Alfred immediately began despatching his young players to various parts of the makeshift pitch with instructions such as "silly mid on" and the like; instructions that none of us understood. Then, having removed his white sweater and tied it around Albert's neck by the sleeves, he drove the stumps into the ground set the bails and scratched out a crease. Satisfied he paced out a pitch drove a single stump into the ground appointed his first bowler and the match began.

For the next two hours we raced around the field in all directions while Alfred hit ball after ball with cries of 'Six,' 'Four,' or 'Well hit,' in praise of his own batting, any request to bat was greeted with disdain and the protester warned that he would be sent off if he did not shut up. On any of the many occasions that he was bowled out he would cry 'No ball!' and replace the bails. At lunch time satisfied that he had upheld the honour of India Alfred pulled stumps and followed by a file of exhausted kids swaggered back to his hut, this Sunday ritual continued throughout the summer with each kid waiting his turn to bat but not once did Alfred relinquish the bat or accept being bowled or caught out.

As regular as our summer cricket was our Sunday morning voyeuristic entertainment obtained by gathering beneath the window of Taffy's hut; his parents had their own regular Sunday habit, they would retire to bed with "The News of The World", that now defunct broadsheet then renowned for its lascivious content and make noisy passionate love. The gang would crouch beneath their open window stifle giggles and exchange whispered comments as the unfortunate couple groaned and cried to the accompaniment of a very noisy brass bedstead.

We held many incredulous discussions about the couple's passion for each other; we could not understand it because Taffy's mother was a tall bony woman with a great hooked nose that almost touched her upturned chin whilst his father was a tiny undernourished man. Taffy explained it by saying that his father was terrified of her and would be beaten up if he did not perform. Our entertainment came to an abrupt end one morning when we became carried away and began cheering the couple on.

Sunday evenings found us kids gathered around the radio in the Griffiths hut. The hut had been subdivided by the older boys into a series of passages and small rooms to accommodate the large family, the focal point of the main room being a large black stove on which a three-gallon ex-army cooking pot appeared to be constantly simmering. Another constant feature was Ma Griffiths, her age was indeterminate but her white hair and deeply lined face bore testimony to years of child bearing and hardship.

I never saw Ma standing on her feet in the hut although she was not disabled as was later proved by her energetic attendance at the Camp Coronation party. Her twenty stone plus form wrapped in what had once been a flowered pinafore appeared to be permanently ensconced in a battered easy chair whose castors had been replaced by books and lumps of wood. She seemed oblivious to the ash from the stove that spread out into the room placing her plimsoll clad feet on it as if it were the softest of cushions. A hand rolled cigarette filled with tarry black shag tobacco drooped from her tight lipped mouth.

She usually ignored us, preferring to sleep as we gathered around the radio deep in the grip of a thriller or western adventure; our favourites were "Dick Barton Special Agent" a cliff hanger with incredibly twisted plots and Geoff Arnold's "Riders of The Range" a straight forward shoot 'em up cowboy series. Sixty years later I can still remember one "Dick Barton" episode where the villains tied Dick and his trusty lieutenant to pipe work in a flooding dungeon using what they described as a new unbreakable wonder product called cellophane. The first cellophane wrapped detective?

Another entertainment was the family's ancient wind up gramophone with its single 78rpm recording of "Twelfth Street Rag". We would play it over and over again tapping our feet and clicking our fingers convinced that it was the last word in sophistication, the wonder was that the brass needle did not wear a hole in the disc.

At intervals one of the kids would cry out, 'Ma's on fire!' and there would be a panic to slap out the spark from a cinder or a dropped cigarette, whereupon Ma would wake suddenly with a grunt and an oath sending the fire crew flying with a belt from her man sized fist screaming obscenities (and her range of swear words was phenomenal) for a moment or two before subsiding back into a noisy sleep.

Towards the middle of the evening Ma would wake and in a voice deepened to gruff masculinity by years of smoking and yelling announce that grub was up, the kids would rush out to the makeshift kitchen to grab bowls or dishes and Ma would ladle out stew from the ever steaming pot.

On my first night I stood and watched them until Ma looked at me and asked, 'Don't you eat?' I nodded, 'Well get a bowl you silly little bugger and get some stew in you.'

I did not need a second invitation and I was soon wolfing into one of the best lamb stews that I had ever tasted, rich, thick and full of meat. Fiercely protective of her brood and with a generous nature that belied her constant cursing and shouting Ma Griffiths was the Matriarch of Hakin Camp feared and respected by all.

In my solitary hours I continued to read avidly and when night fell I went to bed with a candle on my orange box reading until I fell asleep, sometimes I would look up from my book and see my mother sitting in the dark before the glowing stove staring silently into the fire. The life we lived must have been unbearable for an intelligent and talented human being but I never heard her complain. On one occasion I caught the glint of a tear on her cheek but never thought to enquire the reason.

Having read for several hours or until my candle burned out I would fall into a deep sleep and usually kicked my blankets off. One night I was awakened by a cold drop of water landing on my exposed stomach and putting my hand down felt not water but a large insect wriggling beneath my fingers. I shouted and jumped up awaking my mother who brought a candle to find still wriggling on the floor an earwig over an inch in length. She killed the loathsome thing and I returned to bed making sure to wrap the blankets around me. It turned out that the asbestos soaked straw between the roof sheets was a favourite breeding ground for the earwigs and after a while I became accustomed to brushing them off my bare skin during the night.

Although we had been told that we might wait months before the Thomas family vacated the main part of the hut, Mrs. Thomas became pregnant again and it was only a number of weeks before they were given a council house. Moving into the main part of the hut was a simple matter of knocking down the cardboard that filled the interior doorway and dragging our few belongings through.

Now that we had possession of the entire hut our front door was at the opposite end. On our first morning as sole occupants I stepped out of that door carrying our water jugs and took in the new view. On the other side of the concrete pathway was a grassy bank about one and a half metres high. The bank ran the complete width of the area and along it stood a row of huts. On top of the bank opposite our front door was an enclosure made of rough timber and chicken wire in which a dozen or so hens bustled about clucking and arguing watched over by a rooster with a wicked eye and hackles as red as blood.

I crossed the road curious to see more of this feathered harem and was peering through the wire when I heard, 'You stay away from those birds, boy!' in a tone of command so fierce and sudden that I almost dropped my jugs.

The booming voice came from the doorway of a hut that was set on the bank about a hut's width down from ours. I had recently read and reread "Treasure Island" and shared Jim Hawkins's affection for Long John Silver. There in the hut's doorway stood that very same villainous old sea cook, the top of his head brushing the top of the door frame. Apart from his modern dress that incorrigible one legged rogue had come to life. A strong jawed face reddened by wind and weather was crowned by a mane of flame red hair brushed straight back from his forehead to hang over his collar, his shoulders appeared to be almost as broad as the doorway. Where he was missing a leg his trouser leg was pinned up to the waist and he leaned on an old fashioned wooden crutch.

'Do you hear me, boy,' he said, 'you go near them birds and I'll tan the hide off you and I don't care what your father says either.' His accent was like Billy James's broad Pembrokeshire closer to English West Country than Welsh and his voice was a deep baritone.

I drew a breath, 'I haven't got a father,' I said.

'Ahh,' he cleared his throat, 'Well no mind. If the hens are frightened they won't lay. So mark me now,' and he turned and went indoors.

I stepped well back from the chicken wire and went about fetching our water. When I got back in I told my mother of my encounter with Long John and his threats, she was not happy,

'Oh he will, will he?' she said, 'Just let him try.'

'He looks just like Long John Silver, mum,' I said.

'I don't care if he looks like the Old Nick,' said my mother, 'He won't lay a finger on you.'

All that day the vision of the tall one legged man kept returning to me and I looked forward to seeing him again. Such was my first encounter with the amazing man that I came to know as Uncle Larry.

My mother became firm friends with Uncle Larry and his wife, Jean, when she discovered that they owned a piano and they discovered how brilliant a pianist she was. We would spend many happy evenings in their hut with her playing and me turning the pages of her music. Despite having lost one leg Larry was a clever handyman and could outshine any two legged man at physical skills he had made many improvements to their home and it was warm and cosy. Listening to the adult's conversation I discovered that he had been a promising boxer in his youth showing professional potential. His dreams of a professional boxing career ended when he lost a leg rescuing a young child from beneath the wheels of a dockside shunting engine.

The couple had two daughters, Maxine a year older than me and Jeanette several years younger. The girls became part of the gang and Maxine with her father's flaming hair and temper to match was as tough as any boy and not afraid to prove it. Uncle Larry warned me to protect his daughters or face him, such was my admiration for him that I would have defended them to my last breath but it was invariably a case of Maxine defending me.

Winter came and frost painted The Wilderness with a gleaming white brush disguising true nature and turning the area into an iced wonderland. I enjoyed my daily trip to the water pipe imagining that I was a famous Arctic explorer carving out new tracks through a frozen landscape. I had just returned indoors with our water on such a day when there came a loud knocking on our door, opening it I looked up into a weather beaten mahogany tanned face adorned with bushy eyebrows that met above a large nose under which a thick moustache took cover.

The old tramp, for such he was, wore a battered trilby hat a torn jacket tied at the waist with trawl twine and a pair of shiny corduroy trousers. I caught the smell of strong tobacco and stale sweat and jumped back as he threw down a large bundle of fish box planks. He smiled a broad grin revealing tobacco stained teeth.

'Is your father in, lad?' he asked in a broad accent that I later discovered was that of Yorkshire. I replied that I did not have a father and he asked to see my mother. When she came to the door he smiled the grin again. 'You'll be needing firewood, love,' he said, 'two bob a bundle and for half a crown I'll chop it up for you.'

My mother, who collected and fed all manner of waifs and strays without fear or thought, promptly asked him in for a cup of tea. I was not happy with that because, in addition to resenting the dirty old creature sitting on our chair I sensed violence in him. He introduced himself as Bill Matthews - but you can call me Mr. Matthews he told me - and made himself at home by drinking several cups of tea and eating the last of our precious cream biscuits. My dislike increased because cream biscuits were a rare treat and my favourite.

Over the next hour during which time he used up another pot of tea and smoked several hand rolled cigarettes he extracted our life history from my trusting mother. Finally he decided to do some work. 'I'll chop that wood then. Dorothy,' he said, 'can I use your kitchen?'

I followed him out to the kitchen a somewhat grandiose title for a bare concrete floored room that housed a tapless stone sink, a tin bathtub and an old table, cooking being done on the iron stove in the living room. He pulled a large clasp knife from his pocket and spitting on the palm of one hand began whetting the blade on the same leathery surface grinning at me as he did so. Then with a quick slash he cut the twine that held the bundle together releasing the planks. 'You never know when you'll need a sharp blade,' he leered holding the blade before my eyes.

Fish box planks are about one half of an inch thick and roughly two and a half foot long by four inches wide, he picked one up and bending his knee whilst lifting one leg off the floor he brought the plank down on his extended upper leg snapping the wood in two with a loud crack. He held up the two pieces and I noticed that his large thick hands with their blackened fingernails were ingrained with dirt 'You see that?' he said, 'I could snap a man's spine like that if I had a mind to.'

I felt sick. My mother and her kindness had brought a new threat into my life. After he had left I told her that I did not like Mr. Matthews and that I thought he should be kept outside the door. She laughed and told me that I was being silly. 'He's just a poor homeless old man without any family,' she said, 'don't you remember when we were homeless?'

I felt like telling her that we did not go around threatening people with knives but kept my mouth shut. Over the next few weeks the old tramp's visits became more frequent and lasted longer, in fact he was soon arriving every morning and staying until mid evening despite the fact that he insisted that he had what he called 'a nice crib' in an old air raid shelter situated nearby. A neighbour made the mistake of laughingly asking my mother the name of her new boyfriend and received a lecture on charity and dirty minds for her pains.

As he got his feet further under our table Mr. Matthews became more aggressive and demanding. He would complain about the strength of his tea, go to our makeshift pantry and help himself and criticise my mother's liberal parenting. The final straw came when he threatened to hit me when, angry at his presence, I had answered my mother back. She made a joke of it saying how lucky I was to have an old softy for a mum.

I took him to the door that evening in a sullen silence. At the door he turned to me. 'How would you like me for a father?' he asked with what was intended to be a friendly leer. I was horrified and after I had slammed and bolted the door behind him I rushed back in to my mother. 'Mum, you wouldn't marry Mr.Mathews would you?' She told me not to be silly; that she only felt sorry for him and that he would probably move on when the winter became colder. He did not move on and I began to dread his loud knock at the door.

I stopped going out to play being afraid to leave my mother and brother alone with him and began to have nightmares in which he chased me with that wicked knife of his shouting dire threats. I could sense that even my mother was becoming afraid of him but he would not be stopped and would barge in and throw himself into a chair disregarding any attempt to stop him. Then, quite suddenly, he ceased to appear and as the days went by I grew calmer and happier but there was still a nagging fear that he would appear on our doorstep.

Finally I could stand it no longer and asked my pals if they would go with me to his shelter. They agreed to check him out, threatening to beat him silly if he tried any rough stuff; a dire threat considering that the eldest of my supporters was just ten years of age. When we reached the shelter deep in a patch of waste ground I shouted his name. There was no answer and after nerving myself to enter hoping that I would not find his dead body I pulled the old tarpaulin covering the entrance to one side, as I did it fell enveloping me in its thick folds and my heart nearly stopped.

Recovering I saw that my protectors had run away. I struck a match (we always carried matches for incendiary fun) I entered and saw nothing but wreckage, an old mattress half burned lay in one corner and a seat from an old car lay on its side the stuffing torn out. Tin cans and dirty cooking pans were scattered around but there was no sign of Mr. Matthews. I later found out that a gang of kids had wrecked and burned his pathetic home and that must have been enough to drive him away to seek pastures new. I should have felt sorry for him but I could only feel relief that he was out of our lives

Chapter Fifteen

That same winter my sister Marina came to live with us. Alec had taken her out of the epileptic colony and she had lived with him for some months until her boisterous nature and free spirit seeking to taste all that life could offer after years of confinement proved too much for him to cope with.

Marina was a beautiful and affectionate young woman but a stranger to my mother and me. She soon grew especially fond of Peter, who had grown into a perky two-year-old, and would cuddle and hug him constantly spending every spare penny that came her way on gifts for him. One thing that took some adapting to was her epileptic seizures, the French had given us terms for them and the major seizures were called "grand mals" whilst the minor were known as "petite mals". The onset of a grand mal resulted in prolonged and fierce convulsions accompanied by foaming at the mouth and unconsciousness; a petite mal could be unnoticeable to a stranger being a short period of lack of awareness and the twitching of an eyebrow; both types of seizure were accompanied by incontinence and although she never showed it must have caused Marina great embarrassment.

I quickly learned to thrust the bandaged handle of a dessert spoon between Marina's teeth at the first sign of a grand mal, so preventing her biting through or swallowing her tongue. It was difficult to keep it in place as she thrashed and kicked but I had to learn because my mother was no use in such situations being too emotionally involved.

I realise now that I resented my sister's return home and that I was jealous of the attention she received, although to be fair that attention was slight because she was as much a stranger to my mother as she was to me. Marina must have had the patience of a saint because she endured my spiteful tricks and selfish habits with a sweetness that would have endeared her to anyone except the spoiled brat that was me. On one occasion I threw my World War One bayonet - a precious possession of mine - at her, after pausing just long enough to make certain it would not hit her. It appeared, as I intended, to narrowly miss her and embedded itself in the grass bank opposite our hut. My mother promptly retrieved it and sold it to a neighbour teaching me a salutary lesson in anger management and phoney threats.

Christmas arrived with the usual scarcity of gifts and a suitably shaped gorse bush cut from The Wilderness as a Christmas tree. We were luckier than most because although rationing still inflicted a degree of hardship we were the recipients of monthly food parcels from a kind man that my mother had become pen friends with during one of her job searching periods. Every four or five weeks without fail a parcel would arrive containing a packet of tea, butter, sugar, bacon and from my point of view most importantly a bar of chocolate; the Christmas parcel was something special.

With her usual generosity my mother invited Mad Tony to tea on the day we received our parcel. The centre piece of the table was a beautiful Victorian glass ornament comprising of a large cranberry glass bowl from which arose a number of glass barley sugar branches each curving over into a hook from which hung elegant cranberry glass baskets; my mother loved this ornament a gift from an elderly friend and made the mistake of telling Tony to be careful not to touch it.

That warning was a mistake and I watched as Tony's lips pulled back in a lunatic grin and his eyes narrowed fixing themselves on the ornament. Without warning he jumped to his feet and demonstrating his abnormal strength picked the whole thing up. He cackled inanely saying 'look missus' as he threw it into the air and caught it – or tried to catch it. He failed and my mother's beloved cranberry glass hit the concrete floor with a loud crash shattering into a thousand pieces.

A long silence followed, eventually broken when Tony began to giggle but only for a few seconds because he saw my mother's face and in her face murder. Without any further giggles he threw himself at the door and vanished through it leaving it open behind him. She sank into a chair and cried quietly whilst I sat praying for some miracle to turn back the clock and make everything right again. From that day on Tony would run whenever he saw her.

The season of goodwill always gave me a chance to earn some much needed cash by carol singing. I began early and with my boy soprano singing voice and by carefully selecting my target houses (I discovered that the houses with front gardens were the most generous) I earned several pounds in the first week; a figure that shrank dramatically in the second week as more kids took up the game. I also tasted my first sherry and port wine, draining several glasses of both indiscriminately at the behest of kindly householders; the volume if not the quality of my singing no doubt benefiting from the lack of inhibition that the drinks inspired.

Most of the carol singing money went to my mother but she gave me back a few shillings and that enabled me to buy presents for her, Marina and Peter, something that I had never been able to do before. I was so proud that I got a bigger kick from that than from opening my usual gifts of comic annuals and classic books.

The best part of carol singing was gazing up at a navy blue sky sprinkled with stars that shone like iced diamonds and trying to guess which star had shone down on Bethlehem, perhaps my success at carol singing owed something to the fact that I believed in the nativity story with all my heart.

Christmas was all too soon behind us an with the coming of spring the gang ventured further afield. A favourite area was the nearby beach a wide crescent of fine shingle washed by a sea so clear that you could see every pebble on the seabed at depths of ten or fifteen feet; on one peak of the crescent stood a large abandoned Victorian fort, access to this adventure land was easily gained through gaps in the corroded bars of the main gate and it was a great if dangerous place in which to act out our replay of films seen.

On my first visit I was told that I must walk the wall before being admitted to the garrison. The wall, about fifty yards long, was the exterior wall of the fort; some two feet wide with a drop of about forty feet to the rocks on one side. Two feet sounds quite wide but when you are ten years old and when you look down at the jagged rocks below it seems like two inches. Walk it I did, however, to the cheers of the gang. It was not bravery that inspired me but my fear of appearing a coward in front of my gang mates was greater than my fear of falling.

At the other end of the beach a valley of dense woodland some half a mile wide ran inland for a couple of miles, the bottom of the valley being a wide and deep bog. On my first day in the woods we were making our way along a narrow path when a small bird flew into our faces screaming protest at us. The more

Making a small hole in each end with a safety pin Dai put the egg to his mouth and began to blow the contents. All the while the bird was fluttering back and forth in a state of panic. When I saw her egg being destroyed I hated Dai Griffiths and knocking it from his hand I pushed him backwards, he fell heavily and swore loudly. Although I did not regret my action and would repeat it today I instantly realised that I had made a mistake. 'You're dead!' he shouted, 'Get him!'

I turned and ran crashing through bracken and undergrowth until, spurred on by fear, I outdistanced my screaming pursuers. Despite that I carried on running my heart pounding in my chest, I had seen the pain inflicted on kids by Dai and his toughs. Suddenly, I rounded a turn in the path to find myself at the top of a steep bank and as I halted the figure of a grimacing man rose from a crouch brandishing a machete; I had left reason behind me in my flight, the ghost of the murdered boy whose comics I had used appeared before me and I knew that I was about to die.

Yelling in fear I changed direction and careered off towards the bog. The poor man, who I later realised had simply been out cutting sticks for his runner beans, must have been almost as surprised as I and that which I saw as a grimace must have been an expression of shock. The edge of the bog brought me to a halt and to my senses. Collapsing onto a mossy bank I fell back gasping for breath. When I could breathe normally again I listened, the only sounds were the woodland sounds of birds and rustling leaves.

I eventually gathered the courage and breath to move out but decided that I would return home by a different route. I had covered about a mile when I came upon a flat clearing bordered by a small dirt road. On one edge of the space stood a large igloo-like structure made of variously coloured animal skins. A brown and white piebald pony was tethered to a stake and grazed quietly on the grass verge. A group of four kids two boys the eldest about my age and two girls the younger about four or five years old approached me fists clenched.

'Hello,' I said feebly.

'Push off,' said the eldest boy.

'Is that your tent?' was my feeble response.

'It's not a tent it's a bender and you can push off.'

At that moment a tall woman emerged from the bender. Seeing me she approached and enquired of the kids, 'What's going on?' Then without waiting for an answer she came towards me. I shrank back in doubt. 'Oh dear, what's happened to you, love?' she asked and reached out.

For the first time I realised that there were scratches on my face and that I had torn my clothing and scratched my arms and legs in my panic stricken flight from the machete man. The woman led me inside the bender followed by the kids. It was carpeted with multicoloured rugs and I could now see the framework of curved branches that gave it shape. At the centre a small iron stove with its pipe leading up through a hole in the framework held a steaming cooking pot.

Sitting me on a stool she fetched a bowl and pouring water from a large iron kettle she cleaned my wounds. She then brought a jug of home made lemonade and poured me a mugful this was the signal for the kids to clamour for their share. 'Go on then,' she said with a smile and handed the jug to the eldest. I noticed for the first time that her face, although young, was deeply creased and tanned to a rich brown. I drank the lemonade greedily almost choking on the lemon pips and handed the mug back. She smiled, 'So what have you been up to?'

I told her what I had been up to and she said that I was a good boy and had done a good thing. Then she instructed Abraham the eldest to look after me until food was ready, I was happy with that because whatever she was cooking smelled really appetising. Once outside I told Abraham my name and found out the names of Noah, Rachel and Rebecca, I discovered that they were Romany and the fact that all the names I encountered were Old Testament or Hebrew later led me to attach credence to the theory that the Romany are the lost tribe of Israel.

The Johnson family were kind to me on that first day and on every occasion when I visited their summer home (they lived in a remote woodland cottage in the winter). I visited them many times and learned much in the way of Romany lore including their language – sad to tell something that I have completely lost.

I learned how to make a whistle by tapping the bark of a hazel stick until it loosened and could be slipped off like a sleeve whereupon the stick could be cut and notched before slipping the bark back, so forming the whistle; this only works in springtime when the sap is rising. I learned how to place a small peeled stick in a cooking pot to prevent the food tasting of smoke. I learned how to make a glass vase or drinking vessel by running a string soaked in paraffin around the middle of an empty wine bottle lighting it and when it is almost burned out plunging the bottle into cold water so that it cracked neatly around the string mark.

Above all I learned to respect the Johnson family who were amongst the cleanest, kindest, most decent people that I would ever meet. Unfortunately, Didicois or false Romany have given their race an undeservedly bad name but I can recognise a true Romany at first sight and have never turned one from my door. One day in late summer I found the clearing empty, a circular patch of dead grass marking the site of the bender. I felt lost and wandered home despondently. Although I visited the site in hope the following spring it remained abandoned and never in my childhood did I see my Romany friends again.

It was about the time of my woodland escapade that my mother, in a fit of conscience, placed me in the local school. This was no hardship as it was only a short walk across the nearby playing field and along a high walled lane. I made new friends and enjoyed learning new facts. The drawback was the enmity of the Griffiths's gang each of whom consistently mitched from school and all of whom now had a grudge against me. To avoid them I would walk the two mile journey home by lane and road. Entering the camp by way of the undergrowth I would crawl around the perimeter until I was able to make a run for the safety of our hut.

They made my life a misery pelting me with stones or lumps of asbestos sheet whenever the opportunity presented itself. They surrounded our hut, broke windows and screamed obscenities until Larry fearing for his hens chased them off. Emptying night soil or collecting water became a journey of fear and I would run both ways often spilling half of my burden en-route.

A consolation during school hours followed my chance discovery of a talent for drawing. It was during a free period in art class; the teacher who boasted the name R.T.Davies and was of course called Arty by the kids, had told us to draw anything we wished and disappeared in the direction of the staff room. Pencils rasped on paper producing a spate of spitfire pictures from the boys and box shaped houses from the girls. My classmate a respectable non-camp kid named Jeff asked me to draw him and never at that time lacking faith in my own powers I spent the period producing a head and shoulders in profile sketch. The result surprised even me because it was a truly lifelike likeness.

I suddenly found myself the centre of attraction with classmates gathering around asking me to draw their picture or praising the picture of Jeff and I relished this newfound celebrity. When Arty returned Jeff showed him the drawing and I waited in false modesty for his praise; he took one look at it handed it back to my classmate and with a look of total disinterest said, 'You might have found a more original subject.'

Like a spitfire? He failed to crush me because I had found a new love in life and with my unfailing tendency to throw myself body and soul into whatever took my fancy I began my love affair with fine art. I haunted libraries devouring every book on art to be found and drew on any and every subject on any and every surface available. Over the next few years I created a body of drawing in pencil, charcoal, ink and wash that filled a large box that once held packets of breakfast cereal.

I read everything that I could find on the methods and materials of the masters even though oil paints were outside the range of my pocket. I drooled over the drawings of Dürer, Michelangelo and Da Vinci and bored anyone would listen with my opinions on the art of the world. In short, I became an affected little bore.

The bulk of my art studies was, however, in the future, the gang was very much a problem of the there and then. My suffering reached a climax after several weeks of torment; I left school one day and was making my way down the lane daydreaming as usual when, rounding a corner, I saw a blur of movement caught a brief sight of Mad Tony and felt as if I had been struck by lightning. It was like the electric wire shock all over again but this time I lost consciousness, when I came to my head was throbbing and I felt blood on my face and I had a bloody lump the size of a pigeon's egg on one temple. I sat up and saw a building brick lying beside me; Mad Tony had smacked me over the head with it and no doubt run off screaming with laughter.

I sat in the dirt for some time feeling very sorry for myself and then, fearing the return of the psychopathic brat, I made my way home by the shortest route. There was one good outcome of this episode, the gang hearing of it and no doubt fearing that they had gone too far by setting Tony on me declared a truce. I was one of them again and glad to be so. The negative side was the end of my school attendance; I was not going to stop another brick with my head and gave up school for the gang. Tony eventually injured a town kid in one of his rages and was committed to a hospital for the insane. I felt sorry for his parents but personally a lot safer.

As our second summer of camp life began there were noticeable changes parts of the camp began to resemble a wide expanse of concrete wasteland as hut after hut was demolished following the re-housing of the inhabitants. The Griffiths family were given a council house where they promptly wired into the nearest street lamp for free electricity and converted the bathroom into a smokehouse for stolen herring. I took over as gang leader but I lacked Dai Griffiths's inventive talent for thuggery and mischief and the fun went out of gang life.

We kids were saved from total apathy by an event of national importance - the coronation of Queen Elizabeth the Second. Everyone loved the young princess and her handsome husband and every street and community began preparations for the great day. I was even persuaded to return to school, this time to the local Secondary Modern School because I was told that every child would receive a coronation souvenir.

The school was four miles away and a bus was necessary, the snags were that I seldom had bus fare and often overslept and missed the bus. This led to my constant lateness and painful consequences. The establishment was run by a progressive headmaster who ran it on the lines of a poor boy's public school, the inner courts being called quad's, teachers wearing cap and gown and plenty of caning; when the prefect on duty had taken your name as being a latecomer three times you were called before the Head, known behind his back to teachers and pupils as "Boss", and you were caned.

I became a regular visitor to Boss's study and after my third or fourth visit he sat me down and told me in a kindly manner that I was an incorrigible slacker and that he had decided to make an exception to the rules in my case. I immediately thought that he had become tired of caning me and decided to let me off when I was late - such is the sad optimism of youth. He leaned forward across his desk and said without a hint of regret, 'Instead of caning you on every third breach of the rules I will cane you on each and every occasion.'

He waited for a reaction from me and seeing that I was not going to give him one he concluded the meeting by lashing me three times on each hand with his long bamboo cane and calling for the next miscreant. When you had a caning from Boss the cane always caught the first joint of the fingers and as he brought it down with all his force the joint quickly became bruised and swollen making it impossible for the victim to hold a pen.

In addition to the punishment doled out by our Headmaster both I and my classmates were victim to a number of sadistic teachers. Although they were probably in the minority these men and their cruelty played a major role in our school day, on one occasion a woodwork teacher threw a mallet at the head of my pal Jeff and knocked him unconscious, I can still hear the hollow thud as the heavy object made contact with his head. Jeff went down as if pole axed, in panic the man claimed that the tool had slipped from his hand and no more was said. A number of like minded bullies, however, continued generously dispensing beatings that left bruising or red weals on hands and legs.

One consolation for the boys was Miss French an attractive brunette in her early twenties she always wore blouses unbuttoned halfway down the front and never wore a bra. When she bent over your desk to correct your work you not only breathed in her heavy perfume but you had a glimpse of pert breasts with dark strawberry nipples – Jeff reckoned that she used rouge to colour her nipples. Our work constantly needed correcting when she taught us and from the frequency of her displays I am convinced that she was aware of and took pleasure from our interest.

I endured the beatings and enjoyed the company of Miss French for several weeks probably absorbing a little knowledge and earning the gift of a Coronation Souvenir automatic pencil with the Queen's head and crest on it. Considering the number of canings that I took it must have been the hardest won Coronation gift in Britain - I lost it within weeks.

Having received my gift and become involved in my studies I began to enjoy school; circumstances were soon, however, to mar that enjoyment. My one and only pair of school shoes had holes the size of small saucers in the soles; my mother's solution was to insert folded pages from my comic papers, this worked fine until one bright schoolmate spotted the solution and christened me 'comic soles'.

After enduring several days of being followed about by kids chanting my new title, I had taken sufficient ridicule and I terminated my venture into scholastic circles; I remained at home looking forward to the Coronation. It would be difficult for a present day youngster to understand the patriotic fervour generated by this great event but this was before the days of open house for royalty and our queen to be was a beautiful and transcendent creature loved by all with Prince Philip the envy of men the world over.

A vacant hut had been secured and with the interior dividing walls removed this was to be the base for our camp party. People had been preparing for weeks accumulating flags, home made paper bunting and balloons. In the last few days before the party delicious smells drifted from every hut as women tried to outshine each other in the party catering stakes. The big day arrived and it was a big day for us because we had been told and believed that it heralded a new golden age, an age of prosperity and security.

The hut had been decorated throughout with flags, bunting and bright red white and blue balloons. Uncle Larry had loaned his piano, a motley assortment of tables and chairs had been commandeered from people's huts and scarcely an inch of the coronation tablecloths was visible beneath the heaps of food and bottles of drink. A keg of beer for the men stood on a low rack surrounded by small boys hoping to sneak or beg a glass.

Central to the proceedings was the Griffiths's large radio and we listened in respectful silence to the events of the day; a silence broken only by occasional cheers and shouts of "God save The Queen" or murmurs of wonder. None of us owned a television set, such things were for the lucky few. We had seen television through the windows of one or two houses, the owners of which would leave their curtains open and place the set where it could be seen in all its blue flickering glory, but on Coronation Day the select few drew their curtains closed and huddled around the tiny screen congratulating themselves on being among the chosen. We, the less fortunate, would have to wait to see the ceremony on the cinema newsreels.

The great day happened to coincide with my birthday and for the first and last time in my young life I had a birthday party. When everyone sang "Happy Birthday To You" I felt my face burning red but I was still delighted by the attention. After the radio broadcast of the Coronation ceremony had ended I began looking for the dishes of jelly and blancmange - my favourites and a rarely seen treat - but hope faded instantly when I saw the three large white enamel bowls filled with those treats, they had been donated by Ma Griffiths. I had seen those bowls before and recognised them as the family's night time relief vessels. A picture of Madge Williams making her custard slices flashed before my eyes and in my disappointment I decided that I hated Ma Griffiths.

As the party proper got underway my mother began playing the piano and was soon the centre of a sing-a-long, a pile of sheet music lay on a chair beside her and people were rummaging through it looking for favourite melodies. She paused for breath and a young man held a sheet of music out to her. I recognised him as Paul who lodged with a camp family and was known as a bit of a lad and a lady's man. He had once been married to a French woman and claimed a fluency in her language that no one in our circles could test or dispute.

My mother began to play and Paul began to sing in throaty nasal French, the song was "la Mer" and he delivered it with exaggerated gestures and rolling eyes. His mistake was to deliver it in the direction of Alfred Khan's wife, a generously proportioned woman who blushed with pleasure at the attention. Alfred was not pleased and he showed his displeasure by grabbing Paul by the shirt front and head butting him in the face. There was a silence as Paul staggered back against my poor mother spraying her with blood from his shattered nose.

Someone shouted 'Take them outside' and the two men were grabbed and bundled out of the door where they began to fight surrounded by a crowd of cheering partygoers young and old, all thoughts of Queen and coronation departed from their heads. I had never seen two men fight my only experience being film fights where heroes like John Wayne stood toe-to-toe with the villain and manfully exchanged punches. This was nothing like that as the protagonists hugged each other, kicked, slapped scratched and bit each other and spent a great deal of time rolling around in the dirt grunting and panting.

At the end of a few minutes, both parties bloody and bruised, they were pulled apart and told to shake hands. They did so like two guilty schoolboys and everyone returned to the party. The thing that most impressed me was the blood and bruising, something that never occurred in a John Wayne film. After all the excitement the rest of the day seemed dull but it passed into history and into my memory ending with lots of drunken 'Goodnights' and Alfred and Paul leaving arm in arm swearing eternal friendship.

Chapter Sixteen

Shortly after the coronation my mother became ill and was admitted to hospital with pneumonia, this was even more dangerous then than it is today and treatment involved a lengthy convalescence. Because of her epilepsy Marina was not considered capable of looking after my brother and I and it looked as if we would end up in care. The thought scared me, concern for my mother being supplanted by selfish fear, and I thought of running away before the black car arrived.

Uncle Larry and Auntie Jean came to our rescue, agreeing to take Peter and me into their home. Marina was left to maintain the tenancy of the hut as best she could. Our new foster parents had recently moved into a house overlooking the docks. Built on the side of a steep rock face it had two stories at the front elevation but three at the rear, the third being a two roomed basement that supported the overhang of the other two.

We shared the house with their lodger a strange doctor named Dr. Hoe (pronounced 'Who') and because of his name I would think of him later when the "Dr. Who" programme became popular. He was a small man with a shiny bald head and wire framed glasses but he had a long fringe of white hair from just above his ears to his collar as if compensating for the bare ground above. Maxine and I would creep into his room when he was out and examine his instruments playing at doctors and nurses. He was attempting to establish a practise in the town and later succeeded.

So began a major formative period in my life, I had grown to admire Uncle Larry during our months as his neighbours but my admiration for that amazing man - the only father figure in my young life - grew as I watched him perform tasks that would have tested any two legged man.

It was during this period that I developed a serious crush on my elder foster sister, Maxine. She was growing into a beautiful young woman with her flaming auburn hair, china blue eyes, long legs and a figure burgeoning into womanhood. I followed her around like a devoted puppy responding to her every command as if it was holy writ and she took a full advantage of my servility. If Uncle Larry or Auntie Jean noticed my devotion to their daughter they were probably amused by it because they never commented.

Although the house was tall there were only three bedrooms and Dr. Hoe occupied one. Peter and I slept in one of the basement rooms and although it had plain brick walls and stone slab floors it was no hardship after some of our sleeping places.

My education in the Uncle Larry School of The Practical began on my first afternoon shortly after moving to their new home; he had bought a small smokehouse on the docks and he took me to work with him. The smokehouse, built solely of creosoted wood, looked like a Wild West frontier church and its tall chimney tower looked as if it would fall down in a puff of wind but an interior view showed how solidly it was built. There was not much for me to do as he already had a batch of fish curing in the chimney but I did learn how to recharge the fires of which there were several still giving off a pungent oak flavoured smoke.

I watched as he prepared his latest batch of bloaters, as I recall he had already gutted and slightly smoked the fresh herring but had not split them as one does for a kipper. He talked me through the process as he lined the bottom of the first wooden barrel with salt he then placed a layer of fish on the salt followed by another layer of salt and so on until the barrel was filled to the brim. Several barrels were filled in this way and after watching him for a while I was allowed to help. My eyes were watering from the smoke and I discovered that rubbing one's eyes whilst handling salt was not a good idea. After he had bathed my eyes Uncle Larry told me to shut up because crying would make it worse and that it was a good way to learn a lesson. In time I would learn that his favourite adage was "no pain, no gain."

Supper that evening was a pair of fresh kippers with doorstep thick slices of bread (baked by Uncle Larry) heavily spread with butter. Both Peter and I picked nervously at the fish attempting to remove the fine bones until Uncle Larry grabbed my fork stabbed a chunk of kipper and shoved it into my mouth telling me to chew and swallow. The delicious kippers were to form a large part of our diet and Peter and I soon became adept at swallowing them in great lumps. We did, however, draw the line at kipper heads although our guardian uncle did not do so claiming them to be the best part and crunching them eyes and all with relish. Looking back I think that he enjoyed shocking us more than he enjoyed the food, such was his extremely dry sense of humour.

Over the next few weeks I learned the elements of the smoked fish business, how to lay a fire of oak shavings, how to dip the herring in the deep red dye that gave the kipper its distinctive colour, how to climb the rungs of the chimney carrying a long rod with fish hooked onto the small hooks that were called tenterhooks (from which I gather the expression 'on tenterhooks' derives) and hang each rod across from rung to rung until the chimney was filled. The end product was boxed in lightweight wooden boxes and sent off by train. I do not think that Uncle Larry made a great deal of money from the venture but he enjoyed each fresh challenge before boredom quickly set in and he moved on to a new money making scheme.

He was a true renaissance man the possessor of many talents and when the lengthy stone garden wall needed painting he declined to buy manufactured wall paint. I found him one day digging a deep pit in the garden and listened as he explained that we were going to turn the lumps of limestone that stood alongside the pit into whitewash. I could not see how stone could become paint but kept my thoughts to myself and watched as he threw a thick layer of wood into the pit and then touched a flame to it. As it began to crackle and spark he began swiftly to pile on more wood and then to carefully lay lumps of limestone on top of the flames, he then threw on more wood and stepped back to watch his construction that was now smoking steadily.

We left the pit to burn and went off on some other errand; when we returned some hours later he began to dig removing ash with care until he revealed the stone now turned into lumps of flaky white chalk, these he removed and stored in a heap. He repeated this process several times over the following days until he had a substantial pile of burned stone and then he called me to his side. 'Now comes the magic part,' he said.

A bucket of water stood alongside and cautioning me to stand back he picked out a piece of burned stone with a gloved hand and dropped it into the water that immediately began to bubble as if it were boiling. He dropped several more lumps in stirring the mixture with a stick as it thickened and turned white. Finally satisfied he called me forward to look. 'That is white lime, boy,' he said, 'and you must never get it on your skin or near your eyes.'

Over the next few weeks I helped Uncle Larry to coat the old wall with a thick layer of lime wash, watching him make more as was needed and when it was finished it threw the sunlight back in all its blinding splendour. Later when telling Auntie Jean how clever I thought he was I discovered that this remarkable man had engaged in numerous occupations and business ventures even serving as a sea cook on a trawler, something that explained his culinary and baking skills.

I did not see much of my brother Peter who followed Auntie Jean around happily accepting her loving attention and cuddles. She had always wanted a boy and Peter benefited from this with treats small toys and clothing. Uncle Larry was not amused, his attitude towards children was caring but unemotional; providing that we behaved and did as we were told he treated us with kindness but any breach of his rules was dealt with swiftly and firmly.

Another of his ventures was his ferrets. He owned a handsome pair of the polecat variety and lavished care and affection on them as if they were children. Auntie Jean said that they were vicious smelly creatures but I quite liked their musky smell and could soon handle them as if they were kittens. On the first day that Uncle Larry took me rabbiting I was as proud as Mr. Punch particularly when I was given charge of the sack containing the ferret.

We made our way into the countryside with my uncle carrying a large bundle of nets on the carrier of his bicycle and me walking alongside carrying a sack that periodically jumped and wriggled. Onlookers may have been puzzled at the sight of a boy talking to a sack but I felt it my duty to keep the creature within as calm as possible. When we arrived at the overgrown rabbit warren Uncle Larry made his way around the area covering every hole but one with a pegged down net, he explained that the uncovered hole was access for our ferret.

Satisfied that he had covered all escape routes he took me around to one side of the mound and pointed out several nets telling me to grab any rabbit that came out into them. I then watched as he removed our ferret from the sack and buckled a small collar with a bell on his neck or "belled him up" as the saying went. This was necessary in the event of a ferret making a kill underground in which case he would settle down with his meal in what he saw as his new home and need to be dug out; the bell would tell the digger just where in the warren the creature was located.

I watched as he put the ferret down a hole and then ran around to my appointed side. I could hear the distant tinkling of the creature's bell and it sounded as if it were deep in the earth, as it probably was. I did not have to wait long the bell got louder and it sounded as if a herd of stampeding cattle inhabited the warren. Then, without warning, rabbits burst out into the nets kicking and struggling for dear life which not surprising when they were being pursued by one of nature's most vicious killers.

One of the unfortunate rabbits broke out into a net near to me and his size can be gauged by the fact that he tore the pegs out of the ground. I threw myself on him and wrapped my arms around his struggling form surprised by his strength. As we struggled I caught sight of his eyes bulging in terror and a wave of disgust and pity washed over me, disgust at myself for terrifying this innocent animal and pity for his plight. Without hesitation I untangled him from the net and released him, his thanks being demonstrated by the deep scratches left on my bare arm as he leaped away.

I watched him disappear from sight the white flag of his tail bouncing up and down and I felt a great sense of relief. My relief was short lived because Uncle Larry came around the warren just in time to see a couple more rabbits break free of the nets. I cannot recall the oath that he swore because I had suddenly become almost as scared as the escapees but I can remember the whack across my ear that sent me flying into the undergrowth.

I sat and watched in silence as he killed the last of the rabbits, before slitting them open and shaking their blue and grey stomach bags out onto the grass; this was called 'paunching' and had to be done promptly to prevent the meat spoiling. The journey home was also made in silence with Uncle Larry pushing his bicycle and me looking with sad heart at the double brace of rabbits hung from his handlebars noting that every now and then a drop of blood would splatter from a tiny nostril as a head struck against the bar of the bike. I was never taken ferreting again.

Life was not all work, Maxine and I were both avid filmgoers and shared a love of Hollywood musicals our favourite being "The Desert Song". Evicting the chickens from their shed we would sweep it out and stage our own musical shows. We lacked such refinements as musical accompaniment, lighting or scenery but we made up for that with supreme confidence in our talent and energy.

Our audiences, who sat perched on empty kipper boxes, came from the press ganging of local kids and we could always depend on an audience of at least one - Jeanette. The remainder, usually numbering two or three (a full house by our standards), were asked to pay three pennies admittance but as their average

age was five years they usually lacked the price of a ticket and we accepted shells, pebbles, marbles or anything that was offered.

A personal disappointment for me was the fact that Maxine insisted on playing both the Red Shadow and the heroine leaving me to fill in as chorus but such was my devotion to her that I accepted it meekly. My big moment came when she announced, 'The One and Only Al Jolson!' Taking up a position centre stage and going down on one knee I launched into - or more accurately attacked - the song "Mammee" followed by my entire repertoire of Jolson songs learned from my mother.

I can still picture the blank faces of our audience, who had never heard of Jolson or The Red Shadow and sat in stupefied silence until Jeanette prompted them to applaud by taking hold of their wrists and banging their hands together – occasionally one of them would be overcome with fear and wet themselves but we carried on regardless. That tiny group of snotty nosed kids taught me an important lesson namely: do not depend on audience response or let the lack of it throw you but give your best performance regardless of the house.

With the approach of autumn and Guy Fawkes Night we needed money for fireworks, I do not know it was Maxine's idea or mine (probably Maxine's because where she led I followed) but we had what we thought a brilliant idea; we would busk around the pubs to raise fireworks money. Uncle Larry was not one to crush youthful ambition and supported us by providing make-up, a tube of tennis shoe whitener and a tin of black shoe polish. Having seen the films "The Jolson Story" and "Jolson Sings Again" several times I felt qualified to perform as my hero, Al Jolson.

The night of the first performance arrived and Maxine covered my face with a thick layer of shoe polish outlining my lips broadly with shoe whitener. An old waistcoat of Uncle Larry's and a home made bow tie completed the transformation. The whole thing would be totally politically incorrect today and understandably so but we were innocent and this was the early nineteen-fifties just a few years before the television show "The Black and White Minstrels" became popular viewing and brought the minstrel show into millions of homes.

We arrived at our first pub "The Bridge Inn" and with no prior agreement or warning to the landlord Maxine swept into the public bar and in her loudest voice (she had good projection) announced, 'Ladies and gentlemen please welcome the one and only Al Jolson.'

This announcement was (not surprisingly) followed by complete silence and the landlord was probably on his way around the bar to evict this loud child when I entered, or fell in through the door propelled by a hefty shove from Maxine, and went down on knee throwing my arms open as I had seen Jolson do. One or two men began to applaud, soon all were clapping and laughing and I experienced for the first time the thrill of an audience. I have since been privileged to perform before large audiences but nothing could equal that first night in a small public bar.

Without further introduction or accompaniment I launched into my stock of Jolson melodies delivering each number with appropriately stagey actions, I wept for my 'Mamee' I longed for "Swanee" and I grieved for "Sonny Boy" with all the fervour my young soul could summon and despite my ham performance - probably because most people still loved Jolson - I was a ham but I was a hit. At the end of our show Maxine moved among the tables with Uncle Larry's old trilby hat and everyone gave something; one table at which a card school was in progress tipping the kitty an ashtray filled with coins into the hat and we left to more applause.

We could hardly wait to get home and count our takings. Tipping the money out on the large pine table we counted and stacked like junior Scrooges all the while telling the family how great we had been and how loudly everyone had clapped. Over the following few nights we visited several more pubs with similar success excepting the one where the landlord shouted a loud "Out!" before Maxine could even open her mouth. Our run of success was, however, cut short when, after a few evenings, my face turned a bright scarlet and I began to break out in sores from the make-up; Uncle Larry quickly called a halt to the proceedings.

Although we had collected sufficient cash for a small public display I was not to see the fireworks because my mother was discharged from hospital and Peter and I returned to our hut leaving our foster family and the firework money behind us.

Chapter Seventeen

When we returned to The Camp I was surprised to find that little of it remained standing, what had once been a community of a couple of hundred people was now a scattered dozen huts. The verandas had been torn down and the vacated huts demolished only the concrete pathways traced the shape of the past, from early morning until dusk our ears were assaulted by the sound of pneumatic drills as council workmen tore into the concrete foundations and pathways. Our suffering was short-lived, however, because within a week or two my mother was told that we had been given tenancy of a council house and because she was still convalescing I was delegated to collect the key and inspect the house.

I collected the key from the council offices and received directions to our new home. I was disappointed to discover that it was not one of the nice new houses on a clean new estate but a small and tired looking terraced house in a row of ten. The town council was at that time experimenting by installing former slum dwellers or people such as us from places like the camp to streets of "respectable people" in the hope of civilising us. I was, however, unaware of our experimental status and buzzing with excitement as I opened the front door and stepped into the narrow hallway.

The house had three bedrooms, one of them being a small low roofed room built on top of the kitchen and bathroom extension that had been added to the house and accessed down three steep steps. The bedroom that I took a fancy to had a large sash window looking out on the back yard and after the tiny hut windows it was impressive.

As I stood looking out of the window and daydreaming I slowly became aware of a curious sensation on my bare legs (boys wore short trousers until mid teens in those days). I looked down and a shudder of horror ran through me; my legs were literally covered with thousands of fleas crawling and hopping on my flesh like a moving brown blanket. When I was recovered I noticed beneath my feet a loose floorboard and lifted it revealing a dark cavity from which fresh clouds of fleas hopped.

I began to shake uncontrollably and I do not know just how long I stood paralysed with shock but eventually I found the presence of mind to scrape and beat the filthy insects from my legs and I ran from the house slamming the front door behind me. Thankfully there was a small beach nearby and I was able to paddle in the sea washing away the last of the fleas - I threw my socks away.

Despite the trauma of the parasite swarm I returned home excited by the prospect of living in our own house and immediately reported to my mother that it had "real windows!" Then I told her about the fleas. She immediately sent me back to the council offices to report the problem and complain, another five mile walk but I did as I was told and they said that we would have to remain where we were until the house had been fumigated.

Two weeks later we were among the last families to leave Picton Place. Bull Griffiths who worked for a coal merchant borrowed the coal lorry to move our few possessions and as he loaded the lorry the council workmen moved in to demolish our hut. My mother, Marina and Peter were to travel by bus but I was to ride with Bull. I sat in the vehicle's cabin and heard the crash of sledge hammers as they began smashing through the dividing walls. My sadness must have shown on my face because Bull punched me in the shoulder and whispered, 'F*** them.' then he laughed and drove away. When we arrived at the new house we were greeted by the acrid smell of fumigation spray and found that the workers had left all the windows and doors sealed with thick tape.

The council had bought three houses in our new street for their camp tenants: the numbers four, seven and ten and, understandably, the remaining house owners regarded us as a threat that would devalue their properties and turn the neighbourhood into a slum. This fact was demonstrated to me on our first day, naturally, curious about our new territory I walked down the long narrow garden a rough grass patch littered with sawn timber and small mounds of hard set plaster left over from the council's bathroom construction and out into the narrow lane.

The rear garden wall was made of large pieces of limestone held together by the familiar Edwardian mortar of lime and ash but the mortar had deteriorated badly and large sections of wall leaned outward in a dangerous way. I pushed with my hand against one of the leaning sections and felt it give. Thinking that this could fall on Peter and injure him I decided to remove the loose blocks. I took hold of the first and was finding it quite heavy as I carried it into the garden when I heard a loud voice shouting, 'Get out of it, you little scum bag!'

Dropping the block I turned and saw a tall woman standing in a gateway on the opposite side of the lane. 'We have got enough slums in this town without you turning this into another one.' she said. I began to explain that I was trying to make the wall safe but she would not listen. 'Get away, you little pig, before I fetch my hand to you.' she cried lifting her hand as if to hit me.

Having been taught not to answer back to my elders I turned and went into the house to tell my mother about the incident and ask her to explain to our new neighbour why I had been removing the stone but when we went back outside the woman had vanished. As we stood at the gate a young boy rushed out of a house just down the lane and ran towards us screaming for help. Running up to my mother he clutched her apron crying, 'Please don't let her get me. Please. She'll kill me if she gets me

The boy was slightly built, a year or two younger than me and wearing round steel framed spectacles with special lenses to correct a pronounced turn in one eye. He was obviously terrified of someone and as he clung to my mother the someone in question emerged from the same house wielding a long handled broom like a battle-axe. She shuffled up the lane in well-worn carpet slippers that slowed her progress; one reason that the boy had outrun her.

I was about to meet one of the most memorable characters of my childhood, Maggie Beynon, and she warrants a brief description. Not much bigger than the boy, who turned out to be her son, her dark skin was tightly stretched across the pointed features of a face topped by a thick mop of frizzy black hair, her eyebrows had been completely shaved off and replaced with two hoops drawn in black pencil giving her a permanently quizzical expression. Her whole appearance spoke of African or Caribbean origins but, as racial prejudice in terms of status existed even then, no one in my experience was brave enough or stupid enough to suggest or question that. Constant screaming and chain smoking had irreparably damaged her vocal chords and she spoke with a harsh cracked voice.

The boy, whose name we later discovered was Michael, hid behind my mother as she and Maggie stood face to face; Maggie glaring wildly. Then she moved to one side and my mother moved with her; back and forth they performed this strange ballet for several minutes before Maggie paused, saying, 'No one stops me from hitting my own kid.'

'Oh no, well I will,' said my mother, 'You could kill him with that brush.'

They resumed staring at each other but after a few moments Maggie snarled in the direction of the boy, 'I'll get you later, Pinocchio,' and turning on her heel shuffled back to her house muttering all the while.

My mother took the boy indoors where he told us his name – not Pinocchio but Michael - and asked if he could stay with us for a while, 'She'll calm down in a bit,' he said, 'after she has had a fag and a cup of tea,' Ever the mother hen she sat Michael down and fed him. As he ate he told us that they had also come from an ex-army camp and had been in their council house for a couple of months and that there was just him and his mother because his father was 'deep sea'; that was the local term for in the merchant navy as opposed to being a trawlerman.

It was not long before there was a knocking on the scullery door, it was Maggie and she had come to apologise. My mother made the mistake of inviting her in and she immediately ensconced herself in our only armchair kicking off her slippers and tucking her legs underneath her – there she stayed for the next ten years, or so it seemed.

She had a distinctive mode of speech, almost every third word was an expletive and if I had thought Ma Griffiths's range of swear words was large I was soon to rethink. She also had a built in antenna that told her when my mother was serving food and would bounce through the door remarking, 'Something smells good.' Invariably she was invited to share it.

Under Maggie's influence my mother began smoking; something that I had never seen her do, although she never inhaled the smoke simply puffing away happily. This was quite handy for Maggie because from the time that my mother began the habit she never brought her cigarettes with her and she would empty my mother's packet in an afternoon.

The best thing about knowing Maggie was the friendship that was formed between Michael and me; within a short space of time we inseparable and roamed the woodlands and the shoreline chattering away about life like a pair of juvenile philosophers. When the weather permitted we would walk the town until the early hours of the morning discussing every topic under the sun and talking of the great things that we would achieve when we reached manhood. Nobody bothered us during our night time perambulations, today we would probably be arrested.

Our new house was heated by an open fireplace in each of the two living rooms and in each main bedroom; unfortunately we could not afford fuel but Michael told me of the nearby fishmeal factory where he obtained free coke cinders and took me down to meet the manager who turned out to be the husband of the woman who had berated me on my first day in our house; thankfully he was more tolerant of and sympathetic to scruffy urchins and told me that I could take all the cinders I wanted providing I collected them when the factory was open.

Boy

The man then introduced me to his guard dog, Pluto, a large shaggy cross between a collie and a German shepherd. Pluto and I became friends and he would greet me at the factory gates with a wagging tail, tongue lolling from between sharp brown teeth.

Our first Christmas Eve in the house arrived and my mother was in the doldrums. We had nothing for Christmas dinner except a few bits of food left over from the week. I tried to cheer her up, 'Well at least we'll have a good fire. I'll go down to the fishmeal twice today.'

Leaving her sitting in gloomy silence – naturally Maggie was nowhere to be seen when food was scarce – I plodded the half mile to the factory carrying a large hessian sack. Pluto gave me his usual greeting and I climbed the pile of cinders looking for the best ones as he sat watching. Without warning I lost my footing and with a cry slid rapidly back down the heap on my face. I do not know if my cry startled him or my sudden descent kicking cinders in his face frightened him but Pluto dived on to my bare leg and with a half snarl half bark sank his teeth into my calf muscle.

The pain was fierce; even more so as he hung on and began to shake my leg as if trying to tear a chunk out. Unable to move I screamed for help and I heard voices approaching as the manager and several workers responded almost instantly to what must have been an unearthly yell from me.

Pluto was dragged away to his kennel and I was carried into the office where a first aid man poured iodine in to my wounds and bandaged them tightly; despite this treatment and my desire to be brave the blood was soon seeping through the thick bandage and the pain brought tears to my eyes. My one concern was for Pluto, 'Please don't blame Pluto. It was my fault.' I cried, terrified that the poor old dog would be shot.

They assured me that the dog would not be harmed and half carried me to the manager's car where a man was loading my now filled sack into the boot. When we reached our front door the manager leaned over and pressed four half-crown pieces into my hand, 'That is for being a brave boy.' he said.

My mother turned pale at the sight of my bloodstained leg and remained speechless whilst my adventure was explained to her, 'He has always been the most docile of dogs.' He said,' I just don't know what got into him.'

'It was my fault Mum. I frightened him.'

She sat there shaking her head and sighing while the manager fetched my coke from the boot. Whilst he was gone I opened my hands and showed her the money, 'Look, Mum,' I said, 'we can buy food.' In those days four half-crowns or ten shillings could buy a substantial quantity of provisions and I was really proud to be the earner of such a sum.

The manager finally left, apologising again and promising that he would have a couple of sacks of coke cinders delivered each day until my leg was healed and my mother had her outdoor coat on before his car had pulled away. Accompanied by Marina she rushed out to catch the shops before they closed and they returned bent over with the weight of several large bags. With the ten shillings she had managed to buy: a rabbit, vegetables, fruit and other essential food items also - as I discovered on Christmas morning - a comic annual for me and a toy car for Peter. For the second time in my young life Christmas had been saved from disaster at the last minute.

When I was fit enough I resumed my coke collecting and my friendship with Pluto. Whatever had caused him to attack me will remain a mystery and rather than making me scared of him it made the old dog even more special because I felt that I had protected him from the possible consequences of his one misdeed.

Another source of free fuel was the dense woodland at the end of a nearby tidal inlet. Taking a rope and my well sharpened billhook I would walk the two miles inland along a cliff path and once in the woods look for fallen trees about three inches in thickness; by then I had acquired some untaught instinct for conservation that deterred me from cutting down living timber. By tying several long trunks together I could drag them home and chop them into suitable lengths of log. A journey to the woods netted about twenty to thirty short logs and supplemented the coke cinders.

A strange incident occurred whilst I foraged the woodland one bright sunny day in late autumn. Following my routine I would reconnoitre the area, dragging out useable dead trees on my outward trip before collecting my day's load on my return. On this particular day I wandered further than usual, perhaps because I was enjoying the walk; the sky was clear blue and a gentle breeze helped the trees to shed their remaining leaves the sound of its passing being accompanied by happy bird song and the occasional rustle of small animals in the undergrowth.

Daydreaming I pushed my way through an obstruction of bracken and found myself in a grassy clearing; almost perfectly round and about fifteen feet in diameter it was carpeted by short bright green grass that might have been cultivated were it not in the middle of woodland. I paused in the middle of this grassy patch and as I looked around me I became aware of the silence; it was as if nature had paused and the silence was accompanied by a stillness that was just as complete.

I listened; the birds had stopped singing, the trees had ceased their rustling, not surprisingly perhaps because the breeze had stilled. I suddenly felt that I was alone in the woodland world, sole inhabitant of the wilderness and a deep peace such as that occasioned by a mild anaesthetic overcame me. Resisting the strong urge to sit down I stood for what must have been some minutes contentedly breathing in the scent of my surroundings, then for no reason I became scared. Stories of fairy folk and abductions of young people by them rushed into my mind and a cold chill crept up my back.

I finally managed to drag my leaden feet away from the clearing and once back upon the path the woodland sounds began again as abruptly as they had ceased; yet, as relieved as I was to be free of the place, I felt a strong desire to return to that clearing. By the time that I had collected my trees and dragged them home the experience seemed like a dream but I resolved to return to the clearing just to see if the silence was still there; try as I might I never found the spot again and I will never know if I was the victim of a daydream.

Chapter Eighteen

The problem of fuel was easily solved but there were daily crises that could not be answered with a trip to the woods. Maggie began spending more and more time in our house, eating and smoking her way through our all too meagre supplies. When my mother received her benefits allowance on a Monday she would stock up with the best of food and several packs of cigarettes. By Wednesday both food and fags were gone and so was Maggie. This meant that we were on hunger rations or no rations for the latter part of the week.

Peter who, unlike me, attended school regularly and received a free school meal but my mother Marina and I were forced to exist on stale scraps and cups of tea. I quickly learned that even the hardest piece of cheese became edible when toasted under a grill and I invented the fried bread sandwich; a piece of stale bread could be fried in the residual fat left from Monday's bacon and when laid between two slices of dried bread with a little brown sauce it made a filling if not appetizing sandwich.

Several times a week Michael and I would haunt the docks begging herrings as the herring catch was landed or rescuing fish roe from the fish market workers who were about to throw it to the gulls.. How those poor gulls must have hated us as they screamed their resentment at our theft and how odd that the same fish roe is now a highly priced delicacy. Occasionally I visited Maggie's house in the hope of free eats but I was to be disappointed. I would sit and watch her family enjoying a meal without the offer of a crust.

My absence from school gave me the time needed for my scrounging expeditions although it did little for my education. When not scrounging Michael and I had no shortage of kids to play with because our street faced onto large rectangular area of coarse grass banked all around with a set of swings and a seesaw in the middle and kids from the surrounding streets homed in on this unspoiled play world.

In addition to the swings one patch of ground had been trodden bare of grass and formed the marbles pitch whilst one bank had been converted with the aid of borrowed tableware into an alpine roadway complete with hairpin bends and tunnels all to the scale of a Dinky car; the lower end of the rectangle served as cricket pitch in the summer and soccer pitch in the winter.

The rectangle was the perfect unsupervised and unfettered playground for kids. When I revisited the street some years later some local authority genius had levelled the area and laid tarmac to make a large car park occupied by three lonely cars parked well away from each other as if they were not on speaking terms and there was not a single child in sight – they were no doubt all on their home computers. I bemoaned the mentality of local authorities who sanitize our world in the name of progress and as I stood there I could hear the shrieks of laughter from a bygone generation ringing around the area.

One Sunday morning of our first spring on the street named unimaginatively "Brick Houses" Peter complained of tummy ache. By lunchtime he was curled up in agony on our old chaise longue alternating between bouts of screaming and periods of low moaning. Marina was sent up to the nearby phone kiosk to call the doctor and some time later he arrived. Doctor Brissett was a florid faced man well known as an inebriate who displayed a total contempt for the lower orders and was lacking in any bedside manner. His opening remark was, 'I hope that you haven't dragged me out on a Sunday for nothing.' My mother assured him that was not the case and showed him the figure of my small brother.

Puffing with resignation the doctor pulled Peter's shirt up and pressed his abdomen; my brother immediately screamed loudly. Doctor Brissett took Peter's temperature examined the child's tongue and pulled down an eyelid. Finally he sat back let out a long sigh and said, 'This child has had too many sweets, my dear.'

My mother protested but the doctor brushed her protests aside in his usual perfunctory manner saying, 'No food just plain boiled water and a dose of syrup of figs tomorrow will not hurt him.' Marina saw him to the door and when she returned we just stood and stared at each other, it was Marina who broke the silence, 'The drunken old sot,' she said, 'you could smell it on his breath.'

Peter continued crying as my mother began boiling and cooling water for him to drink. Then, about mid-afternoon, he ceased crying and lay there moaning softly; his face had paled to a greenish yellow and his breathing was shallow. This continued until early evening and when my mother made him drink some water he promptly vomited, a disgusting dirty yellow torrent. He continued to retch without speaking, moaning softly and turning his young eyes to us in mute appeal for help. That was enough for Marina, 'I'm getting that swine back.' She cried and without bothering with an outdoor coat she left the house. 'You don't know where he'll be, Marina.' My mother called after her. 'Oh yes I do.' She shouted back.

The next hour was spent watching my mother alternating between pacing the room and sitting holding Peter who was by now semi conscious; then Marina arrived with Doctor Brissett. She grabbed the doctor's arm and shoved him towards Peter saying, 'There, There. Does that look like too many sweets?'

He sat down beside my brother and prodded the child's stomach. Peter moaned. 'Oh my God,' said Doctor Brissett, 'this child has peritonitis.' He had been drunk when he arrived but had apparently sobered up in an instant and without another word rushed out to phone for an ambulance from the nearby public phone box.

Whilst he was out Marina explained that she had found him, as expected, in his gentleman's club. Forcing her way in against the protests of the doorman she had cornered the drunken doctor in the lounge and told him in words peppered with expletives that her brother was dying and if he failed to save him she would have him struck from the medical register. Thankfully her threats had the desired effect and within twenty or so minutes of the doctor's phone call Peter accompanied by my mother was on his way to the local hospital for emergency surgery; unfortunately that hospital was seven miles distant.

It was the following morning before my mother returned. She told us that Peter had survived a long operation and was sleeping quietly. She also told us that a young nurse had approached following the operation and said, 'Please don't say that I told you or I will lose my job but your little boy died under the anaesthetic and he was clinically dead for a quite a time before they brought him back.'

My mother thanked her saying that she was grateful for her confidence but thank God that he was alive and recovering. We were all relieved and when Peter returned home the incident became another traumatic memory. However, about two months after Peter had returned to school his head teacher called my mother in to express concern about his lack of progress. She explained that my little brother who had been one of the brightest children in his class had become inattentive and spent his time in a vacant daze.

The teacher suggested medical investigation and it was ultimately discovered that Peter's brain was not developing as it should. He was to remain a child mentally for the rest of his life. We knew nothing about the effects of oxygen starvation to the brain and it was some years before we associated Peter's problem with his operation. By then the doctor was dead and nothing could be done to compensate Peter for his tragic state of mind.

After Peter's operation my mother informed us that she was changing our doctor and that our new doctor was called Doctor Hoe; having lived with the strange doctor in Uncle Larry's I did not feel greatly confident at this news and I was later to be proved right but I said nothing.

One blessing in Peter's tragedy was the fact that he never seemed aware of his situation, another came in the shape of a classmate who had been asked by their teacher to take my brother under his wing. Graham, the youngest of a large family took the task so seriously that he ended up practically living with us; arriving first thing in the morning in the school holidays or shortly after school in term times he would stay until last thing at night, something that never appeared to bother his parents – perhaps their family was so large that he was not missed.

Blonde where Peter was dark, bold where Peter was shy Graham was the complete opposite of my brother and a perfect companion for him. They would disappear for hours down to the beach or up in the woods and my mother never feared for Peter's safety when he was with his streetwise playmate. There was a slight problem, Graham's passion for adders, that now almost extinct species and Britain's only poisonous reptile.

Located within my wood foraging woodland was an area known as 'the adder bank'; a fern filled valley that was home to hundreds of these snakes. Graham haunted the area and had been bitten so many times that he had apparently developed some sort of immunity to the bite of Britain's only poisonous snake. His favourite trick was to conceal a young adder in the breast pocket of his summer shirt and coax its head out in front of my mother; the resulting scream would send him into fits of laughter as she chased him from the room.

Like a little father Graham would encourage Peter to help himself, praise or scold him when necessary and generally protect him from harm or the taunts of other children. The friendship lasted for years ending when Peter was admitted to a special school at the age of ten. During those years Graham achieved his goal of establishing an adder farm in the hedgerow behind his house by implanting young snakes into nests in the bank and allowing nature to take its course. So successful was he that eventually, in light of numerous householders' complaints and several bite victims, the local council was forced to launch a pest control attack on the area to eradicate the adder population.

Had Graham been born to a prosperous family I believe he could have become a naturalist of note, this was not to be and I later heard that he had died in his late twenties from kidney failure; was this I wondered a consequence of his excessive intake of adder venom?

It was Graham who told my mother about the stone thrower. The nearby promenade known as The Rath was comprised of a large steeply sloping grassy area served by a series of black asphalt paths. According to Graham his brother had been told of mysterious stones crashing to the paths from the sky.

My mother had always had a belief in and a fascination for strange happenings and decided that we would investigate It was said that this phenomenon occurred in the early evening so that evening she led Peter, Graham and myself down to the nearest of the paths; this ran steeply down from the roadway and was bordered on one side by a dense hedge that prevented a person falling down a steep rock face and on the other by the wide expanses of lawn – that were, with the exception of one or two distant couples, devoid of people on that evening.

We were chattering away as we began descending the path and thinking that Graham was making the story up I did not expect to witness anything unusual. We had gone about twenty yards down the path when, with no warning of any sort, a stone hit the path about ten feet in front of us; hit the path is really an understatement it would be more accurate to say exploded onto the path because when we plucked up courage to examine the spot there was large starburst imprinted on the asphalt where what looked like red sandstone had shattered with some force.

There was no possibility of someone hiding in the hedge because it was, as I said, impenetrable and on the other side was a sheer drop of about twenty feet. The only other people in sight were some distance away and from the impression it left the stone must have plummeted straight down from a clear sky. Once these facts sank in I became extremely nervous and told my mother that we should return home; my mother, however, was excited and said that with any luck there would be more stones. This thought failed to comfort me as I imagined the effect such an impact would have on a human skull. A few yards further on another stone exploded on the path and that was enough for me but my mother encouraged by an excited Graham carried on walking.

Finally I persuaded her to turn back and endured taunts of 'big baby' and 'cowardly custard' all the way home. I decided that it would be along time before I ventured down that path again but during the weeks that followed I heard several more stories of "The Stone Thrower" and finally went back to discover several impact marks along the paths, all similar to the ones that we had witnessed. Sandstone meteorites? Bird dropped missiles? I still do not know the cause of the falling stones but what perplexes me is the force with which they hit the path as if fired from a gun.

Many young people go through a phase where they are fascinated by the paranormal and I was no exception. The mentalist Chan Canasta with his mind over matter demonstrations was popular at the time; this 1950's precursor of Uri Geller would move objects simply by concentrating upon them. Naturally I obtained a book on the subject and decided to conduct my own experiment; standing a silver coin upright in a closed matchbox I balanced a match carefully on the edge of the coin, I then placed a glass over the prepared items and sitting about three feet from the lot I began to imagine the red head of the match moving.

I sat there concentrating and after about ten minutes the only result was a headache; then the match began to tremble and after a few seconds of this it turned half a circle before falling off. I was elated and called for my mother who laughed and said that I had probably shaken the table; I knew that I had not but could not convince her and so severe was my subsequent headache that I never repeated the experiment.

I returned to school that spring and found myself in a new class, one ruled by a tyrant named Edgar Beavis. On my first morning I was, as usual, late and after receiving my caning from Boss I found the classroom and knocked on the door. Upon entering I found myself the subject of the stares of about thirty boys and girls and one bald headed elderly man who stared at me over his spectacles that were perched on the end of a red bulbous nose. 'Well?' he snapped.

I introduced myself and said that I had been told that I was in his class. He asked my name and repeating it in a thick Germanic accent stood, clicked his heels, raised a hand in the Nazi salute and shouted, 'Seig Heil, Mein Herr!' The entire class burst into shrieks of laughter at this less than subtle piece of humour and I felt an instant hatred for that nasty old man. When he had sufficiently milked the applause of his audience he directed me to my desk and the lesson continued.

It was not long before I observed a further demonstration of the old sadist's talents; a girl had committed some misdemeanour and become the object of his anger. He poured a stream of invective at the poor child as he dragged her to his desk and bent her over face down onto a clear area of its surface. As she laid there her face turned toward her classmates he threw her skirt up over her back revealing her buttocks almost bare in her small navy blue knickers. He opened a drawer in his desk and took out a large white plimsoll; as he did so the girl, who had seen the lascivious looks on the faces of many of her male classmates, turned her head away. Beavis then began beating her with the shoe bringing it down with all his might until the cheeks of her bottom turned red.

Although I was fascinated by the sight of so much naked female flesh, that which Maggie called 'my soft streak' made me feel a deep pity for the man's victim and an even deeper loathing for him. To the girl's credit she did not cry out only grunting in pain at each stroke but as she walked slowly back to her seat I could see that her face was wet with tears and red with embarrassment. During the time that I was in that class I witnessed many instances of his cruelty to both boys and girls and when people advocate corporal punishment I wish that they could have witnessed it in action.

The glorious month of May arrived and was not only welcomed for the dependable sunshine and flowers but also because it heralded the start of the Pembrokeshire potato picking season. The potato farmers had "Gangers" in the surrounding towns, men and women who could be trusted to recruit gangs of reliable pickers. The position was highly sought after and often handed down from father to son or mother to daughter. The gangers, who were paid a bonus in addition to their picking money, were also popular with their neighbours who sought to earn much needed extra cash.

The potatoes were dug by a tractor towing a revolving fork attachment that threw them up out of the drills and across the ground. They were then collected by the pickers in galvanised steel buckets and then tipped into large sacks. Some tractor drivers would turn at the end of the field and drive straight back down the next drill others would stop and have a cigarette, the latter were popular with sluggards like me but unpopular with the seasoned pickers who would abuse them with cries of "Move your backside." "Get the lead out" or the popular chant "Why are we waiting?" They were eager to fill as many sacks in a day as possible because the normal method of payment was a piecework rate of a half-a-crown per sack and a team of two good pickers might earn several pounds cash in a day when the average national rate of pay was just over one hundred pounds a year; pickers were also permitted to take home a 'feed' or small bag of potatoes each day.

Every now and again a pair of farm workers with a set of scales on a horse drawn sled would weigh and tie the sacks. These men would occasionally tip a sack out on the ground looking for stones or clods of earth put in by crafty pickers to make up the weight. Anyone found guilty of this crime would be sent back to the farm to await the day's end in shame and the ganger would make certain that they were not chosen again.

Maggie was a ganger and I continuously pestered her to take me on her gang until on one magic day she agreed to give me a chance. I could not wait to earn money for my mother for whom life was a struggle and I was up bright and early on the big day because the farm collected the team at around seven o'clock for an eight o'clock start.

The driver heaved me up onto the open top lorry to sit on one of the hay bales provided by a considerate farmer. I was the only male on board the gang being made up of women friends of Maggie's. It was a very tight family group with mothers daughters and sisters forming the pairs required to work a drill. I was to partner Maggie having been warned in her inimitably explicit language just what would happen to me if I failed to pull my weight.

We had not cleared the town boundaries before a sing song began, back in those days you only needed a half a dozen people on a transport for a sing-a-long. The journey to the farm was made shorter by the singing and we were there in no time at all, the lorry dropping us off at the first field. I heard moans and groans from the women and asked Maggie the reason for this; she told me that I would see and I soon did, the field was a coastal one running sharply downhill and ending at the cliff face. As a consequence and because the drills ran down the field for drainage, on every other drill the pickers were working up and down a steep slope and forced to bend over even further than normally. This was a great strain on one's back and these coastal fields were hated, some pickers even declining to work farms bordering the cliff tops.

We collected our heavy galvanized steel buckets and began work with Maggie doing most of it. Her fingers seemed to fly over the fresh dug soil grabbing handfuls of the crop and she filled three buckets to my one. Despite the hard nature of the field once work began the women chatted cheerfully and laughed loudly at each other's jokes, for myself I needed every breath to just carry on and by the time that the morning tea arrived I was pitifully grateful for the short break.

The farmer's wife and daughters brought the large urns on tea on the faithful old sled and it was the best cup of tea that I had ever tasted, hot sweet and milky served in large enamel mugs. I quickly drained mine and went back for a second, a mistake because I was so full of tea when we returned to picking that bending was twice as difficult. By lunch time I was literally on my knees and conscious of the scorn of the neighbouring teams but Maggie remained patient perhaps because she knew that I was trying hard to 'pull my weight'. She did, however, warn me not to kneel as I would suffer for it later – as usual she was right but I carried on kneeling until a horse drawn hay cart arrived to take us to the farm for lunch.

One of the most memorable things about potato picking apart from the sweet scent of the Pembrokeshire soil that gives the crop its distinctive taste was the generosity of the women of the farms. They must have worked for hours preparing the piles of sandwiches that awaited us each day, ham or cheese on thick home made bread with lashings of farmhouse butter followed by great wedges of rich fruit cake. I sat on a bale of hay ignoring the smells of the farmyard and, having wetted my dust dry mouth with another mug of tea, I tucked in as if I had never seen food before. I have enjoyed many alfresco meals but few to compare with those far off farm feasts.

By the time that we returned to work I had stiffened up and the rest of the day was spent labouring against pain from muscles that I was not previously aware of, with Maggie pouring half the contents of her bucket into mine when the farmer came around. Thankfully we completed the steep field soon after lunch and moved to a flatter plain, the mid-afternoon tea break helped to shorten the day and I survived to collect my pay and my feed of potatoes. Thanks to Maggie I had earned a substantial amount of money that I proudly presented to my mother before collapsing onto the settee.

When my mother called me the following morning I found that I could not bend my knees or move my arms, but I was determined not to let myself down in front of Maggie and staggered to the pickup point like a severely arthritic old man. Maggie and her gang found my predicament highly amusing assuring me that the first three weeks were the worst. They were teasing of course and after a few days my body adjusted and I found myself picking as well if not as quickly as most. Thanks to Maggie I earned a very useful wage for my mother, storing up many happy memories of Pembrokeshire potato picking and almost sixty years on I draw curious glances from other shoppers who catch me at the supermarket vegetable counter sniffing the early Pembroke's as if they were exotic orchids.

Chapter Nineteen

Christmas had a nasty habit of occurring at the most inconvenient time and as usual there was no money and little food. Maggie suggested that my mother should send me begging to the manse of the largest church in the town because as she said, 'They have all the money.' I was not to happy about this scheme because although I had begged pocket money from fishermen, that had been done in the company of other kids and had seemed more like a game. Nevertheless goaded by Maggie's, 'You're the man of the family now so get your arse in gear and get your mother some money for Christmas' I put my arse in gear that evening and found myself standing in darkness outside the church whose great tower loomed over me disappearing into the night sky.

The church was famous locally as the one in which Lord Nelson had worshipped with the Hamiltons when living with them in their nearby mansion house and it dominated the end of the town's main promenade; Nelson held the town in such high regard that he presented this church with the truck from the mast of L'Orient the French flagship sunk at the battle of the Nile. The adjoining manse was no less imposing than the church and my footsteps crunched loudly in the frosty air as I made my way up the gravelled drive.

Climbing the stone steps that led to the tall oaken door I took a deep breath and tentatively pressed a bell push, there was no response and determined not to be thwarted after coming this far I lifted the heavy iron door knocker and banged it down several times. This had more effect and within moments a light shone through the stained glass panels at each side of the door and the door was opened by the vicar himself.

Although I had attended church whilst in the children's homes and chapel with my Auntie Eileen I held the high church and its clergy in deep awe, regarding them as God's police force put in place to watch upon and report upon us sinners, so the sight of this tall man clad in his black cassock and staring down at me filled me with the urge to turn and run. Before I could act on my instinct the figure stared at me with one of the coldest looks I had ever received and snapped out, 'Well?' The conversation that followed was almost Dickensian.

At thirteen years of age I was quite a large boy but the vicar towered above me and totally intimidated I blurted out my prepared speech, 'I am sorry to bother you, Sir, but we have no food and my mother thought you might help us with some money from the poor box.'

'I don't know you. You are not one of my parishioners.'

'No, Sir.'

'How dare you come to this door? Do you know that you are begging?'

'I'm sorry.' I felt a lump in my throat and knew that I was about to burst into tears so I clamped my jaws tightly together and took a deep breath.

'What does your father do?'

'I don't have a father, Sir.'

'What does your mother do?'

'She looks after us.'

A long silence followed whilst he decided whether this brat was being facetious or was merely simple minded and if my legs had not turned to water I would have fled; instead I stood there and for the first time in my young life felt the fire of shame light in my stomach and spread throughout me.

Eventually the vicar uttered a clipped, 'Wait there,' and left me standing alone on the step. He returned a short while later and thrust something at me, it was a ten shilling note, ' Don't ever knock my door again,' he said and as I stood there with my Thank you and Merry Christmas' stuck in my throat he slammed the door leaving me in darkness.

That was when the tears came, blinding me so that I almost fell down the steps, accompanied by great gulping sobs that took my breath away. Once outside the gate I thrust the money into my pocket not wanting to touch it and I began to run through the frosty night burning with shame and hate; hate for the vicar, hate for the church, hate for my mother, for Maggie and for Christmas. When I reached home I handed my mother the money without a word, Maggie gave her an 'I told you so' look and said, 'You should try the Catholic Church next, they're not short of a bob or two.'

The ten shillings from the poor box went on food and did nothing to ease the fuel problem but Maggie came to the rescue by telling my mother where she could buy a lorry load of railway sleepers for next to nothing. As soon as the money could be had the deal was done and the lorry arrived at the top of our back lane; there it stopped because it was too wide for the narrow passage.

Maggie had spoken the truth regarding quantity because the load consisted of fifty to sixty creosote impregnated railway sleepers each about nine feet long and twelve inches by nine inches in section; weighing about one hundred and fifty pounds apiece.

My mother asked the driver if he would unload and carry the sleepers the twenty five yards to our garden and was told politely but firmly that he drove but did not carry. It was down to me and I began the work; thankfully the driver did help by pulling each sleeper out over the tailboard so that I could get my back under it and lift it, which was a struggle as I was despite my strength only thirteen years of age. I then staggered (there is no other word for it) the seemingly endless distance to our garden before throwing the sleeper off with a sigh of relief.

I was on sleeper number fifty something or other and looking forward to completing my labours when I suddenly felt as if my chest was being torn apart, found it almost impossible to draw a breath and saw the my surroundings spinning around. When I came to I was laying on the ground beside my load with my mother and the driver leaning over me. My mother was calling my name but I was too absorbed by a terrific cramp in my chest to reply. 'You'd better get a doctor, Missus,' said the driver.

They carried me indoors and Marina was despatched to find Doctor Hoe; whilst the driver guiltily unloaded the remainder of his load. When the doctor had examined me he informed my mother that I had pulled a heart muscle and should rest until it had repaired itself; meanwhile I should take aspirin for the pain – the pain was so intense that I would have cheerfully accepted cyanide if it could ease it.

My mother thanked him and he left, whereupon she began treatment. Knowing my mother's previous addiction for aspirin I should have been wary when she fed them to me almost on the hour but I was trusting and in pain and so spent the next week or so in a happy and relatively pain free torpor; by which time my mother's excesses seemed to have worked because she had me out in the garden hacking the sleepers into useable logs with my billhook.

Despite my recovery my mother insisted that I paid a visit to Doctor Hoe's surgery. It was dark when I entered the Regency period house from which he dispensed his care and I found myself in a large hall facing a wide staircase that swept upwards into the gloom; I say gloom because the only light came from a series of candles set in niches up the stairway. Venturing upwards I saw more candlelight coming from an open doorway, 'Hello' I said in the direction of the doorway and Doctor Hoe's voice instructed me to, 'Come in.'

There was no waiting room or receptionist and upon entering the surgery I saw the doctor sitting behind a large desk lit by candle light and almost obscured by a cloud of cigarette smoke. Seating myself on the chair that he indicated I saw that, in addition to the usual filing trays a large ashtray brimming over with cigarette ends occupied centre place on his desk. He saw my look and asked. 'Do you smoke, son?' I shook my head, 'Good,' he said, 'It's a filthy habit.' Breathing tobacco fumes in my face he examined me and pronounced me, 'Fine.' Many years later I was told by a specialist that the left ventricle of my heart was damaged; was that the price of cheap timber?

Following "the cheap firewood" stunt my thirteenth year also saw the birth of "the great get rich lodger scheme." It began one day as Maggie sat at our table helping me to eat my dinner, pausing between mouthfuls of my sausage egg and chips (it was the affluent front end of the week) she took a puff on her

Woodbine cigarette and said, 'You know, Dolly, you ought to take in lodgers.'

My mother was always open to suggestions and, unfortunately, Maggie was never short of them; she had a mind like a mantrap, razor sharp and quick to snap onto any opportunity to make money. She thought that my mother shared this gift when in fact she was the most unambitious and least grasping person that I ever met.

Maggie always had at least one lodger and she had put a new slant on the term 'taking in boarders' because she 'took them' for every penny they had without a hint of guilt or a sign of scruples. She would empty the pockets of any lodger who made the mistake of rolling home drunk, taking that which she regarded as a safe portion of any money in the certain knowledge that when sober the man would remember nothing.

On one occasion she found an elderly lodger dead in his bed and thoroughly searched his belongings before contacting the authorities; as she later told my mother, 'It was a good job I did search because the old bugger had three hundred pounds hidden away.' A small fortune in those days sufficient to buy a terraced house but it was just another perk of the job for Maggie.

My mother was horrified, 'Oh Maggie, you didn't.' she cried. Maggie was unabashed. 'What good is money to him now?' she asked. 'It would only go to the state and I need it more than they do.' Such was her outlook on life and lodgers; on the day of her brainwave she truly thought that my mother could follow her example and clean up financially.

Whilst she waited for her suggestion to sink in Maggie took another puff of her fag and blew smoke over my food; food never interfered with the business of smoking and I do not think that I ever saw her without a cigarette in her mouth - one of her lovers (they never seemed to regard me as a child) told me that she even smoked during sexual intercourse, 'True as I'm here,' he said, 'as I'm banging away she's puffing away.' This was the same young man who told me that on one occasion she had a paper packet of fish and chips on a bedside chair and ate from it as they made love. When I told my mother about this she laughed and said, 'Perhaps she kept the salt in her belly button.'

A silence followed Maggie's lodger idea during which I looked at my mother and she looked with raised eyebrow at me while Maggie stole my last sausage. Finally my mother said, 'I don't think that I would like strangers in the house; they might be violent for all that I would know.' Maggie gave her a look of scorn and said, 'You get them from the police station; they keep a list. That way you know that they are safe.' At this point I was more concerned with my lost pork sausage than the conversation – such treats were scarce in my life and I felt like stabbing Maggie with my fork but she had taken that along with the sausage.

A few days later my mother told me that she had placed her name with the local police station as a landlady and, the town having a constant flow of itinerant seamen; it was not long before she welcomed her first lodger.

Early one evening a few days later there was a knock on the door and I opened it to find myself looking up at a large black man; I stared because I had never seen a black person before. He dropped a seaman's kitbag from off his shoulder and I got a better look at his face; his appearance inspired misgivings, his face was heavily scarred with a nose that appeared to have found something interesting on his left cheek by the way in which it was bent over. 'The police sent me.' said the man, 'I'm looking for digs.'

As he spoke he twitched suddenly to one side and straightened up just as quickly; I twitched with him instinctively and then felt stupid. At this point my mother appeared and I soon found myself studying this stranger in the light of our living room; I saw that, in addition to his broken nose, his one ear was badly misshapen proclaiming his long years in the boxing game more loudly and graphically than any fairground barker and his face bore many scars.

He introduced himself as Taffy Price and in the course of conversation we discovered that, although he was now seeking work as a deckhand he had until recently earned a living as a boxer in a fairground boxing booth, a career that had left him punchy and resulted in his habit of involuntary ducking and weaving.

Having agreed terms and charges – charges that were in my opinion far too low – my mother told me to show Taffy to his room. After tea although his speech was slurred and sometimes difficult to understand we spent a pleasant evening listening to his stories of the boxing world and fairground life until bedtime arrived. My mother wished our lodger goodnight and said that she hoped he would find his bed comfortable. 'I won't need no bed, missus.' He said, 'I'll sleep on the mat in front of the fire.'

Despite my mother's pleas he refused to budge and curled up like a large pet dog before the fire. Having little choice we left him there and when my mother arose the next morning he was up washed and shaved with a kettle on the boil. There was, however, a major snag to the arrangements, Taffy Price perspired heavily and sleeping fully clothed before a fire turned him into a bath of sweat causing the room to stink. He bathed frequently and my mother's laundry basket bore testimony to his regular change of clothes but every morning resulted in the ritual airing of our living quarters. My mother appealed to Maggie for advice and her solution was to drop in and berate the poor man in such an abusive manner that he eventually walked out of the room with the comment, 'You are not a nice woman, missus.'

Taffy only stayed for a couple of weeks; whether it was Maggie's frequent abuse or his failure to find a berth I don't know but one day he told us that he was going to try the port of Fleetwood, saying, 'They're not so choosey there.' I am sure that it never occurred to him that there might be a racist element involved in his failure to find work; it certainly never crossed our minds, the word 'racist' had not entered everyday thought and conversation at that time. So Taffy disappeared from our lives and we were once again lodgerless.

It was some time before our next lodger appeared; meanwhile Maggie maintained a steady stream of them and at least one new lover. Our new lodger was an elderly man named George Fryer, a smartly dressed man in his sixties was the next referral from our local police station. He was a ship's cook and quietly spoken and thanked me politely when I showed him to his bedroom.

As she prepared tea my mother chatted about the pleasure of having a respectable lodger and when all was ready sent me up to call him down. I knocked softly on his bedroom door, there was no response; I knocked louder, still no response. After several attempts I became worried and reported my concern to my mother, 'Perhaps he is dead, mum.' I said dramatically. 'Don't be silly,' she said, 'you will have to open the door.'

I duly went up and turned the knob of his door (there were no locks on our inner doors at that time.) As I cautiously opened the door I called his name but without any reply and opening it further I peeped around its edge; I immediately yelled for my mother because laying straight out on the bed was a body covered completely by the merchant marine ensign, known to seamen as "the red duster;" there was no sign of breathing or movement from the prone figure.

My mother came running up the stairs and recoiled at the sight, 'Oh My God, he's dead!' She gasped. We stood leaning together for support and then she said, 'You had better touch him to make sure,' a suggestion that did not appeal to me in the least. We stood for a while and then she pushed me forward with a, 'Go on.' Thinking 'why me?' I crept towards the bed; leaning over I touched the nearest foot, no response. 'Is he cold?' my brave mother enquired and I believe that my look conveyed my feelings to her because she said no more.

Finally, in desperation, I grasped the foot and shook it; to my horror the body, still covered by the flag, responded by bending at the waist into an upright position. My mother screamed and I leaned against the bed's footboard my knees shaking. As we remained frozen in our terror George pulled the ensign from his upper half and enquired with a beatific smile, 'Is supper ready?'

'Yes it is.' Was my mother's weak reply and we both crept downstairs leaving the resurrected George to lower the flag. When my mother plucked up courage to ask our lodger about his strange sleeping mode he replied that he liked to be prepared for his Saviour and so adopted the manner used to cover a seaman's corpse aboard ship.

I liked George who would approach me at a crouch, playfully punch my arm and burst into the old music hall song, 'Whenever I go out you can hear the people shout, "get your hair cut..."' he would pause and sing, '...George Fryer.' He would then burst into loud laughter at his own joke. I was still, however, apprehensive about his morbid habits and was not wholly dismayed when this most gentle of men, who conversed with The Lord Jesus at any time without warning as if Our Lord was sitting unseen beside him, did not stay for any length of time being called to the bedside of an ailing relation. I later had several moments of amusement as I imagined him draping the patient in a red ensign ready for the off.

My mother registered once again with the police and it was only a few days before we had a response. I was happy with this because, due to her spending every penny the lodgers paid on food, there were no hungry days when we had a paying guest.

The problem was that our next lodger having paid his initial deposit failed to honour his weekly debt having spent all his money on alcohol. Unfortunately his stay was lengthy because my soft hearted mother would not evict him. Another George he was as unlike the first as possible; his drunken moods varying from loud and abusive to morbid and self pitying.

My mother once again sought Peggy's advice which was, 'Kick the bum out.' Remembering our homeless days she could not bring herself to do that but George Two provided the solution, although it was not one we would have wished.

We were used to him disappearing to meet his fellow sufferers on the railway lines that were a part of the dock's railway, there they would pour the brown liquid from tins of metal polish into bottles of methylated spirits and drink themselves into unconsciousness on the resulting cocktail. George would eventually crawl home swearing but one day he failed to return and we received instead a visit from the police. They reported that he had fallen into a drunken stupor on the docks railway lines and that a passing shunting train had severed both legs at the thigh; he was dead from loss of blood when they found him but they knew where he lived because they had sent him to us.

When the police officers who had been most graphic in their description of the scene left with our late lodger's belongings my mother sat silently for a moment and then began to sniff; I knew that tears were coming and decided to leave her alone. When I returned her eyes were red and she said in a flat tone of voice, 'No more lodgers.'

Despite my mother's determination not to accept boarders she relented when Maggie, who was now separated from her husband and living with a lover asked her to give the estranged husband a few nights board whilst he visited his children. He was not a nice person, a short dark man of North Wales origin he had the usual contempt of his type for the South Wales people and he was a heavy drinker aggressive in his cups.

Because my mother had disposed of our spare bed Maggie helpfully suggested that Ifor should share mine; a suggestion that I did not welcome but was persuaded to agree with. On the first night I went to bed early, hoping to be asleep before my bed mate retired and I succeeded because I do not recall him climbing in beside me. A heavy sleeper I slept blissfully unaware of my loss of privacy until an odd sensation awoke me; I felt hands probing the cheeks of my bottom. Consciousness and realisation of Ifor's intentions occurred simultaneously and with a yell for my mother

I leaped from the bed, pulling up my pyjama trousers that the filthy old beast had loosened to achieve his aim.

I threw myself down the stairs with the pervert shouting after me that I was having a nightmare and I found my mother and Marina enjoying a bedtime cup of cocoa; thankfully Peter was tucked up in bed. Never having experienced such a personal assault I was in shock and was still stuttering a tearful explanation when Ifor came into the room. He was laughing and said to my mother, 'The boy is mad. He has had a bad dream.'

I hid behind my mother and my loathing for the man calmed me sufficiently to tell her what had occurred. My mother stared at him speechless but Marina called him a filthy old bastard. He laughed again, obviously still drunk, and muttered something in the Welsh language. 'I am going to get your wife,' said Marina and left.

All three of us sat in a silence broken only by his Celtic mutterings until Marina returned with Maggie. I told her of my narrow escape interrupted frequently by the sardonic laughter of her ex-husband. She looked at him and then at me. 'You must have been bloody dreaming, you silly little bugger,' she said. 'I wasn't!' I yelled, 'he tried to put his thing in my arse!' By now the combination of anger at the assault and frustration at being called a liar had reduced me to near hysteria.

Accusation and denial bounced back and forth until, finally, Maggie turned to my attacker and said, 'Get your arse down to Number Eight and don't disturb Alan.' He left and my mother thanked her for her intervention. 'Well, whatever, there's no real harm done,' said Maggie and followed her ex-husband. I was still shaken and, afraid that my mother and sister would not believe me, repeated the truth of the incident over and over again. Then, after a hot drink, we locked any threats out and went to bed.

No further action was taken and Ifor left the following day. We never saw him again but a few months later Maggie told us that he had died of a particularly nasty form of syphilis; I had come close to being infected by him with the most virulent form of the disease and close to a painful death.

In the weeks that followed I suffered a recurrence of my infant nightmares; I would dream that I was being chased by fearsome monsters or inanely cackling lunatics intent on killing me and awake soaked through with sweat. The climax came one night when I dreamed that an insane Ifor was chasing me, clawing at me with sharp talons. I screamed and headed for what I thought to be an open window. How my mother reacted so quickly I will never know but she heard my screams and ran into my bedroom in time to see me diving through the closed window.

As glass and frame shattered under the impact of my head and shoulders she grabbed the tail of my pyjama jacket and hung on as I fought to escape her and plunge head first onto the concrete paving ten feet below; in my dream state it was soft grass and the distance two feet. She later said that she did not know how she held me and believed that desperation gave her strength whilst she hung on and prayed to God that the fabric of the jacket held. After a struggle that left us both exhausted I came to and realised my danger; when my mother examined me my only injury was a large bump on my forehead. This episode seemed to cure my nightmares but taking no chances my mother insisted that for some time I should sleep with one ankle tied to a bedpost.

Without the lodgers we returned to our 'eat for three days, survive for four' living pattern; my mother just could not manage money and it never occurred to her that when food was on the table she was in addition to feeding us also feeding Maggie, Maggie's current lover, her children and Peter's friend Graham. Little wonder that supplies ran out quickly.

As usual Maggie had a solution, my mother could borrow money on her allowance book, 'Everyone does it,' she said, 'and Cecil Paul never refuses you a loan.' By a coincidence the money lender, or more accurately loan shark, was the son of the toyshop keeper who had been so helpful to us on our first Christmas in the town. 'His mother is a nice woman,' said my mother, 'so he must be a decent man.' Oh dear, how wrong could she be; the man known simply as Cecil was an out and out rogue the black sheep of a family of grey sheep.

Not surprisingly, I was nominated to perform the deed and my mother having signed the appropriate pages of the book I took it to the large and forbidding house named The Gables. I rang the bell and waited; at the sound of the bell a chorus of howls began, sounding like a hungry pack of wolves.

Visions of Dracula's castle popped into my over imaginative head. Eventually the door was opened and I looked up at the biggest man I had ever seen; dressed in, army battledress trousers, a dirty khaki vest and size thirteen army boots he was over six feet six inches tall and he towered above the door frame as I leaned forward and peered up at him.

He was, however, unlike the forbidding vicar of my previous begging expedition, quite friendly and his look was benign as he waited for me to speak. I held out the allowance book, 'My mother would like to borrow some money, please, Mr. Cecil.' He leaned out and looked up and down the street, 'Come inside boy,' he said, 'and don't go waving that book about.'

Once inside the house I became aware of an unpleasant smell and saw that the large entrance hall, with its oak panelling and wide staircase lit by stained glass windows, was obstructed by a number of large bulging sacks, the source of the smell. I later discovered that these were filled with uncooked sheep's heads for his dogs. He took the book from me and examined it, his eyes narrowed, and 'Who told you that I lend money?' he asked. 'My Auntie Maggie.' I replied and told him where we lived.

'Well she had no right to. He said and examined the pages of the book. 'How much do you want?' I told him the figure that Maggie had suggested and he snorted, 'I couldn't do that. How about?' and he quoted a lesser figure. Not wanting to go home empty handed I agreed and saying, 'Come on then.' he led me past the sacks into a long panelled room whose bay window featured yet more stained glass.

A woman sat in an armchair nursing a baby, she did not say a word as we entered but simply removed one large breast tipped with a nipple the shape and colour of a big strawberry from her blouse and began to feed the child. I had never seen a woman's breast before and flushed with a mixture of lust and disgust; she saw me staring and leaning her head to one side she smiled at me. I immediately thought of the Duchess in "Alice in Wonderland" and instinctively smiled back. As Cecil took the money from a desk he explained his rate of interest to me but it fell on deaf ears, pleased to be getting some money and confused by Mrs. Cecil's display I just wanted to get out of there.

When I returned home with the money my mother asked about repayment, something that I had not thought to ask, and I could not give her an answer; Maggie who was naturally waiting to see how I had got on said, 'Don't worry, girl, you just pay him and borrow on the next week's money.'

So it was to be and every week when I returned to The Gables I would collect my mother's book for her to sign and then hand it back for a lesser amount. According to Maggie, Cecil would take handfuls of books to the post office each week and no one ever queried it. After a couple of months of borrowing and repaying there was no surplus left after payment, my mother simply signed her allowance over each week and received a bag of basic food from our friendly loan shark, this was usually not even enough to last a few days and she became desperate.

Finally my mother accompanied me on a trip to The Gables and told Cecil that when her new book arrived she would not give it to him. At this he flushed a deep red and turned his back on us clenching his fists. When he turned to face us he was calm, 'You can't do that.' he said.

My mother, who never lacked courage when pushed, looked him straight in the eye, 'Oh yes I can.' she said, 'and I will.' They had reached an impasse and he recognised it. Changing his tone he led us into the study (now vacant of mother and baby) and began to outline a plan. Cecil's plan was simple; he would employ me at an unpaid wage of five shillings a week to walk his four greyhounds twice a day, he would take that off my mother's debt and she would also pay him five shillings a week. In return he would not ask for her book and the debt would slowly decrease. We agreed and I became an unpaid dog handler.

I turned up at eight the following morning to meet my charges; they were four handsome racing greyhounds perfect specimens of their breed and I was instantly converted to a greyhound fancier. Each of the four had kennel names but Cecil referred to them and called them by the title 'dog' and told me to do the same; I was to walk them a set route at a steady walking pace and not to allow contact with any other dogs or permit people to pet them, 'They're not bloody pets, they're working dogs,' he said.

On our first walk I was surprised at their tremendous strength and, although I succeeded in following the route given me, it could be said that they walked me. Nevertheless I enjoyed the task and quickly grew fond of the dogs, each of whom was an individual. After a week or so Cecil asked me if I would like to go to the track with him, I jumped at the chance because I had never been to a dog racing track and the next evening found me crushed between the dogs in the back of Cecil's smelly transit van.

The nearest local track was not on the "A" circuit but it was a respectable venue with floodlighting and a good sized grandstand. In the kennels Cecil handed me a long white coat and a white cotton panama hat. I looked at him, 'You have to walk the dog around the track before the race,' he explained. The coat was a good fit which was surprising because on receiving it I must have grown three feet in height and when I walked around the floodlit track in procession with the other handlers I felt like a star.

Cecil's dogs put up a good showing and he drove us home in a happy mood explaining along the way the different tricks pulled to nobble a dog including the one of forcing several pints of water down the beast just before a race. When I said that anyone who would do such things to another man's dog was sick he laughed and said, 'Don't be stupid, boy, they fix their own dogs.' Although times must have changed I have never and never will bet on a dog race, my time with Cecil and the things that I witnessed and heard at the track disillusioned me for life.

The situation with Cecil and his dogs continued for several months, during which time I became thoroughly acquainted with Mrs Cecil's breasts, both right and left. She would pull either out without warning when she decided her baby was hungry and for some odd reason I always thought of the Duchess scene, something that would have no doubt shocked Charles Dodgson. I decided that the right breast was larger than the right but when I ventured to question this with Maggie all she could say was, 'You shouldn't be looking at women's tits you dirty little git. If I catch you looking at mine I'll kick your arse.' There was little danger of my doing that as the objects in question were apparently non-existent.

All went well with my dog job until one wet evening, when as they used to say locally 'the rain came straight down' overwhelming drains and gutters and rushing down the street like a river; lacking protective clothing and having the usual large holes in my shoe soles I decided to cut short the usual walk and call in on Maggie.

Her front door was as usual unlocked and I made my way down the hall pulled along by my charges and opening her living room door I called her name but I do not think she heard because at that moment the dogs saw Maggie's cat sleeping on the hearth rug. The dogs headed for the cat and the cat headed for the curtains, shinning up them at rocket speed with a furious screech.

I had no choice but to follow the dogs as they proceeded to tear Maggie's curtains to shreds while the poor cat clung to the curtain rail in terror. At that moment Maggie entered from the back room realised what she was seeing and collapsed into an armchair; the one and only time that I saw her at a loss.

I ceased my attempts to control the dogs and stood there watching them fight over pieces of curtain. Maggie came to within seconds and began screaming obscenities at me and my charges, she had lost all reason. Her words became gibberish as she grabbed her trusty broom and began beating the dogs with its head. This sudden onslaught had the desired effect and with yelps of pain they retreated. I dragged them out of the room saying over and over again as I went, 'I'm sorry. I'm sorry,' whilst praying that she had not injured Cecil's beloved dogs.

It was still raining and with my nerves as shredded as Maggie's drapes I allowed the dogs to drag me in whatever direction they would. Gradually I became aware of my physical state, I might have been standing naked under a shower for all the protection my scant clothing gave me and I began to shiver from a combination of cold and shock. Seeing a bus shelter I led the dogs into its cover and stood there numb in body and brain. How long we sheltered I do not know but I was awakened from my trance by Cecil's voice yelling, 'My dogs! What are you doing to my dogs, you little shite?'

He ran into the shelter grabbed the leads from me and hit me across the face; when you are hit by a six foot six inch man with hands that were literally the size of shovels you feel as if you have been struck by lightning and I fell to the floor half stunned. 'If these dogs get pneumonia I'll kill you!' he screamed, 'Be at my house tomorrow morning.' He then bundled the dogs into his nearby van and drove away leaving me lying on the wet floor, a floor that bore unmistakeable evidence of the local lad's use of the shelter as a urinal.

When I got home smelling like a public urinal and feeling that I would be better off dead, my mother began ranting at me about Maggie's cat and telling me that I stank did not improve my moral. I slunk off to bed to dream about great beasts devouring me and crowds of people screaming abuse at me because I was a murderer. The next morning I told Cecil about the cat and he promptly sacked me for my honesty; as a result my mother's debt just went on and on.

Chapter Twenty

Although my mother's days as a landlady had ended, whenever Maggie's newly established common law partner returned from the sea her current lover would become our lodger for the duration of her his shore leave (it was not uncommon for her to have two lovers at one time and although I failed to appreciate her attractions she undoubtedly possessed attractions in plenty.) Our ground floor front room would be converted to a bedroom and usually there was little problem with the exercise. On one occasion however there was a problem that bordered on the bizarre.

The boyfriend involved was a young Derbyshire man by the name of Billy Rose a handsome and superbly fit specimen he possessed a natural charm that endeared him to all and I looked forward to having his company for our evening card games; a large feature in our lives in those pre-television days.

Billy moved in and I noticed that he was not his naturally sociable self at the tea table, eating little and grunting monosyllabic replies when spoken to. Shortly after the meal he announced that he was going to bed and retired. It must have been about an hour later that we heard bangs and shouts from his room.

Marina took hold of young Peter whilst my mother and I went to investigate these strange noises. Listening at Billy's door we heard him holding a fierce argument with himself raising his voice at intervals to a shout or a cry of rage; the odd phrase such as, "I will. I will," or, "She'll be sorry then." filtered through.

My mother knocked timidly on the door, 'Are you all right in there, Billy?' she asked; there was no answer. Throwing me a worried glance she opened the door and we entered. Billy stood in the centre of the room, the chairs lay where he had kicked or thrown them and the bed clothes had been torn from the bed and flung around the room; his face was deep red and his eyes were bulging from his head. Without warning he burst into a fit of maniacal laughter.

'Oh God, Billy, what is wrong with you?' she asked.

'Wrong! Wrong! There's nothing wrong. Everything is right.'

'But you look ill, dear.'

'Oh no, I'm fine because I am going to kill her.'

He laughed again and my mother looked at me and rolled her eyes. I was both scared and fascinated; I had seen maniacs on film but never in the flesh. My mother pushed me back towards the door, 'I'll go and make you a nice cup of tea, love.' she said as she steered me from the room closing the door behind us. She whispered, 'Find the key,' and within a few minutes we quietly locked the door on our mad lodger. I was then sent down to Maggie's with instructions to get her alone and tell her about Billy's state of mind. Her response was typical, 'Silly bugger is having a brainstorm, just lock him in overnight. He'll be OK in the morning.'

I relayed this comforting reply to my mother and we all crept quietly to bed; the front room was silent and I hoped that the storm was over but that was not the case, in the early hours of the morning Billy discovered that he was locked in and began kicking and pounding the door screaming dreadful threats at our family; thankfully, the house being old, the door was strong and held. As the hours passed the outbursts became intermittent and eventually ceased.

The next morning, my mother quietly unlocked the door and we sat down to breakfast waiting for an eruption that never came, Billy emerged from his room and greeted everyone as if nothing untoward had occurred. He did look a little pale but we all looked the worse for wear after our night of terror.

The day passed uneventfully without a sign of Maggie who never visited our house while her husband was home. Towards midday Michael called in and handed my mother a small box containing a red light bulb, 'Mum says that a red light will calm a looney down. They use them in loony bins,' he said.

Later that afternoon my mother sneaked into Billy's room whilst he was in the bathroom and changed the light bulbs; I did not think this was such a good idea imagining how I would react to finding myself in the conning tower of a submarine when I switched on my light.

My misgivings proved to be well founded when Billy, who had been quiet all day, said goodnight and retired. Within seconds we heard an enormous howl from him and rushed in to find out what was wrong; he was sitting on the bed gibbering. My mother sat beside him and held him to her saying, 'There, there. It's all right. I am here with you,' patting him as she uttered baby comforting words and explained that the red bulb was to save electricity.

He gradually calmed down and began to cry. 'I thought that I was dead and in hell,' he said. I felt sorry for him at that moment but my pity evaporated quickly as he pushed my mother aside, stood and began to pace around the room; a difficult feat as the bed filled most of its small area. He then began to breathe heavily and grunt, 'That's where I'll end up, Hell,' he said, 'Thanks to her I will but it will be worth it when she is dead.'

'Come on now, Billy, that's no way to talk. You have got your whole life in front of you.' My mother's attempt to restore his wits failed and grunting like an animal he reached into his open kit bag and drew out a wicked looking sheath knife with a six inch blade. 'I'll cut her throat,' he grunted, 'She won't make a fool of any other man.' He laughed and I sat down on the bed as I felt my strength drain out through the soles of my feet.

I had to admire my mother's bravery as she took him by the shoulders and, ignoring the knife, eased him down onto the bed beside me but I was not happy with the fact that this placed me in close proximity to the blade that was gleaming blood red in the glow of the coloured light bulb. She reached over and took down the rosary that Billy, being a devout catholic, had hung over his bedrail; she held its crucifix up in front of his eyes saying, 'Is she worth your soul, love? Is any woman worth that?' He turned away from the crucifix and began stabbing the bed viciously.

I wished that my mother would show some sense and get us out of there, instead she handed me the rosary saying, 'Talk to him and keep reminding him that he is a catholic. I'll go and get Maggie.' Had I not been frozen with fear I might have laughed out loud at such a daft suggestion but before I could react she left closing the door behind her.

I heard the key turn in the lock and I was left alone with a homicidal maniac who was now alternating between stabbing the bedclothes and tearing at them with his teeth. I looked at the crucifix thinking that if I was stabbed to death holding it I might at least have a good chance of going to heaven. I thought of following my mother but remembered that she had thoughtfully locked the door.

How long we sat there I do not know; I do know that whenever he paused his mad exertions and might have turned his attentions to me I thrust the crucifix in front of his face telling him that he was a good catholic and breathed a sigh of relief when he resumed his attack on the bedclothes. After what seemed like a lifetime I heard voices and my mother entered with Maggie who immediately snatched the knife from poor Billy and threw it across the room before giving him a backhanded slap across the face and screaming at him. 'You stupid bastard. What are you playing at?'

I heard his sharp intake of breath as he recoiled from the slap. She slapped him again, 'I've had to leave himself on his own down below. What if he follows me and sees you?' Billy began to cry like a child, big chest heaving sobs 'Another episode like this and we are through, Boy.'

He sobbed, 'I'm sorry Maggie,' he cried over and over again. 'So you should be you daft ****. Now if this good woman has any more trouble with you I'll take that knife and stick it up your arse. Do you understand?' He nodded understanding and Maggie led us from the room apologising for causing such trouble and we closed the door on her pitiful and chastened lover.

The next morning it was as if nothing had happened, Billy was his old cheerful self and proved to be good company when sane before returning a week later to Maggie's arms; just another day in the saga that I would call 'knowing Maggie.'

Life was not all gloom, doom and drama and on the whole our days were happy; there was no television in the house but the radio provided great entertainment with music, drama and comedy and in the evenings when we were not listening to the radio we played cards for pennies and half pennies, the most popular game being Newmarket a simple sequence game that a child could play but still provided great fun and a lot of excitement.

On most evenings Michael and I were at the cinema, we earned our ticket money by selling kindling door to door; my share of this extra money also bought a modest supply of art materials because I was still drawing at every opportunity and building up the sizeable portfolio of work that I stored in a large cardboard box. My hero was the great German engraver Albrecht Dürer and I dreamed of achieving a standard approaching his.

Our kindling supplies came courtesy of Milford Docks. In the middle of the docks was a large box dump where broken or discarded fish boxes were tipped and, as the life of a wooden fish box was short, the mound was usually about twenty feet high humming with swarms of flies. We would tie together as many of the broken staves as we could carry and cart them off home where we would chop them into kindling and bind the sticks into sixpenny bundles. The worst side of this routine was the smell and the box-tip rats, they were large, ugly, numerous and not afraid of humans.

On one occasion I disturbed a heap of wood and found my face about eighteen inches away from a particularly ugly rodent; its fur was wet and matted, one ear was chewed off and it was baring its ugly yellow teeth in a snarl – or maybe it was a grin. We stared at one another and I remembered stories of how cornered rats were supposed to leap at your throat; in fairness to this unfortunate creature I do not think it had a leap in it but that did not occur to me at the time.

Michael had noticed my frozen posture and came across to see what was wrong; seeing my rat he immediately threw a lump of wood at it causing it to scramble out of sight. I have always had a loathing for rats, tempered by sympathy for a creature that is persecuted by all; despite that sympathy the incident made me take more care when sorting wood.

Another source of income was scrap-metal, using an experienced eye gained in my camp days I would dive on a piece of non-ferrous metal like a vulture upon its prey and it was surprising how quickly a saleable weight was collected. On weekends and summer evenings I would defy the efforts of the elderly watchman at the nearby Thomas Ward ship breaking beach and sneak aboard newly arrived vessels; not only was scrap metal there for the taking but also marine charts left in pigeon holes in the wheelhouse; I was fascinated by these depictions of far off seas and harbours and I would take them home and play with them for hours steering my vessel through stormy waters to discover treasure.

It was on a summer evening that I climbed aboard one large merchant ship and began to explore. I had recently begun smoking and always carried a box of matches, (the era of the throwaway lighter was still to come) with these I began exploring first noting an attractive bundle of charts to be collected later. Striking matches as I went I descended down several decks and then...horror...burning my finger I dropped the match and also my box of matches; I believe that my breathing and heartbeat ceased in terror because I found myself in total blackness, darkness would not adequately describe the complete absence of light.

Those first seconds in that steel tomb return to me vividly when I hear of or see film of a marine disaster because I realise the terror that strikes when the generator fails and the blackness begins; the story of the Titanic distresses me even more deeply when I think of those trapped below decks when the lighting flickered out and recall that long ago moment aboard the empty ship.

After an age my heart began thumping in my chest and my lungs remembered to do their duty recovering lost time by causing me to pant almost to the point of hyper ventilation. Dizzy with fear and a surfeit of oxygen I sank to my bare knees on the cold steel deck and began to grope around for my matches; they were nowhere to be found.

I sat back on my haunches and felt the tears filling my eyes; I knew that no one would hear my shouts from this deep in the ship and could not hope for rescue the following day because I knew from observation that the first week or so of scrapping concentrated on the superstructure some three or four decks above me.

In desperation and praying for help from God I began my fumbling search anew and God heard my prayer because my hand fell on that wonderful box of vestas. I clutched them to my chest with such passion that I could easily have set them off in one fierce blaze. Thankfully that did not occur and weak kneed and shaking I made my way up into the daylight.

I sat on the upper deck for some time thanking God and making extravagant promises for future good behaviour and then, forgetting about sea charts or scrap metal made my way home. It was some time before I ventured aboard another empty ship, this time armed with two boxes of matches and a stump of candle (electric torches were outside my budget.) As for my promises to God, they were rapidly forgotten and broken but I know that I was forgiven because he has been so good to me in so many ways since.

As I mentioned, I had begun smoking in that, my fourteenth year. For some reason, probably through one of my mother's many odd contacts, she and I were invited to a house party held to welcome the officer's of a Canadian destroyer that had docked in the port. It was a pleasant event and although I was only a kid the officers treated me as an equal and made certain that I was made to feel a part of things.

Halfway through the evening, as I sat sipping my first ever glass of cheap sherry and attempting to appear grown up, a young lieutenant sat beside me and offered me a cigarette. I declined politely saying that I did not smoke and he leaned back in amazement. 'You don't smoke?' he exclaimed. 'How old are you?'

I told him and he sat silently for a moment before looking me straight in the eye with, 'You aren't a man until you smoke, son.' He produced his cigarettes again and insisted that I try one; to my surprise it was pleasant and I felt only a slight light headed effect, I later discovered that Canadian cigarettes are much milder than the British brands.

By the end of the evening I had acquired that terrible addiction to nicotine something that I was not to throw off until middle age. I also sewed the seeds of my first hangover at that party by creeping into a corner with a bottle of sherry and drinking myself silly for the first time in my life. The combination of tobacco and cheap sherry made me wretchedly ill and I spent half the night with my head down the lavatory pan.

`Cigarettes were relatively cheap in price at that time but they still cost money that I did not have. The solution came from Maggie's current boyfriend; a trawler man; because larger trawlers carried duty free drink and tobacco that would be sold to the crew once the vessel was outside the three mile limit he was able give me regular gifts of quarter pound tins of "Pirate" brand shag tobacco at little cost to himself. This hand rolling tobacco was so strong that, upon breaking open the inner foil lid a whiff of tar would assail the nostrils and after hand rolling a cigarette from the shag I would have tar stained finger tips.

Once addicted to "Pirate" I found all other tobacco tasteless and was eventually obliged to turn to a brand of cigarettes called "Capstan Full Strength"; probably the strongest and in terms of nicotine content undoubtedly the most health threatening brand available. As one whose health and pocket were ravaged by tobacco I applaud every measure to prevent young people becoming enslaved by it and wish that my mother had declined that party invitation.

Whilst I was dipping my toe into dissolution's pond my sister, Marina, had grown into a vivacious and beautiful young woman; she attended local dances and she had made a small circle of friends with whom she enjoyed shopping, partying and all the other activities of youth. Her friends were aware of her illness and were patient and supportive; she was enjoying life and we could not have foreseen how suddenly and unfairly her innocent pleasures would end.

It was a quiet afternoon; my mother was playing with Peter at the table, Marina was upstairs doing whatever young women do at their mirrors and – as usual – I was buried in a book. When the front door was knocked I jumped up to answer it and found myself facing a tall man wearing a trilby hat and a long gabardine coat; on each side of him as if guarding him stood a man in a white hospital uniform. The tall man spoke, 'May I speak with your mother?' he asked.

I turned and found my mother standing behind me at the foot of the stairs with her hands on Peter's shoulders; at that moment Marina called down asking who was at the door. 'It's alright, love. It's for me,' my mother replied.

'Do you have a daughter named Dorothy Marina?' the man asked without any preamble.

'Who wants to know?' asked my mother, instinctively on her guard.

'I am Doctor ... from the local Health Authority,' he said, 'and I have an order committing your daughter under the Mental Health Act.' We stared at him, I was not certain of his meaning and my mother was nonplussed. 'I beg your pardon?' was all she could manage.

'We have had complaints from neighbours that she has been falling in the street and frightening their children.'

'She has epilepsy,' said my mother, 'Of course she falls when she has a fit.'

Ignoring me the man stepped into the hallway followed by the men in white. 'Please get Marina ready. We have an ambulance waiting.' He said.

Marina, who had been listening from the top of the stairs screamed down, 'No, mum, send them away!' 'Don't worry, love, I won't let anyone hurt you,' replied my mother and pushing Peter behind her she stepped forward to stop the doctor from moving further into the hallway. I was at the front door with all three men between my mother and me and I saw the doctor grasp her by the shoulders and firmly pin her against the wall saying to the men as he did so, 'She's upstairs.'

The men pounded up our stairs and I heard Marina slam her bedroom door screaming repeatedly, 'No, mum, don't let them get me!' We had no locks on the flimsy upstairs doors and I heard a crash as the men broke Marina's door open; then came the sound of a struggle with my sister screaming for help all the while. I looked to my mother for directions but she was standing white faced and silent held by the doctor. Peter began to cry but everyone ignored him.

Then, apart from Peter's whimpering, there was a silence. My mother called out to Marina but there was no reply. I felt physically sick; this could not be happening, these people could not break into our house like this. The whole thing was so unreal that for one of a rare few moments in my life I closed my eyes and told myself it was a dream but when I opened them I could hear Peter whose crying had turned to sobs as he clung to my mother.

I saw the doctor push my mother back into the living room with my little brother stumbling between them and heard the sound of the men coming back down the stairs; their footsteps were slow and so heavy that I felt them as much as heard them. When they came into view I saw why; they were carrying Marina one at her feet and the other at her shoulders. She was trussed up in what I later realised was a strait jacket a gag or mask obscured most of her face and she appeared to be unconscious. I believe that they had drugged her but will never know the truth.

As they shoved past me carrying my sister I stood frozen with disbelief and heard a half cry half moan from my mother that did not appear to have come from a human throat as it sounded more like the groan of a wild beast. The doctor released her and quickly followed his helpers through the front door. She stood leaning against the living room door frame gasping guttural moans of, 'No, no,' over and over again.

When I looked out onto the street the men were slamming the rear door of the ambulance and as I watched they climbed in and drove away. Neither my mother nor I could have imagined that Marina was beginning over forty years of incarceration in mental hospitals, all because epileptic seizures had caused her to fall in the street. We never found out who had filed the complaint and consequently with the exception of Maggie regarded all our neighbours with suspicion from then on, resulting in our virtual isolation from the small community.

Leaving my mother calling my sister's name I ran down to fetch Maggie and she immediately ran back with me. She instructed me to make my mother a cup of tea and having been told what had happened tried to reassure her with, 'The buggers can't get away with that,' and other comments about a free country and so on but my mother remained in a state of shock until with the assistance of several stiff whiskeys supplied and administered by Maggie she was led to bed.

The next day saw the start of a family campaign that was to last for many years beginning with a visit to Doctor Hoe who explained that Marina's abduction had been quite legal providing a sufficient number of neighbours had complained. He advised my mother to phone the county mental hospital and enquire about Marina and taking his advice we discovered she had been admitted to a large mental hospital about thirty miles from our home. My mother was told that Marina was fine and asked not to attempt to visit her until she had undergone tests, a process that took two to three weeks.

During the waiting period my mother wrote to our Member of Parliament and received no reply; she could not afford a lawyer and there were no Citizens Advice Bureau in our area so we just waited hoping that the hospital could tell us just how we might obtain Marina's release.

When the time was up my mother took the train to the hospital town leaving me to care for Peter. She returned that night in a state of distress and told me that my sister was on a large ward with patients of all types, some continually screaming others banging objects on the walls and some who ran around clawing at everyone in reach. All that Marina could do was hug her and whisper pleas to be brought home before she went mad and it took all of my mother's courage bolstered by love of my sister to remain there for the permitted hour. Finally, covered in spittle from inmates and shaking with nerves, she left having promised Marina that she would get her out of there; she was still shaking when she arrived home.

The hospital authorities were unhelpful and would only say that Marina would be kept until she was considered fit to return to the community. This situation continued for almost a year with my mother making the few visits she could afford and then we received a letter from the hospital saying that my sister had been transferred to Rampton Hospital for the Criminally Insane, this same hospital was notorious for housing murderers and rapists and was later to house the infamous Yorkshire Ripper. We knew of the institution by repute and, horror struck, my mother left for my sister's previous hospital to find the reason for this action, as none had been given in the letter.

On her return that night my mother told me that she had been informed by the management that Marina had assaulted a nurse and broken her arm but on her way out a young nurse had taken her aside and told her the true story. Marina had been winding wool for an elderly patient when a nurse, well known for her lack of patience, had told her to drop it and get into bed. Marina had replied, 'O.K. nurse, just let me finish this skein,' whereupon the nurse without any warning had grabbed my sister by the back of her hair and began to drag her towards her bed.

The sympathetic nurse explained that Marina had recently fallen on several occasions during seizures hitting the back of her head which became bruised and cut. She said that the pain must have been unbearable when my sister's hair was pulled and that Marina had struggled and hit out causing her assailant to fall against a bed and break her arm. Having told my mother this - just like our informant regarding Peter - she begged her not to repeat it because she would lose her job if they knew she had told her the story; my mother promised not to and in her distress failed to ask for the nurse's name.

It took five years to obtain Marina's release from Rampton and by the time that this lovely intelligent young woman was returned to a Welsh Mental Hospital both she and we had accepted that she would remain incarcerated indefinitely. She would be in her mid sixties, confined to a wheelchair and totally reliant on carers before she was discharged into sheltered accommodation with only a few years left of a life that had been cruelly destroyed by thoughtless people and a heartless bureaucracy and to this day I carry a deep guilt that I did nothing to stop her abduction. After Marina was taken away I found myself questioning the existence of God and wondering about the world and its ways more deeply than I had previously done.

Chapter Twenty One

Despite the poverty and tragedy that marred our happiness we were fortunate in living close to a long promenade; with a large open air swimming pool as its crowning glory its green lawns and curving paths led down almost to the cliff edge. On a warm day I would climb through the hedge and lay flat on my back in the long grass that topped the low cliff for hours gazing up into the blue sky; it was during one of these meditations, as I lay listening to the grass grow, that I was hit by the realization that the earth was a living thing and that humanity was a parasite upon the planet. I later discussed this at length with Michael and we agreed that it made sense; I believe, in addition to being junior philosophers we must have been budding conservationists long before the idea became popular.

Sometime that summer I rushed as usual to be first to answer a loud knocking at the front door and found myself nose to nose with a gnome wearing a flat cap, tweed jacket tied at the waist with trawl twine, collarless striped flannel shirt and corduroy trousers held at the ankles by bicycle clips. It wasn't a gnome of course but the figure had all the attributes of one; in height he was slightly shorter than me, his shoulders were over developed giving him the appearance of having a hump on his back (what locals called 'a joey), his legs were bowed and his face was tanned to a mahogany brown with a prominent red nose and rosy cheeks; he looked to be in his early forties.

He spoke and his accent was so broad that the only word I could decipher was 'rabbits.' I asked his pardon and he reeled off his speech once again, remaining incomprehensible to me; at that point my mother came to the door and the man removed his cap with a courtesy that would have been more natural in a Victorian era revealing a bald head as red as his cheeks.

He appeared to modify his speech to almost intelligible for my mother and as he did so he stepped to one side and pulled forward an ancient black bicycle which had several brace of rabbits hanging head down from the handle bars. Twisting one of the creatures free he held it up slapping its flank and I caught the price of 'one and six,' (one shilling and sixpence.)

Against all my instincts my mother invited the rabbit seller in and as he pushed past me I almost groaned on inhaling a body odour that filled my nostrils and forced its way down my throat causing me to gag. Leaning his bicycle in the hallway he lifted a brace of rabbits from the bars and holding them up as if proud of them said, 'O.K. Two bob for two, Missus.'

My mother told him that she would buy them but wanted them skinned and he grunted something that sounded like, 'Urrrll do that,' within minutes the chenille tablecloth had been whipped off our living room table revealing its scrubbed top and the rabbit man, who I later discovered was known as Toddy to the locals, had removed his jacket rolled up his shirt sleeves and set to skinning the rabbits.

I had often skinned rabbits with my Romany friends and seen Uncle Larry do it but to watch Toddy was to watch a master. He opened a large clasp knife and with the sureness of a surgeon drew the blade around each leg; he then took each foot and snapped it cleanly off. Looking at my mother he offered her the feet which she politely declined; he shrugged and laid them on the table, his offer was not strange because many people set great store by a rabbit's foot as a bringer of good luck.

I watched marveling at the delicacy of the operation as he removed the fur from flesh in one piece first from the torso and then from each leg ('Taykin uz coat orf,' he called it) leaving it hanging from a naked body still attached to the head; finally he cut around the neck and we had our rabbit ready for the pot.

Toddy soon became a regular visitor, my mother would feed him and bought him a new shirt with a collar, she even offered discreetly to let him use our bath but he said that he bathed every week in the tide near his home; unfortunately he never appeared to change his clothes and carried a pungent cloud of body odour with him. As his visits became more frequent and I began to think that I could not look another rabbit in the eye it became obvious that my mother's kindness was being construed as an invitation to courtship. After my mother had given him his money and a meal he would sit in the armchair following her movements with soft eyed puppy-like adoration; then he would begin to sing a quiet and croaky rendition of the popular ballad "Give Me Your Love".

Maggie spotted this and told my mother to be careful or she would be stuck with her admirer. She also told us that he lived in an old cottage near a beach with all its windows shuttered up. According to Maggie his mother had died and he had kept her body for weeks shut up with a halfwit sister until neighbours broke in, buried the old lady and placed the sister in care. She would taunt him whenever she could, calling him a dirty old git and telling him to get a bath; that did not, however, stop her begging cigarettes from him at every opportunity.

Things came to a head on the day that he followed my mother out into the kitchen, grabbed her, planted a big kiss on her cheek and in a garbled dedication of love asked her to marry him. My mother tried to laugh it off and led him back into the living room where she attempted to change the subject until; faced with his persistence she lost her patience and bluntly rejected his proposal, telling him to grow up and not to be so stupid.

I had never witnessed such a transformation in a human being. He stood and paced around the room wringing his hands and moaning quietly; he then began slamming a fist into the opposite palm so fiercely that it sounded like the crack of a whip. By this time his face, normally bright pink, had turned purple so that I feared that he would explode or drop dead with a stroke.

Even the mad Billy Rose had not scared me as much as Toddy; I knew his strength and also his lack of intelligence, a dangerous combination in any creature. I watched as beads of sweat popped out on his forehead where swollen purple veins were vying with his skin for vividness and was convinced that my mother and her soft heart had finally done for us. I felt like screaming, 'you stupid woman!' at her but my fear robbed me of the energy to do so, all I could whisper was, 'Oh, mum.'

After several circuits of the room Toddy sank down into the armchair put his head in his hands and began to cry; eventually his sobs subsided and we sat in silence. Then, without warning, he jumped to his feet and pausing enroute to grab his bicycle left without a word; my mother called after him but he ignored her. We never saw him again. Shortly after this that horrible disease myxomatosis reached our area and I thought of Toddy and the affect it must have had on his meagre livelihood but soon forgot him as new interests demanded my attention.

My old friend Jeff had introduced me to the Army Cadet Force and throwing myself into cadet life with my usual obsessive commitment, I lived, ate and breathed army. When I received my battledress uniform I lavished care upon it pressing the creases into blouse and trousers until they were the sharpest on parade and after saving enough to buy my two pairs of army boots I spent countless hours with spit and polish on the parade pair until they gleamed like black glass. I was a proper little fanatic and I am sure that, had I been born in Nazi Germany, I would have quickly become a brainwashed Hitler Youth; such was my blind adherence to my new found military doctrine.

My favourite cadet activity was manoeuvres or war games. Armed with fully serviceable Lee Enfield .303 rifles but given only blank ammunition we would march out into the surrounding countryside and create mock military havoc amongst the poor farmer's crops and livestock.

This was a time in which the IRA were quite active and we would be told that should a man with an Irish accent ask to see our rifle we should smack him over the head with its butt and run; pity any poor farmhand of Irish origin who passed the time of day with us and shame on the fool who decided to instruct children to oppose one of the most ruthless of terrorist organizations. Nevertheless, I longed for a confrontation with a terrorist, creating lurid fight scenes in my head each ending with me leading a cowed captive back at the point of my rifle.

When not contemplating a single handed attack on the Irish Republican Army I would often walk the nearby promenade with its grassy slopes and commanding views of Milford Haven and spend many hours just sitting on a bench watching the passing world or, if lucky, the takeoff or landing of one of the handsome Sunderland flying boats that were based further up the haven. I sat and watched such a landing one sunny day in early spring, transfixed by the grace of the great plane.

Following the subsidence of the great spume of water after the plane's touch down I walked along the promenade. Had I turned for home my life would have remained as it was with its small stresses and simple pleasures, regrettably I turned away from home; on such simple decisions can life change dramatically and permanently.

As I continued my stroll I saw amongst the people watching the Sunderland, now surfaced, and coasting back to its base a figure in a long gabardine raincoat studying the scene through binoculars. The man lowered the glasses and I realised that it was an old friend from my camp days, the man known as Circus; I was about to make one of the greatest mistakes of my young life.

Approaching the man I greeted him as Circus to be told that his name was Stanley. I apologized saying that I thought he was my old friend from the camp and he laughed saying that he was but that he now preferred to be called Stanley. We talked for a while and he told me that he was sailing as a Deckie Trimmer on a trawler – the larger of the steam trawlers carried deckhands who, when not on deck gutting the catch, were required to periodically 'trim' or shovel the tons of coal from the rear of the coal hold to the end nearest the fires a hard and dirty job but well paid.

After a chat and a couple of his cigarettes it occurred to me to invite him back to our house for tea and he accepted. As usual my mother saw nothing odd in a strange face at the tea table and made Stanley welcome. It was the beginning of the week so food was plentiful and he ate as if he had been starving for weeks; this brought out my mother's maternal instinct and when he told us that his landlady hardly fed him she filled his plate over again and beckoned me out into the kitchen. 'Shall we offer him lodgings?' she asked.

Circus had always been a minor hero for us kids and the thought of having him as a lodger appealed to me. We returned to the living room and my mother made the offer, one that he accepted eagerly saying that he could move in that day and so Stanley became a part of our household. He left after tea and returned that evening carrying two large suitcases; hung about his person binoculars, cameras and various small packages suspended from string. As I was to discover Stanley was a childlike collector of gadgets and novelties and not particular from where or from whom he obtained them, having little respect for other people's property rights.

He sailed the day after moving in and we did not see him for twelve days (trawlers were usually at sea for ten to twelve days and in port for two or three) when he returned he was carrying gifts of a pillow vase full of cooked king prawns for my mother and a tin of fifty cigarettes for me. During his time ashore he took my mother shopping for little luxuries and played games with Peter and me and his lodging money was always paid on time. He would entertain us in the evenings with stories of his life in the circus, claiming to have been a clown in the famous Billy Smart's circus and then after two days he was back to sea.

This pattern continued for a couple of months and Stanley became a fixture in our life; even Maggie liked him, probably because he always passed his cigarette packet around. It must have been just after he sailed for his fourth or fifth trip as our lodger that my mother sat me down and told me that she had something to tell me, 'Stanley has asked me to live with him,' she said and seeing my puzzlement she went on,' as man and wife.'

If she had slapped me hard across the face it could not have given me such a shock. I looked at her, understanding but not believing what I had just heard; nothing that they had said or done had prepared me for this. 'He will make you a good father,' she attempted by way of comfort; she might as well have slapped the other cheek. Speechless I jumped up and ran up to my bedroom, slamming the door behind me.

I threw myself on my bed and lay there trying to remember any sign of affection that Circus (I could no longer bring myself to think of him by his name) and my mother had exchanged, nothing; I had noticed him putting his arm around her shoulders and her giving him a hug on his returning from sea but my mother was naturally affectionate and demonstrative and I had thought nothing of it.

Despite my mother's entreaties I remained in my room for the rest of that day staring at the ceiling and cursing my stupidity at introducing that man to my mother; she did not know anything about him except the stories that he had told and I knew that she had rejected a number of suitors, so why him.

As usual Maggie had the answer, 'Your mother has reached the time of life when she needs a man in her life. You're no good to her, you're only a kid and she needs more.' I looked at her with disgust, I had an idea of what she was alluding to and the thought of my mother and Circus disgusted me. 'You'll understand one day,' she went on, 'that we women have needs.' I knew all about her needs and resented the fact that she classed my mother with herself but I began to accept that I could do nothing to change things.

I was out playing when Circus returned from sea and I came home to find him seated at the table tucking into a meal; he did not say a word and continued eating. My mother nudged me. 'Say hello,' she said. He looked up from his meal and grinned revealing blackened teeth and a mouthful of food; any appetite that the smell of cooking had inspired died instantly. 'Go on,' she prodded, 'say hello.' I managed a reluctant greeting and the rest of the day went quietly I retreated to my bedroom early and remained there. When my mother and Circus went to bed I pretended to be asleep in order to avoid saying goodnight.

It began the next day, a steady stream of power flaunting and humiliation. I came down - late as usual - to find Circus seated in the best chair drawing heavily on a cigarette and reading the daily newspaper whilst my mother could be heard singing contentedly from the kitchen. I ignored him and shouted, 'Good morning, mum, what's for breakfast?' Before she could answer he snorted a laugh, 'At this time of day? You'll be lucky,' he said.

I gave him what, in my fourteen year old imagination was, a look of scorn. 'I didn't ask you.' I snapped.

'Well you should have, you should have asked the boss.'

'You're not my boss.'

At that moment my mother came into the room with my breakfast and the small storm blew over but the calm was not to last as Circus became bossier each day and took to ridiculing me at every opportunity; he even made fun of my beloved drawings, leaning over my shoulder and making scathing remarks such as, 'I've seen three year olds who could do better than that.'

I had never seen such a change in a human being, it was as if he detested me and wanted to make me suffer (in fairness, the feeling quickly became mutual.) He appeared to lose pride in his appearance, gone was the smartly dressed jovial companion that I had invited into our home. He quit his ship and lay around the house smoking cigarettes bought for him by my mother; he became more slovenly as the weeks passed, going days without shaving and left his hair uncombed.

I spent more and more time away from the house and on a walk with Michael I told him of my problem. 'I think that Circus hates me,' I said, 'he keeps on and on poking fun and making me appear small.' Michael said that the man was probably jealous of me and to ignore his spiteful ways, '...that's what I do.' he said and I thought that with Maggie's long list of boy friends he should know.

Weeks passed and things got steadily worse. Circus took to stealing from the little money I earned from my kindling sales and began smoking my tobacco as if it were his own. When I complained to my mother she made excuses for him such as, 'It's difficult for him at the moment it will be O.K. once he gets a ship.' I immersed myself in my books, my drawing and the Army Cadet Force in order to forget my troubles; I failed, however, and began sleep walking again. Fearing for my safety my mother persuaded the council to fit a mesh of steel bars over my window and allowed Circus to fit bolts on my bedroom door and drill a spy hole.

Each night he would shout at me to get my arse upstairs, 'Time for you to be banged up.' He would say and laugh; I later discovered that he had served several prison terms and liked to picture himself as a warder. He would close the door on me and slam the bolts home loudly, then he would peer through the spy hole and say, 'Don't forget that I can see you but you can't see me.'

Because of my fear of the dark I slept with the light on and I would lie in bed feeling his eyes on me as I read my bedtime book.

Regularly without warning he would shout, 'I can see you playing with yourself, you dirty little shite.' My hatred for him grew greater each day as did my contempt for my mother who permitted him to treat me in such a way.

I felt totally unloved and unwanted; my one consolation was my cat. Tommy had come to us as a stray, a skinny scruffy tar ball of a creature but with love and care he had grown into a handsome feline with shiny black coat and eyes that shone like green diamonds. It would be true to say that he was my cat; I was the one who fed him, visiting the docks on a regular basis to obtain fresh fish with which to supplement his cat food and stealing milk from the pantry for him when Circus had dictated that cats should drink water.

Tommy became my close companion as I descended into a slough of self pity; whenever I sat down to read a book or listen to the radio he would appear on my lap purring and rubbing his head into me. He would respond to my stroking by purring so loudly that it could be felt as well as heard, he would then fall asleep with a tiny pink tongue protruding between his sharp white teeth. Circus was not an animal lover and insisted that Tommy should be locked out each night regardless of the weather and each morning after being released from my bedroom I would go looking for my cat with a saucer of milk.

One morning Tommy failed to turn up. I spent the morning going back and forth to the garden and calling his name but he did not appear. It was about mid-day and I was sitting immersed in a book when I heard my mother calling me from the garden; there was panic in her voice and I ran out to find her leaning against the garden wall with her hand over her mouth. Looking down the garden I saw my beloved cat on his stomach at the bottom of the path, he was attempting to crawl towards me but making no progress. I ran to him and knelt beside him, his teeth were drawn back in a snarl and he was trembling violently.

I tried to pick him up and he clawed at me giving out a cross between a growl and a scream; it was the most chilling sound that I have heard before or since and my blood froze. The scream and the clawing caused me to drop him and he hit the concrete path with a thump. I looked at my mother panic stricken, she stood there muttering, 'Oh, my God.' over and over again. I turned back to Tommy and as I did he began to retch, convulse and gasp for air; this lasted for about half a minute and then he gave one almighty convulsion that bent his back almost in half and with a shuddering intake of breath he fell still.

I looked down at my once beautiful cat now disfigured by the ugliness of death; a snarl was fixed on his face and his eyelids were half open showing his beautiful green eyes turned back in his head. I took a breath. I could not believe what I was seeing and I picked him up half hoping that he would recover in my arms but his body was already growing cold and stiff and the truth finally struck me. Leaning back on my heels and holding him to my chest I threw my head back and howled, 'No. No,' to the heavens. I then began to yell at God, calling him every filthy name I could think of and asking him why he had allowed my cat to die; at the same time hating myself for my inability to save him.

I carried Tommy into the house whereupon Circus told me to take him back out, 'You don't know what germs are on that thing,' he said and I was too grief stricken to argue. Taking my cat to the garden I laid him down on a patch of grass and returned to the house to fetch a bath towel to wrap him in. I could not leave him laying out there so I immediately began to dig a small grave and when it was done I laid him in it. After I had filled in the grave I prayed to the God that I had so recently cursed to take care of my cat and illogically comforted myself with the belief that he would.

When we told Maggie about Tommy's death she said that she knew of a neighbour who was putting down meat laced with strychnine for the rats but despite my pleading refused to name the culprit; that was probably a good thing because in my state of mind I might have done something drastic to them.

After the death of my cat my nightmares became more frequent coming to a head when I woke the household convinced that, although wide awake, I had seen two six foot tall pillars of pearlescent shimmering white at the foot of my bed and heard them discussing me. One asked, 'Is this the boy?' and the other replied, 'Yes.' The odd thing was that I heard the voices in my head as if they communicated without talking out loud. When one of the pillars said, 'Look on the wall,' and I saw on the wall the image of a grey bearded old man with a hooked nose that was enough for me and I began to yell for my mother. Please don't think me crazy, dear reader, but I now see that same grey bearded old man every time that I look at myself in a mirror.

My mother had been begging the doctor for help with my night time problems and soon after the white pillars incident I was asked to attend the local hospital for an electro- encephalograph. I found the experience amusing particularly when they asked me if I liked Marilyn Monroe, as if any male able to draw breath could do otherwise. When we were called into to discuss the result the doctor said that I had an overactive brain and that when my body slept my brain kept working. 'Don't worry,' he told my mother, 'it is a sign of intelligence and will correct itself with age. He was right, no one could accuse me of having an overactive brain today; sluggish would fit the bill better.

I was desolate in my grief for Tommy; grief felt as only a child can feel that emotion. In my experience every feeling and emotion is much sharper in youth but they are dulled with advancing years. It is almost as if nature dilutes our ability to feel year by year, drop by drop in preparation for the inevitable total relaxation; heart wrenching grief becomes poignant sorrow, joy becomes quiet pleasure and so on. I was brought back to near normality by the annual summer camp of the Army Cadet Force.

Once a year cadets from all over Britain gathered for two weeks at army camps across the country to live the military life to the full with Spartan conditions, parades, assault courses and all the rigors of army life - or so we imagined in reality we were protected from hardship and harm. The camp that year was near Blackpool, the weather was perfect and I threw myself into the activities winning my "First Class Rifleman" badge with a Lee Enfield on the firing range.

At the end of the first week we were given leave to see the sights of Blackpool and we climbed aboard a coach wearing our best uniforms and full of excitement. Like most provincial boys I was impressed by the lights, the music and the sound of this great resort. The weather was good and after taking in the funfair and the other attractions I went shopping with a fellow cadet named Robert. Why we had become friends I do not know because he was from a well to do middle class family and a pupil at our local grammar school, a totally opposite background to mine; perhaps it was my ability to assume a civilized persona gained from my years of wandering.

We found ourselves in a Woolworths store and were wandering around looking for souvenirs of our visit when a pair of men accosted us with, 'OK, boys, you'd better come along with us.' I had no intention of going anywhere with two strange men and told them so. Their response was short and sharp, 'Suit yourself, son, if you don't come to the manager's office now we'll call the police.'

I realised then that they were store detectives and complaining loudly I followed them with a silent Robert alongside me. Once inside the office we were asked to turn our pockets out on the manager's desk; from both sets of pockets emerged our pocket money and the usual junk that boys collect but in addition Robert's pocket contained a small trinket. There followed a long interrogation during which we were accused of working as a team and Robert admitted that he had stolen the trinket without my knowledge.

The manager berated Robert telling him that he was a disgrace to his uniform and reducing him to tears. My chivalric idea of loyalty prompted me to interrupt and using my persuasive talents acquired from my begging ventures I told the manager of Robert's distress at being away from home and his poor health from asthma; the first a total lie and the second a half truth. Either the man was moved by my pleas or he was sick of the sight of a blubbering youth, whatever the reason he evicted us with a warning and we made for a sea front bench to recover.

Robert later said that he did not know why he had stolen the item and told me that he would never forget how I had helped him, 'I thought that I would end up in prison,' he said. Years later Robert the almost thief joined the police force and rose to senior rank whilst I, who had never broken any law, was refused entry because my mother was living with Circus an ex- convict.

On the last night of camp there was a party and a talent contest. My ever encouraging friend Jeff persuaded me to enter and although the hall lacked even a piano I inflicted my a cappella version of the old music hall song "Burlington Bertie" complete with grand gestures on my audience. To my surprise (after such a ham performance it should have been to my shame) they loved it and applauded loudly making me the winner of the contest. Once again I felt the thrill that comes from hearing applause and a further seed of the instinct to perform was planted in me.

I returned home from camp revitalized and, ignoring Circus sprawled in the armchair, went straight up to my bedroom. Throwing my kit bag down I looked around taking in the familiar objects: my books stacked in piles along one wall, my pin up pictures, my art materials on the old kitchen table; then I felt a chill, something was missing. The large box containing years of my art work that usually lived underneath the table was nowhere to be seen.

I ran down the stairs calling for my mother, 'My box! What have you done with my art box?' My mother looked at me speechless, she had no idea what I was on about. Then I noticed the wide grin on Circus's face, 'Do you mean that junk in the cornflakes box?' he said, 'That went to the rubbish tip.'

I sat down and stared at him, 'It was a fire hazard,' he sneered, 'useless bloody crap.' All the pent up hatred in me burst out in a torrent of abuse for that pig of a man; I called him every obscenity and ended by making reference to a turn in one of his eyes and calling him a cockeyed bastard. Then I sat there breathless and empty.

As I gasped for breath he stood and crossed to me; I suddenly felt as if I had received an electric shock to my head, he had punched me full in the face without warning. I felt and heard the bones in my nose break and tasted the rusty iron of the gush of blood in my throat. I fought for breath and choked on my blood gasping and coughing at the same time.

My mother rushed me and shielded me from further assault. 'My God what do you think you are doing' she cried. 'He's tasted "the little adder" now,' he said, 'maybe he'll keep his trap shut in future.' Within minutes my nose began to swell and by evening I had developed two black eyes to match my bulbous nose; more hurtful than the broken nose was the fact that with one spiteful gesture Circus had destroyed years of art work and with it my ambition to obtain a place in an art college.

Following the breaking of my nose something odd occurred; instead of hating Circus more deeply I developed a contempt for him and although I vowed that should he hit me again I would pick something up and brain him I found that he ceased to have the effect on me that he had previously. It was as if I felt that he could do little worse than he had done and that he had fired his best shot and missed.

He must have sensed something of this because he ceased to provoke me and we ignored each other speaking only when necessary. This uncomfortable truce continued for some weeks without my consideration of the effect it had on my mother; Peter, being occupied with his pal Graham, had been blissfully unaware of the friction in the household.

Later that year on an autumn morning my prayers were answered and Circus disappeared from my life. There was no warning, no preliminary argument or discussion; he simply got out of bed one morning telling my mother to lay on and rest because he was meeting an old friend about a job and he left. The day passed uneventfully and with the approach of evening my mother became concerned, her concern becoming anxiety as ten o'clock approached. She sent me down to fetch Maggie who expressed her view that Circus was probably drunk and afraid to come home; an unlikely scenario as drink was not one of his vices.

Midnight came and there was still no sign of him so my mother asked me to accompany her to the nearest public telephone from which she phoned the local police station (in those pre-electronic days you could phone your local police be answered almost immediately by a local Bobbie and enjoy a prompt response, unlike today when you progress through endless options dictated by an mechanical voice and often end up being told that no one is available and asked to leave a contact number.)

The policeman, however, simply echoed Maggie's 'drunk with pals' idea and assured my mother that Circus would turn up the next day; as a rider he gave the cheerful information that no bodies had been found that day. When we returned home Maggie - experienced in all things male - suggested that my mother check his suitcases, they were missing. 'He's done a bunk, our kid,' said Maggie, and so it was.

Lacking any sympathy for my mother, who could not understand what she had done to receive such treatment and went around in a mood that alternated between misery and anger, I was on top of my little world. Once again I was the man of the house with my mother seeking my opinion and advice and, best of all, I was free from abuse and ridicule (Maggie excepted of course but then she ridiculed and abused everyone within her reach.)

For a few happy months life was uneventful; autumn gave way to winter and the infamous Atlantic gales that lashed the Pembrokeshire coast each year. I had built up a good stock of logs and coke so heating the living room was not a problem and at bed time my mother would heat building bricks in the oven and wrap them in towels to act as bed warmers; you discover a new meaning to 'awoke with a start' when you kick a building brick out of bed in the early morning hours. As for the winds I loved them although my mother hated them.

I often left the cinema to be picked up at the entrance by a gust of wind from a gale and thrown yards down the road; I must have been a little lacking in common sense because I found the experience exciting and could hardly wait for the next gust. On such nights people could be seen pulling themselves from shop front to shop front to prevent being blown away. Occasionally a roofing slate would sail past spinning as it went and crash to a shattering end on the ground or, worst case, smash through a shop window; it was best to make yourself scarce when you saw these because the loss of one slate would trigger a chain reaction and you would often see whole sections of roof lifting off.

Despite the menace of wind and slates I welcomed the thrill of danger that came with them; I had developed a philosophy of my own that refused to be afraid of any natural hazard, concluding that there was no malice in nature such existing only in humanity or rarely in the animal kingdom. Consequently, I sought out or welcomed dangerous gales, lightning and high seas and because God protects fools I survived.

The uneventful and peaceful life was too good to last; after all Maggie was only a few doors away. She breezed in one day accompanied by a tall woman with two young children and introduced the woman as her sister Iris, recently divorced. Iris was a tall dark skinned woman a few years younger than Maggie and could be called handsome rather than beautiful; with all the candour of her sister Iris revealed in conversation that she had once earned a living as a prostitute in Cardiff's notorious Tiger Bay.

Over time I heard her tell many tales of that life, all really unsuitable for my young years but each of which I relished. One tale involved a famous celebrity, an entertainer whom Iris claimed to have known when they were in their teens and although I relished every salacious detail I will not repeat the story out of respect for that personality.

After tea, sandwiches and a lot of chat on that first day Maggie came to the point, Iris was homeless. I looked at my mother because I knew what was coming, sure enough Maggie asked my mother to take the family in. I said nothing, not wanting to incur Maggie's anger but prayed silently that my mother would say no…she said yes. 'It will only be for a few weeks, love,' said Iris,' I've heard of a house that's going to come empty soon.'

So it was that Iris her young son and her daughter moved in with us. In some ways it was like having Maggie living with us because Iris had many of her ways but were Maggie was hard Iris was merely hardened and still retained the softer edges of womanhood. In fact I enjoyed her company and quickly developed a schoolboy crush on her.

Christmas was approaching and like children everywhere we were excited (I do not know why because from experience we could expect little). Iris's boy Tom was near Peter's age and quickly bonded with him and Graham making the duo into a trio of which we saw little. Her daughter Vivienne was a precocious ten year old and followed Michael and me everywhere making childish attempts at coquettishness.

One day when just the three of us were at home Viv' stood by our table watching us play cards; juvenile banter flowed easily and the Michael asked me if I would like to see Viv's fanny. I laughed at him and told him not to be stupid. 'You'll frighten her,' I said. 'No I won't,' he replied, 'Go on Viv' show him your fanny.' Without hesitation the child smiled broadly, pulled down her knickers and pulled up her cheap cotton dress; thrusting her tummy out she turned back and forth from Michael to me. 'You can feel it if you like,' Michael said, 'she won't mind. All the boys do.'

Viv approached my chair and thrust herself towards me. On seeing this poor abused child behave so wantonly I felt a fierce wave of pity sweep over me and I wanted to take her in my arms and comfort her. I realised, however, that such a gesture would be misunderstood so I simply said, 'Put your knickers on, there's a good girl,' in what I hoped was a grown up tone. She stared at me for a moment and then looked at Michael with a puzzled expression. 'Go on,' he said, 'do as you are told,' and she did.

Neither Michael nor I mentioned the incident again and I took care not to be alone with Vivienne from then on; not wishing to get Michael into trouble I said nothing to my mother or Iris.

There was a curious footnote to the Vivienne episode. Some twenty-five years later when working as an insurance manager I called at a house in a middle class suburb of Cardiff and left with a policy on the young housewife. That same year when visiting

West Wales one of Maggie's children told me that Viv' sent her love and that she had been the young housewife in question; I had not recognised her but she had me and found it highly amusing. I was only too pleased that life had been kind to the little waif that I had once pitied.

About a week or so from Christmas I answered the door to a smartly dressed young man who clutched a thick document case in both arms. He was a council official and he followed me into the living room in which both my family and Iris's were having tea. He came straight to the point, 'We understand that you have taken in lodgers without permission and may be overcrowding,' he said. There followed a brief silence in which we all looked at my mother awaiting her reply.

'I've given this lady and children shelter,' she said, 'because I know what it is like to be homeless but I am not taking any rent from her.'

The young man who had been scribbling on a pad looked up and said, 'You do know that lodgers are forbidden without our permission.'

'I do,' she replied, 'but I thought that only applied to paying lodgers.'

The young man scribbled again then offered the pad to my mother, 'Will you sign your statement, please,' he asked and she did so without a word. After he had left my mother dropped her mask of calm and turned to Iris her jaw slack with fear, 'What are we going to do,' she asked. 'Don't worry, chuck,' said Iris, 'Maggie will know what to do.'

Maggie's first comment was, 'I'd like to know what dirty bastard shopped you,' followed by, 'You don't want to worry they're only trying to scare you, it happened to me once. You'll get a snotty letter and a warning not to do it again. I just ignore them.' The following week, a few days before Christmas, my mother received an eviction notice. My first instinct was fear, fear of a return to homelessness, and I was angry with my mother for putting our home at risk but would not add to her distress by telling her so.

Taking the eviction notice my mother, accompanied by Peter and I, went down to the council offices. In a cold bare office she faced interrogation by a pimply youth to whom she explained her ignorance of the tenancy's lodger clause and said how sorry she had been for that poor family with nowhere to sleep just before Christmas; she concluded by swearing that not one penny of rent had changed hands and then she began to cry. When I saw her in tears I wanted to hit the young council clerk but he was obviously embarrassed and suggested that my mother put her statement in writing and he would then present it to the Housing Committee. She went home and wrote the letter which I delivered by hand and we waited.

The specter of eviction hung over Christmas and the New Year but my mother and Iris tried bravely to create a festive atmosphere and the younger children were protected from our gloom. Early in January a letter dropped through our mail box, it informed my mother that, provided Iris and her children left our house and my mother gave an undertaking not to take any boarders in future, the eviction notice would be suspended - not cancelled, suspended.

Luckily Iris had been offered a rented house by an old friend and she moved out within days. Her new home was a large detached house on the outskirts of town that sat like a square concrete box on what appeared to be wasteland; within a few months it became notorious for her entertaining of men friends and earned the nickname "The Ponderosa" after the ranch in the popular television series "Bonanza".

The next couple of months were pleasantly uneventful until, upon answering the front door one morning, I found Circus on our doorstep. He resembled a second rate one man band because in addition to a suitcase he was hung about with a drum kit, the parts suspended on string. He gave me the friendliest of gap toothed grins and asked politely if he could come in. Stunned by his sudden and unexpected appearance and bemused by his musical accoutrements I stepped back and he struggled past me. I heard my mother's loud gasp of, 'Oh, my God,' as he entered the living room and I followed to find him attempting to hug her, an attempt thwarted by his bass drum.

After he had divested himself of his drum kit, and sat in the armchair sipping a cup of tea, he explained that he had left home because he was guilty of failing to provide for us and wanted to earn good wages in pastures new; his aim, he explained, had been to return with lots of money. My mother, of course, believed him and, despite the fact that there was no sign of any new found wealth, welcomed him back. It was life with Circus again but with a difference; his attitude had changed and this was a new contrite man.

He no longer ridiculed me and, although he did not find work, he helped around the house and treated everyone with consideration. Maggie was sceptical, 'You should have kept the git out,' she said, 'he'll never be any good to man nor beast.' She insulted him at every opportunity but he accepted it with a smile saying that he knew she was only joking.

The winter ripened into spring with me counting the weeks because this was the summer that I was to leave school (although I had seldom attended) and I could, at last, become a working man. May heralded the potato season and both Circus and I joined Maggie's gang, Soon after this my friend Jeff called to tell me that the end of term exams were about to begin; Jeff who always had my interests at heart said that although I had missed these in the past he thought that I owed it to myself to sit the last ones of our school years and encouraged by his faith in me I dragged myself back to school. I met with the usual sarcasm from teaching staff and, resigned to the frequent canings (I still found it difficult to get there on time) I sat through the examinations.

The last day of term arrived and we received our report books; bound in royal blue buckram their cover embossed in gold with the school crest these thin volumes recorded a pupil's progress. I opened mine to the latest page expecting the usual, 'No position because we never see him,' comments from the various teachers to find instead a long list of first place marks. In a class of more than thirty pupils out of twelve subjects I had achieved first place in nine.

At the bottom of the page 'Boss' had written 'This boy has the intelligence for higher education. It is a pity that his poor attendance record has held him back.' I showed the book to Jeff who was as delighted as if it had been his own. 'I told you that you could do it,' he said, 'Oh boy, if I took a report like that home my dad would buy me a new bike.'

All the hours of reading at home and studying in my own time had paid dividends but I told Jeff that I had simply been lucky with my answers and tried to play down my achievement. Nevertheless I was filled with an unfamiliar sense of pride and ran all the way home to show my mother, who read the report and commented that it was very nice - not quite the praise I had hoped for. Maggie further deflated my ego by remarking that I was probably in a class of dunces and that was that. I stored the book away in a cardboard box and it was later thrown out with the rubbish. I could not remain disheartened for long because, joy of joys, I was finished with school for ever.

Shortly after my final school term ended my mother, with Maggie's help, found me a job as a van boy with Jenkins The Pop – a local mineral water factory; fifteen shillings for a six day week of twelve hour days and my first step on the journey of adulthood, a journey dominated by a fear of permanence and a loathing for continuity but that is another story.

So the seasons of my childhood came and went; marked not by calendars and dates but by events large and small, people nice and not so nice and all the trivia that makes up a childhood and I stood at the open door of adulthood blissfully unaware of trials and tribulations to come and stepped through.

Boy